THE PHILOSOPHY OF
JOHN STUART MILL

THE PHILOSOPHY
OF
JOHN STUART MILL

Alan Ryan

SECOND EDITION

MACMILLAN
PRESS

First Edition 1970
Second Edition 1987

Published by
THE MACMILLAN PRESS LTD
Houndmills, Basingstoke, Hampshire RG21 2XS
and London
Companies and representatives
throughout the world

Printed in Hong Kong

British Library Cataloguing in Publication Data
Ryan, Alan
The philosophy of John Stuart Mill.—
2nd ed.
1. Mill, John Stuart
I. Title
192   B1607
ISBN 0–333–43562–1 (*hardcover*)
ISBN 0–333–43563–X (*paperback*)

CONTENTS

CONTENTS

PREFACE TO THE SECOND EDITION

The Philosophy of John Stuart Mill was first published in 1970. Reading it fifteen years later arouses the mixed feelings usual in such circumstances – the conviction that the author was formerly altogether cleverer, more imaginative and more enthusiastic than he has become alternates with embarrassment at his ignorance, disorder and clumsiness. The object of this preface, however, is not to review my own work but to say a little about the subsequent condition of some of the subjects the book addressed.

The Philosophy of John Stuart Mill was in part a work of propaganda; its aim was to show Mill as a much more systematic thinker than had previously been thought, and in particular to present his *System of Logic* as a key to ambitions which give a unity to all his thought. The argument of the book was that the ultimate object of *The System of Logic* was to establish the scientific credentials of the social sciences, and that Mill's discussion of induction, causation, the nature of mathematical knowledge, the nature of natural laws and the rest was intended to show that the social sciences could be nothing other than the natural sciences of social life. For Mill, this was not a "neutral" philosophical truth, for it seemed to him that if there was to be rational social and political reform, it could only be on the basis of a scientific understanding of social and political life. Nor is this simply a plausible inference from the structure of Mill's work as a whole;

his *Autobiography* explicitly declares the polemical purpose of his attack on the intuitionism of Whewell and Hamilton and on the exaggerated empiricism of Macaulay.[1] The philosophy of science and of social science in turn lays the foundations for the defence of utilitarian ethics. In my view of Mill's programme, he saw utilitarianism in ethics as uniquely consilient with, if not strictly implied by, the rational understanding of society which the new social sciences would yield. But one of the many ways in which Mill was unusual among the nineteenth century utilitarians, and indeed would still be unusual among their twentieth century successors, too, was in combining this stress on the role of timeless natural laws in science and of general principles in morals with an equal emphasis on the historical development of society and personal development in ethics. It was this which made him so eager to do what would have seemed inconceivable to the early philosophical radicals, namely to incorporate the insights of Coleridge into an enlarged utilitarian morality and theory of government.[2]

This view of Mill is now widely accepted; the dismissive view of Mill as a good natured but slack-minded eclectic is no longer widely held. It is not only a more careful attention to Mill that has made him seem intellectually more impressive than hitherto. The philosophical climate has changed, and since 1970 logical and epistemological naturalism has ceased to be as unpopular as it was in the 1960s. So far is this true that *The Philosophy of John Stuart Mill* now seems too quick to dismiss Mill's view that the propositions of arithmetic and perhaps even those of logic were empirical truths. Mill, it will be recalled, suggested that propositions such as "2 + 2 = 4" ought to be understood as empirical truths about "collections"−e.g. that the collections *oo* and *oo* could be rearranged as the collection *oooo*. To this, Frege asked mockingly whether the truths of arithmetic would cease to hold in a universe where everything was bolted down. But this is scarcely conclusive. Frege's question insinuates in our minds the thought that the truths of arithmetic are conceptual or *a priori* truths by mocking out of contention the thought that arithmetic has to be "about" empirical objects. Mill may have been right, however, to doubt whether there could be arithmetical truths about a world in which there were no "collections". For there hardly could be a universe even in imagination in which every discriminable object (consider the case of discriminable events and discriminable thoughts about events) was bolted down. This no doubt means, as Mill admitted, that even if the laws of arithmetic are empirical generalisations, it is beyond the limits of our imagination to give a coherent account of what it would be *like* for the laws of arithmetic to break down. This does not imply that the suggestion that somewhere in the universe the laws of arithmetic *might* break down is incoherent in itself as well as unintelligible to us. That we cannot give any coherent account of what it would be like to experience such a breakdown is a fact about *us*, not the laws of arithmetic.[3]

Whether we can extend the claim to the laws of logic is a moot point. W. V. O. Quine has popularized the thought that our beliefs form a system which confronts the world only "at the edges", so that we possess a sort of entrenched core of beliefs which we do not treat as empirical, even though in some extended sense they are such, and the truths of logic and mathematics belong to this "core". This image is one which Mill's naturalistic account of "the laws of thought" certainly matches. Other writers, too, have suggested that the laws of logic are empirically justified, that they, so to speak, sophisticate and clarify the procedures which as a matter of fact have been successful in securing the transition from truth to truth. This suggestion is in line with what Mill suggested in his *Examination of Sir William Hamilton's Philosophy*. As with the truths of arithmetic, we are faced with the difficulty that we seem unable to make much sense of the thought that there could be some conditions under which the best way to respond to experience would be to say that the laws of logic were false and to revise them rather than our other beliefs about the world. Here too, it is possible to reply as Mill does, that this is a fact about *us* rather than about logic or the world. Unconvinced critics of Quine argue that such a view really is incoherent, not just hard to come to terms with. The idea that we *ought* to give up some portion of the laws of logic is parasitic upon the idea of there being good reasons for believing one thing rather than another; but good reasons must be logically good reasons, so that the one thing we cannot treat as empirical and revisable is logic. We cannot evade the distinction between beliefs which we can envisage giving up and beliefs which it seems impossible to give up because their being true is what structures everything else we believe.[4]

If recent arguments in these areas would have made Chapter V more sympathetic than it is, other topics would have been treated more clearly but perhaps more critically. Two subjects central to what follows which have been greatly clarified in the past fifteen years are the analysis of causation and the understanding of the relationship between causal and "rational" explanations of human action. On the first, the work of John Mackie and the analysis of counterfactuals by David Lewis and others has enabled us to see in what ways Mill's belief that all causal claims are implicitly general is false. Many causal claims rest on and imply no generalizations; I do not mean by this that their truth does not in fact depend on physical laws, but that Mill's view that all causal statements imply covering laws is false. Suppose I throw a shoe at a window and the glass breaks; it may well be that I have thrown my shoe at the window dozens of times and that this is the first time it has broken the window. Whatever I do imply when I say "the shoe broke the window", it cannot be "whenever I throw my shoe the window breaks". Nor does there appear to be any generalization to which I can be compelled to give my assent less vacuous than "whenever anything exactly like this happens, this happens". When we set philosophical pre-judices aside, there seems little reason to think that there are any laws of nature couched in terms of shoes and windows. If there are none, then there are no laws which strictly *cover* the singular causal claim. This is doubly relevant to Mill's analysis of causation, because once we see causation in this light, we not only have to reject Mill's most treasured beliefs about the way all causal claims invoke general laws, but we see that the logical gap between everyday singular causal claims and the genuine laws which we invoke in explicating them is very much wider than Mill ever noticed.[5] We may well continue to believe in a law-governed universe, and believe that every causal claim is explicable by some set of natural laws and some account of the nature of the participants in the events we explain; none the less, we cannot sustain that belief merely by appealing to the idea that all causal claims are implicitly general. The gap between the non-generalisable terms in which ordinary causal claims are made and the special languages of the sciences tailored to the task of generalization suggests that in ordinary causal contexts the role of regularities is not to provide covering laws so much as to provide evidence for hypotheses about what would have happened in other circumstances.[6]

The analysis of singular causal claims is, for all that, problematic still. The suggestion has been made that "the shoe broke the window" ought to be analyzed counter-factually.[7] The thought is that the shoe's impact was an indispensable part of conditions which under the circumstances were sufficient to break the window; this implies that but for the arrival of the shoe the window would have remained unbroken. The difficulty is that it is not difficult to imagine cases in which it is true that the impact of the shoe broke the window but false that the window would have remained unbroken otherwise. Suppose you throw a brick which arrives a split second after my shoe has gone through the glass; it was my shoe which in fact caused the damage, but your brick *would have* done it. The singular causal claim is true while the corresponding counterfactual is false.

Whatever the way forward in analyzing singular causal claims, a concentration on their analysis and their independence of laws which genuinely "cover" them has revealed ways of reconciling what twenty years ago seemed to be utterly hostile positions on the place of causal and rational considerations in rendering an account of human behaviour. Mill's account of the explanation of behaviour has often been taken as a paradigm of misapplied causal analysis.[8] Mill certainly held that actions were caused by volitions and volitions by the combination of beliefs and desires; he was deeply hostile to any suggestion that the causal ties between desiring and acting were in any way "special" or different from those holding between any other pairs of events.[9] But Mill's critics have commonly held that the explanation of behaviour in terms of beliefs and desires is not causal at all, that "rational" explanation is something distinct from causal explanation. In arguing this, they have invariably relied on Mill's own assumption that causal explanation is always law-governed; for they have pointed out that a man who does something for one reason – goes to the post-box to post his letters, say – might equally well have done the same thing for a different reason – gone to the post-box to keep a rendezvous with his mistress, perhaps. It seems intuitively obvious that there are no causal laws linking reasons and the actions for which they are reasons; it is concluded that since we do cite reasons in explaining actions we are rendering actions intelligible rather than providing causal explanations of them.[10]

This, however, falls foul of the objection that there is an important distinction between saying that someone has a reason for acting in a certain way and saying that this was the reason for which he acted. Suppose I go to the post-box and post my letters, but also keep an assignation with my mistress at the same time. Having letters to post gave me a reason to go, but that was not in fact the reason which got me to go; the reason which got me to go was my wish to keep my date. Very frequently, somebody offers as a reason for their actions what would be a perfectly adequate reason so far as conferring intelligibility goes – "I went to post my letters" secures that; but their account is challenged on the grounds that it does not offer their "real reason". The "real reason" is the one which is causally effective. The point is worth making much of, because there are two central issues in the social sciences which almost everyone cares about a good deal, but which can hardly be advanced unless we maintain this causal understanding of the role of reasons in action. One of these issues is self-deception, the other the operations of ideology. I may in all sincerity say that I rebuked a student because she had done no work; it may be that she had done no work and that a rebuke would have been in order and that a disinterested observer would have agreed that a rebuke was in order. None the less, it may well be that I in fact rebuked her because she reminded me of my mother, against whom I had some grudge which I wished to settle. Again, a government may say – sincerely or not – that it is acting in the public interest when its critics maintain that this is either self-deception or an ideological blind, and that the "real reason" for the action is to line the pockets of the bankers or to secure re-election. It is true that uncovering the "real reason" makes the behaviour intelligible in a different way from the way it was intelligible before; none the less, what is important in uncovering the real reason is not that we have made the world more intelligible, but that we now know what caused the events in question.

Just as in the case of singular causal claims in the non-human realm, a counterfactual analysis of what the causal claim amounts to will be partially but only partially successful. That is, an appeal to the "real reason" for an action will commonly be backed up by the claim that the person would have done the action in the absence of the proffered reason but not in the absence of the "real reason", i.e., that even if this policy had not been in the public interest the government would still have pursued it, so long as it lined the bankers' pockets. Sometimes this will not do, because it may be that I would have gone to the post-box to post my letters even if it is true that what actually made me go was the desire to see my mistress. So it may be that even if my pupil had not reminded me of my mother I should have spoken harshly to her and that even if the measure had not lined the pockets of the bankers or increased the chances of re-election the government would have done it. The claim being made must be that even if that is true, it was the other reason which was in fact causally effective. We may justly complain that Mill did not advance the analysis of the notion of causal efficacy very much, and indeed that he was so hostile to any such notion that he hardly could have done much with it; but we ought to count it in his favour that he never lost sight of the centrality of causal considerations in all explanation, human and merely physical

In these areas, hindsight would have led me to a more complex account of both Mill and the subject under discussion. The area in which the degree of sophisticaion with which Mill's work is discussed has changed most strikingly, but in which I should not wish to alter the content of my own account very much is the treatment of utilitarian ethics. Later accounts have added a good deal to what appears here, but the consensus has been that the considerations which appear below are very largely those which ought to be taken into account. To take the point on which I rest a good deal in my discussion of *Liberty*, it has become a commonplace that Mill did not think of the principle of utility as a *moral* principle, but rather as the supreme principle of all practical reasoning. Thus, as he explained, it is utility which constitutes, though certainly not as a moral matter, the nature of good practice in architecture as much as it constitutes good practice in any other activity. Good architectural practice is determined by the requirements of commodious building; the attractions of commodious building are explained by utility. The difficulty is less in such claims as this, which show what it is like to have non-moral practical principles than in determining the features which make moral principles *moral*.[11]

It is not that Mill offers us too few clues, rather that he offers us too many and offers us too little advice about how we should reconcile them. For instance, Mill sometimes seems to confine morality to the realm of our dealings with others; morality is a matter of duties, we have no duties to ourselves strictly speaking, and whatever considerations bear on what one might loosely call our obligation to make the most of ourselves, they cannot strictly be held to be moral considerations.[12] Again, he says that morality is a matter of punishment. We only call an action wrong if we mean that it ought to be punished, either by law, or by opinion or at least by the reproaches of the agent's own conscience.[13] It is easy to see that these criteria *might* naturally coincide, because it is easy to see that the threat of punishment is a natural way of reconciling each person's interest in doing just as he chooses with the interest of others in being protected against his ill-will, carelessness and stupidity, and that punishment might "grow" as a social practice out of our natural resentment at mischiefs done to us and our desire to revenge ourselves on the miscreant. But there is no necessity that they should coincide; and if we make the reproaches of *conscience* a salient element in the story, it is equally natural to suppose that "self-regarding immorality" is what conscience is particularly calculated to suppress.[14] I argue below that Mill's conception of morality is generally one in which its other-regarding elements are central, and that he does link punishability and regard for the interests of others in the way just suggested, and that he is committed to the view that there is no such thing as self-regarding immorality. But there is no avoiding the fact that he also criticises Bentham for limiting morality to "business" matters and the realm of our duty to others.[15] Again, supposing this difficulty is overcome, it is difficult in an account which emphasizes duties to others and the realm of the punishable to provide a clear distinction between moral obligation in general and the obligations of justice in particular. Mill insists on the need to make such a distinction, and provides an account of it in the final chapter of *Utilitarianism*. Yet what is offered as the central "very simple principle" of *Liberty*, the proposition that individuals and society may only coerce the recalcitrant to prevent harm to others, blurs, or any any rate ignores, the distinction. In *Liberty*, Mill writes of coercion being restricted to the defense of those interests which "ought to be counted as rights", and in *Utilitarianism* the sphere of justice is explained precisely as the sphere of rights. Yet in *Liberty*, he draws only the diitinction between self-regarding acts of imprudence, folly and lack of self-respect on the one hand and "wrong" properly speaking on the other.[16] Not all wrongs done to others are injustices, nor is it clear that it is only injustices strictly speaking that a utilitarian would wish society to repress.

A major reason for supposing that the principle of utility justifies moral principles but it not itself a moral principle is that only such a view can avoid collapsing the distinction between prudence and morality. It has long been recognised that we need to draw such a distinction if we are to avoid reducing utilitarianism to absurdity. Suppose I watch a footling television programme and am utterly bored by it; I have failed to do the optimific thing, because I have gained less utility than I readily could have done. I have acted imprudently. If the principle of utility was a moral principle and I had a genuine duty to maximize utility, watching the wrong programme would have been a breach of duty, and would therefore have been immoral. That seems absurd; it has seemed absurd to everyone except William Godwin who happily embraced the thought that prudence, justice and morality at large all collapsed into a duty to maximize utility.[17] Mill plainly had some sense of the need to avoid such absurdities, but it is quite unclear how concerned he was with such issues. But one indispensable element in what we can plausibly see as his response to the need to keep familiar distinctions alive was his explanation of morality in terms of the realm of the other-regarding; self-regarding conduct requires the application of utilitarian considerations to our own welfare, other-regarding conduct requires the application of utilitarian considerations to everyone's welfare.[18] It is a further element in the argument, moreover, that brings us to the excessively familiar question whether Mill was an "act-utilitarian" or a "rule-utilitarian". Mill frequently wrote of the need to apply the principle of utility by way of *axiomata media* or "secondary rules". He also—and this has been less frequently noticed— drew a distinction between prudence and morality by claiming that prudence calculated consequences in particular cases whereas morality dealt with "classes of cases" and produced rules rather than single instructions.[19] This makes morality a matter of rules in some fashion in which prudence is not a matter of rules—the difficulty is to elicit an account of that fashion from Mill's own writings.

Critics have found it impossible to tie Mill down to a particular view of the relationship between rules and morality. Sometimes he seems to have in mind the need for rules of thumb—this is certainly what he suggests in *Utilitarianism* when he treats moral conventions as utilitarian calculations done ahead of time, just like the calculations of the *Nautical Almanac*. But rules of thumb are at their most useful in prudential contexts, and the rule prohibiting murder just does not look like even a social and impartial rule of thumb. For a prudential rule of thumb such as "don't generally drink more than three glasses of wine at dinner or you'll have a fearful headache" cries out for adjustment in particular conditions—weaker wine, more absorbent food, less vulnerability to headaches in old age; but "don't murder" does not at all cry out for adjustment in the light of the fact that one's victim is a pest, that nobody will miss him, or that nobody will notice your doing it. Mill explains the difference by denying that any of us has the right to adjust moral rules; but then that must make them quite other than rules of thumb. Mill must be claiming that *having a rule* on which we can all rely is what produces maximum utility, and this has nothing to do with rules of thumb. What promotes utility is having rules against murder, depriving individuals of the right to revise those rules off their own bat, and assuring everyone that they are safe from attack– even if they are dreary, boring, unloved and unlikely to be missed.[20] It is sometimes suggested that this analysis implies that morality is essentially a matter of submission to rules, and it is then claimed that this is a form of "rule worship"; but there is no question of "rule worship" in Mill's account of the role of moral rules, since he is insistent that the merit of utilitarianism as opposed to all sorts of intuitive ethics is that it enables us to revise our moral principles in a rational way.[21]

This is not the occasion, nor is there space here to embark on a full analysis of Mill's position and that of his interpreters. But I should acknowledge that if I do not wish to revise much of the content of the last three chapters of what follows, I do wish to modify the context and therefore the tone of the discussion. In particular, I now wish to be more sensitive to Mill's own conception of what the utilitarian philosophy could do and to his conception of what his own writings on ethics might achieve. Two heuristic observations are in order. The first is that it is implausible to suppose that we shall discover in Mill a precise answer to questions he never posed in the form in which we have got in the habit of posing them.[22] Mill never wrote a treatise on ethics to stand alongside his *Logic* and *Political Economy*; his writings in moral philosophy are much slighter and more polemical–much more "public" too–than his writings in epistemology and logic. The best one can say for some of the more complex contemporary reformulations of Mill's views is that they achieve the kind of thing he wished to achieve. There is not much sense in asking how far they match his ideas.[23] Secondly, and more importantly, we should consider whether we have not been misled, by Mill himself and by later moral philosophy, into expecting something from utilitarianism that he never expected it to produce (even if Sidgwick did). Mill insists on the need to derive practical injuctions of all kinds from one ultimate principle

by a process of deduction this suggests, and it is an analogy; made
much of below, that a rational ethical theory is a mirror of a
rational scientific theory, and aims at the kind of comprehensive
and impersonal perspective on moral matters that a physical
theory aims at in its realm. Since such a theory depends so
heavily on the plausibility of what it sets as its ultimate goal it is
this quasi-scientific quality which makes the "proof" of the
principle of utility such a central problem. Recently, it has been
argued that it is a disastrous mistake to try to construct a moral
theory with the aspiration to discuss our duties "from the
standpoint of the universe".[24] But Mill may not have had quite
that ambition in mind, and it may well be that that explains why
he was much less interested in proving the utilitarian standard
than we have supposed, and much less interested in trying to
deduce moral principles from it than we suppose. Mill was
characteristically concerned to pick off contrary accounts of
morality on a piecemeal basis; so, he rebuts Carlyle's assault on
"pig philosophy", or tries to show that a sensible Christian will
find nothing repugnant in the dictates of utility, but ought to
acknowledge that there is much more to morality than the
dictates of moral authority. His critics have all been scandalized
by the lackadaisical quality of the "proof", and nobody has ever
suggested that Mill's accounts of the utilitarian merits of, say,
private property, non-government provided education or intellectual *laissez-faire* have much in common with proofs in formal
logic. It may be, however, that the critics and Mill have simply
been at cross purposes.

Mill's concern was for the most part to show that moral
principles are subject to rational discussion insofar as they can be
connected with utility and not otherwise; in some cases, utility
will warrant not so much a particular injunction as the strategy of
enforcing a line of conduct in all cases, and thus, paradoxically,
the strategy of ignoring utility for the sake of utility. Some of our
moral beliefs will emerge unscathed from the sort of enquiry Mill
has in mind, and some will turn out to be superstitions which
ought to be discarded. Nor will the principle of utility itself
remain untouched by this process; our conception of what
happiness consists of will alter as we bring the principle and our

best defended moral attitudes into an acceptable relationship. Mill thought that reading Hegel had a tendency to debauch the intellect, but he knew that this kind of dialectical interplay was typical of both science and practice. It cannot be said that he made this "give and take" process central to his discussion of rational inquiry and rational practice, but it is at any rate latent in what he does make central. Mill does not, of course, emerge triumphant on this interpretation. *A Theory of Justice* has so familiarized everyone with the thought that utilitarianism cannot cope with "the separateness of persons" that I need do no more than refer to the anxieties expressed here about Mill's difficulties with both justice and personal identity.[25] But Mill is more understandable and more impressive when he is read with a greater concern for his own view of what he was doing. *The Philosophy of John Stuart Mill* was sympathetic to its subject, but there are many places where it would have been better if it had been more so.

NOTES

1. *Autobiography*, p. 158.   **2.** *System of Logic*, VI, x, 5.   **3.** *Examination of Hamilton*, Chs. XX, XXI.   **4.** Quine, "Two Dogmas of Empiricism" section 6; Hollis, *Models of Man*, pp. 53-5.   **5.** See below, pp. 62ff.   **6.** Mackie, *Cement of the Universe*, pp. 58ff.   **7.** *Ibid.* p. 30.   **8.** Winch, *Idea of a Social Science*.   **9.** *System of Logic*, III, v, 11.   **10.** Lessnoff, *Structure of Social Science*, pp. 83ff.   **11.** See Berger, *Happiness, Justice and Freedom*, pp. 105-120, and the references there cited; Gray, *Mill on Liberty: A Defence*.   **12.** *Utilitarianism*, etc., p. 135.   **13.** *Ibid.*, p. 45.   **14.** *Ibid.*, p. 45.   **15.** *Dissertations and Discussions*, I, p. 361.   **16.** *Utilitarianism*, p. 135.   **17.** Godwin, *Political Justice*, pp. 84-90.   **18.** Below, pp. 220ff.   **19.** *Dissertations and Discussions*, II, p. 475.   **20.** *Ibid.*, p. 476; cf. *Happiness, Justice and Freedom*, above.   **21.** *Dissertations and Discussions*, II, pp. 471-2.   **22.** Sumner, "The Right and the Good", p. 114.   **23.** e.g., Wollheim "John Stuart Mill and Isaiah Berlin", pp. 260-66.   **24.** Williams, *Ethics and the Limits of Philosophy*. **25.** Rawls, *A Theory of Justice*, p. 29; below, p. 229.

ACKNOWLEDGMENTS

A great many people have helped me with this study of Mill over the last several years; to credit them with the results may seem to many of them a mixed blessing, when I have so often persisted in adhering to what they thought was error. But, for all their help I thank Professor Richard Wollheim of University College, London, Professor Ron Atkinson of the University of York, Professor Anthony Flew of the University of Keele, and Patrick Day, also of Keele, all of whom have read and commented on drafts of the whole·or part of this study. For informative conversation and argument I am indebted to H. L. A. Hart, Alan Montefiore, and Steven Lukes, all of Oxford, John Grundy of Keele, and Alasdair MacIntyre of the University of Essex. It would be ungracious not to thank three generations of undergraduates at the University of Keele for the stimulus of their questions and objections. My final debt is recorded in the dedication; it is a dozen years since Michael Cherniavsky suggested that I might find *On Liberty* more sustaining than my schoolroom diet of motoring journals. I have been grateful ever since.

A.R.

INTRODUCTION

The aim of this book is to present John Stuart Mill as the author of a philosophical system, a system which I shall call "inductivism"—the philosophy of what Mill himself termed "the inductive school." In general Mill has not been thought of as a systematizer; both his admirers and his detractors have seen him as an eclectic, a man who tried to do justice to the multifaceted nature of truth, without concerning himself with the consequences for his general philosophical position. Yet, this view of Mill belies his own utterances on the subject; his *Autobiography* tells the story of his search for a systematic philosophy of knowledge and action. His father and Bentham had created an excessively narrow, abstract system; in Kant and Hegel he could find no recognition of the psychological discoveries made by Locke and his empiricist successors. In his own day the alternative positions seemed to be the misguided extreme empiricism of Macaulay, on the one hand, and the Anglicized Kantianism of men like Whewell on the other. Yet, system there must be; his diary for 1854 contains his credo concerning the importance of a systematic approach to philosophy: "In the moral and psychological department of thought, there is hardly an instance of a writer who has left a considerable permanent reputation, or who has continued to be read by after generations, except those who have treated or attempted to treat of the *whole* of some great department of speculation. . . . few of the systems of these systematic writers have any permanent value as systems; their value is the value of some of the fragments. But the fragments (the parts which are excellent in wholes which are inadmissible) if published separate would probably have attracted little notice. This is a tribute which mankind unconsciously pay to the value of theory and systematic thought." [1] Mill's view of the common dislike of self-consciously systematic thinking was very similar to that of Keynes; men who said they had no system almost always were in the grip of unexamined prejudices which blinded them to the facts every bit as effectively as the most metaphysical of systems.

The goals, method, and characteristic style of Mill's philosophy are to a great extent intelligible in terms of his dislike of the intuitionism of Whewell and his colleagues at Oxford and Cambridge. The domination of these institutions, which seemed to Mill to be engaged in nothing more than the defense of privilege, by philosophical doctrines which seemed to him calculated to enshrine and sanctify reactionary social and political views, gave to his attacks on intuitionism the aspect of a crusade. Arguing in the *Autobiography* that the *System of Logic* might serve a valuable, if minor, social purpose, he says: ". . . whatever may be the practical value of a true philosophy of these matters, it is hardly possible to exaggerate the mischiefs of a false one. The notion that truths external to the mind may be known by intuition or consciousness, independently of observation and experience, is, I am persuaded, in these times, the great intellectual support of false doctrines and bad institutions." [2] Indeed, he says, "There never was such an instrument devised for consecrating all deep-seated prejudices." [3] As the name suggests, the central doctrine of the intuitionists was that the test of truth was whether a proposition was self-evident, whether the contradictory of a belief was inconceivable. It was, therefore, not surprising that the intellectual stronghold of intuitionism was mathematics, where appeals to inconceivability had long been in constant employment: "And the chief strength of this false philosophy in morals, politics, and religion, lies in the appeal which it is accustomed to make to the evidence of mathematics and of the cognate branches of physical science." [4] To deprive it of this base, Mill devoted great efforts to showing that the apparent necessity of mathematical and geometrical truth could be accounted for in inductive terms, for, as he saw, "to expel it from these, is to drive it from its stronghold." [5] But, as the quotation above suggests, it was not only mathematical truth which the intuitionists thought to be necessary though not analytic; in the first place, the law of universal causation was supposed to rest on the inconceivability of an uncaused event. Mill, therefore, had to show—and it is one of his more striking efforts—that although the law of universal causation does lie at the heart of causal inference, it is for all that a law which we discover empirically, and which we prove by induction. Not merely this major law, however, but lesser laws also were held by intuitionists to be cases of natural necessity; the purpose of scientific inquiry was supposed to be to purge the mind of confusion, until it could perceive these necessities. But Mill denied that there were any such necessities to be perceived, and his account of induction is the alternative account of just what inductive reasoning does establish. On the analysis of causality, the intuitionist view of causation was that it involved something more than uniform succession; a real cause *produced* its effects, it did not just precede them. Mill attacked the view that causation was *efficient* at its strongest point, the doctrine that the archetype of a causal relation is that holding between oneself and one's actions. In the form in which Sir William Hamilton held this doctrine, Mill criticized it both in the book which he devoted to Hamilton's philosophy and also in the *System of Logic*. Even if it is true that we come to form the concept of causality as the result of the experience of performing our own voluntary actions, it is nonetheless false that this experience is of efficient causation. The relation between volitions and the actions that they precede is one of physical causation. Volitions cause actions in precisely the same way that a spark causes an explosion of gunpowder or cold turns water into ice.[6]

This view of the type of causation involved in human action was closely bound up with the problems of personal identity and free will. It was a tenet of intuitionism both that we intuited our own identity and that we intuited that our will was free. Mill, of course, denied that we did anything of the kind. For an atomist of Mill's persuasion, all identity is inferential; the percipient subject feigns or creates the identity of physical objects by assimilating one perception to another, and it seemed to Mill that this phenomenalist account of the identity of physical things ought also to hold of the identity of persons. Again, over the issue of free will the intuitionists wished to draw a sharp line between nature, which was subject to causation, and man, who was not. To Mill this seemed to put an end to both individual psychology and social science, and it set him the task, which in any case was one he found emotionally compelling, of accounting for our consciousness of freedom in a way which would save the truth both of free will and of determinism.

Finally, of course, Mill objected very strongly to the intuitionist account of moral belief. To claim that moral and political principles were self-evident was merely to enshrine prejudice as the ultimate court of appeal; it was to encourage men who always resented having to give reasons for their actions in the delusion that they need give none, that their feelings, their conviction that no sane person could think other than they did, were sufficient grounds for their moral beliefs. "By the aid of this theory, every inveterate belief and every intense feeling, of which the origin is not remembered, is enabled to dispense with the obligation of justifying itself by reason, and is erected into its own all-sufficient voucher and justification." [7] One consequence of this was that the liberty of the individual was an uncertain gift from the crowd, for where the majority of men had no guide other than their feelings, they were unlikely to have any clear understanding of where they were, and where they were not, justified in interfering with a person's freedom of action. Where the likings and dislikings of an untutored crowd were taken for the dictates of morality, there liberty was in danger. In some ways, it is this danger that underlies almost everything Mill writes in opposition to the intuitionists, and the result is to give his treatment of such seemingly remote topics as mathematical reasoning an unusual emotional intensity.

Mill's positive goals, as I have tried to explain them in what follows, are the establishing of a correct theory of scientific explanation, human action, and social science, in order to provide the basis of a rational ethics. A rational ethics is one which employs the same standards of rationality as are current in natural science, and the logic of Mill's case drives him to spend a long time on the basic problems of scientific explanation. It is worth remembering, in this connection, that the *System of Logic* was not written in the order in which we have it; in particular, the final book, "The Logic of the Moral or Human Sciences," grew out of Mill's thinking in the essays on the methods and scope of economics which he wrote four or five years before he was able to see any distance into the problems of inductive reasoning which form the core of the work.[8] In other words, Mill had a rather clear idea of what was the truth about practical reasoning and about the methods of social science before he could link this to the account of scientific explanation which supported this truth.

Mill's system, then, is in its broadest extent an account of human rationality in the areas of scientific explanation and moral action. Mill starts from the fact that being rational is intimately connected with having reasons for one's thoughts and actions, with being able to explain and to justify. On Mill's account, to proffer an explanation is to perform a deduction; we deduce the particular case to be explained from laws and initial conditions; we deduce laws of a low order of generality from laws of a higher order; and we deduce policies from general principles in the same way. This emphasis on deduction is accompanied by an almost equal emphasis on the goal of scientific progress, which is held to be the reduction in the number of laws involved in an explanation together with an increase in the number of phenomena the laws will account for. This deductive theory is one with many famous adherents, and with it this account of Mill's philosophy opens (cf. Chap. I).

But such a view had its difficulties for Mill. These spring from his atomism; if all there are, are particular facts, particular, individual events, if these are all we can actually observe, then what are general laws *about?* Mill's answer is that general laws are to be understood as rules of inference, rules which license us to infer from "particulars to particulars." [9] This—discussed in Chapter II—is "real" inference, which is the process of induction, and in the light of which deduction is seen as a process not of proof but of the testing of proofs. Mill then goes on to develop the canons which govern inductive reasoning; these have always been thought of as deductive, eliminative canons, but it is part of my case that they are rather more than this, and that this raises some interesting questions. One of these is how far we can understand them as genuinely *inductive* canons, once we appreciate the force of Mill's claim that the law of universal causation is not part of the *proof* of causal laws (cf. Chap. III). Another point which emerges from the consideration of the canons is that Mill's account of causal connection contains several important ambiguities; it is usually thought that he believed a cause to be a sufficient condition in time, but closer inspection of what he says shows that it is at least as true that he thought a cause was, properly speaking, both necessary and sufficient; such a doctrine clearly rests on the underlying belief, rarely stated very explicitly, that the universe is made up of a vast chain of atomic events or facts, linked in a determinate order (cf. Chap. IV).

The last element in Mill's defense of inductivism in the natural sciences is his account of mathematical truth, where he attempts to show that it is a form of inductive truth. This is a part of Mill's philosophy which no one has ever greatly admired. Mill himself never made such confident claims for it as for many other parts of his philosophy, and there is little cause for surprise in this. But, as the attempt to drive the intuitionists from their stronghold, it has an interest which is more than sufficient to justify our spending some time trying to make something of it (cf. Chap. V).

Part of Mill's rationalism and one ground of his hostility to the intuitionists was his belief that there is, properly, only one *nature;* he would never use the expression "natural sciences" to distinguish the physical from the human sciences. The "physical" sciences were distinguished from the "moral" or human sciences, but all were equally natural sciences. But this brought Mill up against the problems of personal identity and free will. Mill's atomism was coupled with the doctrine that many terms which seemed to refer to unobservable entities can be reduced to ways of talking about our expectations and beliefs concerning observables. So, for instance, words like "force" or "tendency" were to be construed as labels for our belief in the truth of certain counterfactual propositions. Mill carries this to the length that even the identity of physical objects is a matter of our beliefs about future and hypothetical sensations. But if the identity of physical objects is parasitic upon the mind of the percipient who, so to speak, builds his expectations into things, what of the identity of the percipient? Are persons also susceptible of this reductive analysis? (Cf. Chap. VI.) One reason why Mill more or less supposes that they must be, in spite of his self-confessed failure to show anything of the kind, is that an atomistic psychology is the only one compatible with his account of what it is to explain a human action. This psychology in turn raises another problem, that of determinism and its apparent incompatibility with human freedom. Mill has an avowedly polemical purpose in maintaining that men are as much governed by natural laws as is any other part of nature; Mill's aim is to change society on the basis of our sociological and psychological knowledge. Yet if this knowledge presupposes that everything is determined, then it looks as if the practical aim is futile, while, should men be free to choose what the future is to be like and the practical aim is thus not futile, can there be any scientific certainty about the way they will behave? Mill's account—analyzed in Chapter VII, below—of how the dilemma is to be resolved always seemed to him one of the most successful parts of his philosophy; whether or not it is so, it has certainly been a popular and long-lived view.

Once it is established that there can be a science of man, it follows for Mill that there can be a science of man in society: sociology. Mill sets out to answer the question of what are its methods and aims. His reply reflects the influence of Newtonian physics on British philosophy ever since the days of Locke—of whose school Mill counted himself a member. Mill considers and rejects the extreme empiricism of what he calls the "chemical" method, a method associated particularly with Macaulay; he rejects also the excessively abstract and hypothetical approach of economics, which was typified by what he named the "geometrical" method of James Mill's *Essay on Government* (cf. Chap. VIII). Unsurprisingly, physics is the model for sociology, though with several modifications which are necessitated by the difficulty of securing the verification of sociological predictions and explanations (cf. Chap. IX). And the aim of sociology, at its grandest, is to reproduce in the social world the achievements of astronomy, Newtonian celestial mechanics, by plotting the trajectory of social progress (cf. Chap. X).

On the basis of the social sciences, Mill hopes to erect the "Art of Life," the rational ethics, prudence, and aesthetics.

The "Art of Life" is the prescriptive counterpart of the philosophy of scientific method; it is the philosophy of action rather than that of thought. In Mill's account of how this art is to be established, brief though this account is, it is plain that the same criteria of rationality are involved as are involved in the account of scientific explanation. The hallmark of rationality is to be able to deduce as many consequences as possible from as few principles as possible—ultimately indeed from the single principle of utility. But Mill makes it clear that ethics is not a science but an art, not a set of truths but a set of rules or prescriptions (cf. Chap. XI). This distinction between science and art makes the question of what Mill understood by proof in ethics an extremely difficult one. Nonetheless, Mill's belief that rationality in ethics involved deducing all one's principles from the single principle of utility can certainly be criticized both because it is impossible to perform some of the deductions, and also because there seems to be at least one other independent principle with which utility may conflict—a principle of justice (cf. Chap. XII). Ethics, in any event, was thought by Mill to consist only in the social portion of the Art of Life, and this leaves us with the question of what Mill thought were the ultimate goals of the art; the point of ethics is to maintain social life, but for Mill there were individual goals which it was the purpose of social life to leave us free to pursue. The relation between Mill's account of ethics and his conception of the individual's proper goals is the burden of the account of *On Liberty* with which I conclude this book (cf. Chap. XIII).

By way of introduction, it remains only to emphasize that the program is Mill's program; nothing in what I say is meant to answer the question whether any such attempt to link scientific rationality and moral rationality on the basis of an empiricist—or any other—metaphysics can be successful or not. I am clear in my own mind that many of Mill's arguments are inadequate; more importantly, one of his greatest failures, that over personal identity, lies at the heart of the metaphysics on which his system of ideas rests. Nor do I think that there is any obvious way of patching up Mill's system which will make it both systematic and persuasive. But I cannot persuade myself that it is incumbent on me to try; for in conformity with Mill's own experience I think that although much of what Mill says is best understood by placing it in his system, its value is that the parts are never less than interesting and are frequently both illuminating and correct.

NOTES

1. *Letters* (ed. Elliott), II, p. 375. 2. *Autobiography*, p. 158. 3. *Ibid.*
4. *Ibid.* 5. *Ibid.* 6. *System of Logic*, III, v, 1 ff. 7. *Autobiography*, p. 158. 8. *Ibid.* 9. *System of Logic*, II, iii, 4.

THE PHILOSOPHY OF
JOHN STUART MILL

I

THE DEDUCTIVE
CONCEPTION OF
EXPLANATION

It is not an original observation that Mill's account of what
it is to explain an occurrence or a natural law closely resembles what is probably the most popular current account,
that given in terms of the "hypothetico-deductive" model.
Hempel and Oppenheim, for instance, say of their own (itself
by now classical) statement of this position that: "The account
given above of the general characteristics of explanation and
prediction in science is by no means novel; it merely sum-
marises and states explicitly some fundamental points which
have been recognised by many scientists and methodologists." [1]
And the first name they cite is Mill's. Nicholas Rescher, criticizing the deductive model, places Mill among its defenders:
"According as naturally as it does with the mechanistic approach of classical Newtonian physics, the deductive conception of explanation rapidly established itself after the be-
ginnings of methodological consciousness in the second quar-
ter of the nineteenth century. Such illustrious thinkers as
Comte, Whewell, Mill, Jevons—in short most major nineteenth century theorists of scientific method—all supported
this conception of the nature of explanation." [2] This is quite
in keeping with the common view of Mill's place in the empiricist tradition, temporally between, and intellectually

rather below Hume and Russell. This placing of Mill in the "deductivist" tradition usually leads to two kinds of criticism. The first is of Mill's confusions and inadequacies by the standards of the best versions of this theory of explanation; the second is of this view of explanation itself and of Mill by implication. A more interesting criticism is of the placing itself, namely, that it fails to square with a good deal of what Mill said about inference and the role of generalizations.

But let us first characterize the basic tenets of the "hypothetico-deductive" account of scientific explanation. The only *essential* tenets are concerned with the deductive requirement; but a number of other views are commonly held concurrently. The essential tenets are these: to explain an individual occurrence it is both necessary and sufficient to produce a lawlike general statement and a statement of initial conditions which together entail the statement describing the occurrence to be explained. This is the requirement of formal adequacy. The material adequacy is secured by the requirement that the premises be true[3]—or at any rate well corroborated.[4] To explain a law, it is necessary and sufficient to find a more general law or several laws which entail the law in question. Popper summarizes the position: "To give a *causal explanation* of an event means to deduce a statement which describes it, using as premises of the deduction one or more *universal laws*, together with certain singular statements, the *initial conditions*.[5] A set of law statements is in turn to be explained by their deduction from a "new, a more general system of hypotheses."[6] This is substantially Braithwaite's definition of a science: "A scientific system consists of a set of hypotheses which form a deductive system; that is, which is arranged in such a way that from some of the hypotheses as premises all the other hypotheses logically follow."[7]

Mill's own account resembles that of Hempel[8] so closely that they even speak of the same example—save that where Hempel talks of a haystack being set on fire Mill talks less specifically of "a conflagration."[9] Mill's account is this: "An

5

individual fact is said to be explained by pointing out its cause, that is, by stating the law or laws of causation of which its occurrence is an instance. Thus a conflagration is explained when it is proved to have arisen from a spark falling into the midst of a heap of combustibles; and in a similar manner, a law of uniformity is explained when another law or laws are pointed out, of which that law itself is but a case, and from which it could be deduced." [10] To this Popper has objected that although "Mill's account of causal explanation is in the main quite acceptable," [11] Mill fails to distinguish between laws and initial conditions; but the passage cited [12] by Popper does not show this, even if it does show that Mill was careless in his use of the term "cause" when distinguishing them. For when Mill talks of the possibility of deducing all actual and future phenomena of nature from as few natural laws as possible, he is quick to point out that we should need to know not only the laws but "the collocations consisting in the existence of certain agents or powers, in certain circumstances of place and time." [13] In any case, Mill would hardly forget that a syllogism requires a minor premise.

Commonly, if not essentially, this account of explanation is accompanied by several further doctrines. One of these is that there is no such thing as inductive inference; that there is only one logic, and that is the logic of deduction. Popper takes perhaps the firmest stand on this, holding that there can be no "problem of induction," because there is no such thing as inductive inference. Braithwaite, more tolerantly, equates the "problem" with that of choosing sensible hypotheses, knowing how to reject bad ones and so on. Mill, of course, is notorious for having held idiosyncratic views about induction, as for example the view that there was no *non*-inductive inference. But before we tackle this issue, it is worth pointing out what Mill's views on this matter were when he reviewed Whately's *Elements of Logic* in 1828, at which time he came very close to endorsing the sort of view put forward by Popper. In his review Mill roundly denounces the Scottish

philosophers who had disparaged the value of the syllogism.
He says of them that they "fancied that it (the absurd part
of scholastic philosophy) was produced by the employment
of the syllogism in lieu of induction, and concluded that, in
order to avoid similar errors, it was necessary to discard the
syllogism, which they thought was one form of reasoning and
confine ourselves to induction, which they imagined was another." [14] But in this they were wholly mistaken, and fell
into an error which the schoolmen had avoided. For the
schoolmen saw clearly "that the process of philosophizing
consisted of two parts, the ascertainment of premises, and the
deduction of conclusions. They knew that the rules of the
syllogism concerned only the second part of the business
(which alone is properly called Reasoning), and could only
prevent them drawing conclusions which their premises did
not warrant, but could not furnish any test of the truth of
those original premises which were not deductions from any
prior truths. The evidence of these . . . was derived from
experience, and the process of the mind in attaining to them
was termed *induction.*" [15] The interest Mill had in maintaining this distinction sprang from two sources. In the first place
he was at that time arguing for the importance of deduction
in economics, where he thought its role was all-important;
and second, he had to champion the cause of his father's *Essay
on Government* against Macaulay's claims to inductive rectitude in the face of Mill's scholastic adherence to deductive
methods. But whatever the reasons behind it, Mill's adherence
to the view that there was no such thing as inductive reasoning was unswerving. "Syllogistic reasoning is not a *kind* of
reasoning, for *all* correct reasoning is syllogistic; and to *reason
by induction* is a recommendation which implies as thorough
a misconception of the meaning of the two words, as if the
advice were, to *observe by syllogism.*" [16] He praises Whately
for his attempt "to refute the error (fostered by the prevailing language on the subject) of supposing that mathematical
reasoning, and theological, and metaphysical, and political,

and moral, are so many different *kinds of reasoning*. Whereas what in reality is different in these different cases is not the *mode* of reasoning, but the nature of the premises, or propositions *from* which we reason." [17] To hold such a view is to be committed to a deductive account of explanation, since explanation is a form of reasoning, of evidential reasoning. If there is only one form of reasoning, then there can be only one form of explanation, and, we may add, of justification, however many ways there may be of arriving at the premises by means of which we explain or justify.

A second position, necessarily linked to the deductivist thesis, is that all causal explanations are implicitly universal. That is, the explanation of an event in terms of its cause makes implicit reference to a universal law. To explain the catching fire of the haystack in terms of the lighted match dropping onto it is to subsume this case under a law covering all cases like it. Behind all singular causal statements of the form "a caused b" is a general statement of the form "A-type events cause B-type events." Hempel states this lucidly: "the assertion of a causal connection between individual events seems to me unintelligible unless it is taken to make, at least implicitly, a nomological claim to the effect that there are laws which provide the basis for the causal connection asserted. When an individual event, say b, is said to have been caused by an antecedent event, say a, then surely the claim is intended that whenever 'the same cause' is realized 'the same effect' will recur. This claim cannot be taken to mean that whenever a recurs then so does b; for a and b are individual events at particular spatio-temporal locations and thus occur only once. Rather a and b are viewed in this context as particular events of certain *kinds*—e.g. the expansion of a piece of metal or the death of a person—of which there may be many future instances. And the law tacitly implied by the assertion that b, as an event of kind B, was caused by a, as an event of kind A, is a general statement of causal connection to the effect that, under suitable circumstances, an instance of

A is invariably accompanied by an instance of B." [18] The final sentence of this statement seems to equate causation with constant conjunction; but this is not a necessary concomitant of the deductive account of explanation, even if they are to-day constantly conjoined. In Mill's lifetime Whewell provided an example of one who both believed in the requirements of deductivity and held that causation involved more than constant conjunction. Mill, however, seems to subscribe exactly to Hempel's statement; while discussing the utility of syllogistic inference, he points out that a valid inference "will hold not merely in some individual case, but in all cases of a given description. . . . the experience which justifies a single prediction must be such as will suffice to bear out a general theorem." [19] And his initial statement about causation backs this up: "To certain facts, certain facts always do, and, as we believe, always will, succeed. The invariable antecedent is termed the cause; the invariable consequent, the effect." [20] Mill constantly talks of induction as a process of generalization, or establishing generalizations: "Induction may be defined, the operation of discovering and proving general propositions," [21] or again, "we shall . . . conformably to usage, consider the name Induction as more peculiarly belonging to the process of establishing the general proposition." [22] Of course, I wish to argue ultimately that this apparent identity of doctrine between Mill and later writers is *only* apparent; but it is important to see both that there are large areas of genuine agreement, and also that there is ample reason why most writers have been ready to assimilate Mill into the ranks of the deductivists without demur.

A feature of the deductive account of explanation which is certainly to be found in Mill is the emphasis that so many of its supporters place on the systematic character of science. It is not easy to characterize this emphasis briefly, for it consists in part of reports on what some areas of scientific inquiry have already achieved, in part of aspirations for other areas of inquiry, and in part of a metaphysical presupposition about what the universe must ultimately be like. But, roughly, the view is that a science aims at explaining as wide a range of phenomena as possible from as few initial assumptions as possible; these assumptions feature as axioms from which all more specific laws are to be deduced. This is not, as Nagel suggests,[23] a Laplacean dream from which Mill suffered unusually badly. It is the stated ambition of many of the most articulate and successful scientists. Nor does it seem to be an ambition contracted from unwise mingling with philosophers; it seems, rather, to have been an ambition which philosophers have made canonical after its realization by scientists—or at any rate its partial realization. The metaphysical view behind the ambition seems to be that a perfect theoretical structure would mirror the universe exactly, and that the universe must be so ordered that this is true. Mill says in this connection that the question which is the essential problem of the investigation of nature is: "What are the fewest assumptions which being granted, the order of nature as it exists would be the result? What are the fewest general propositions from which all the uniformities existing in nature could be deduced?"[24] Similarly, we find Einstein saying: "The supreme task of the physicist is to arrive at those universal elementary laws from which the cosmos can be built up by pure deduction."[25] In part this is *only* ambition, a hope that successful explanations for a wider range of phenomena can be found within an ever-simpler theory. But in part it *defines* scientific achievement; in Braithwaite's account, for instance, the existence of a system of logically linked hypotheses (with at some point testable conclusions) is what makes a science a science. It was a dominant attitude in Popper's *Logic of Scientific Discovery*, although he has now moved on to an ideal of change and constant progress which "may to some extent be contrasted with the current ideal of science as an axiomatized deductive system. . . I now believe that these most admirable deductive systems should be regarded as stepping stones rather than ends. . . ."[26] Curiously enough, his reasons for regarding them as essential stepping stones are very much the same as Mill's reasons for casting explanation in a syllogistic form: it is thus, and only thus, that we cast our theories into a testable form.[27]

Most of Mill's problems concern us later; in particular his account of causation and of inductive inference. But it is already time to raise some objections to his deductive theory, even at this simple level. The first is that Mill's account is *too* simple. He represents explanation as consisting in a straightforward deduction of *explanandum* from *explanans*. But it is doubtful whether it is often the absence of a covering law as *explanans* which holds up explanation. More often, surely, it is our ignorance of what factors are relevant, of what sort of explanation we want, even our inability to say quite *what* we want explained. It is not fair to state that Mill had nothing to say about this, for he discussed problems of classification, to take one example, at considerable length. But it is fair to say that he did not put the weight on such problems that he should have done; his discussion is tacked onto an account which it should modify but does not. There are two obvious explanations for this. In the first place he never met with any logic beyond that of the syllogism. Hence he never supposed, and could not have supposed, that any account of, for example, the derivation of one natural law from another should be given, more formal than the requirement that the explaining law should be "more general" [28] than the one explained. Again, he says that the law to be explained should be "a case of" the explaining law;[29] and this leaves it unclear whether the relation between them is an analytic one, or whether the transformation which makes it clear that one is a case of the other employs some non-analytic rule. The second point is that Mill has nothing much to say about the role of theories in science. Because of this he talks as if the question of what the circumstances are is always to be settled by more and more precise inspection; he ignores the fact that the way we describe them may depend on the theory we adopt to explain them. It is at least odd to regard the inverse square law, for example, as a straightforward generalization from observable phenomena such as the rising and setting of the sun; yet these phenomena are cases, if not *of* the law, at any rate governed *by* it. Later and more complicated accounts of deductivism avoid this sort of criticism; in presenting a rather elemental account Mill is persuasive of its merits—lucidity and simplicity—but extremely vulnerable to attack on its weaker flanks.

We may also object to Mill's insistence that to explain something is always to assign its cause. It is certainly true that in everyday explanation we want, for obvious reasons, to be told about causes; though even here it is not universally true. For instance, an explanation in dispositional terms is hardly a causal explanation and may nonetheless be satisfactory in the circumstances. Moreover, the relation between a more and a less general law is certainly not that the more general law is in any sense a cause of the less general. And in the physical sciences which were Mill's paradigms of what an explanatory system of laws should be, it is commonly the case that the causal explanation of singular events is not at issue. It would be silly to insist very strongly on this point, since Mill's use of the word "cause" is so varied that a charge of this kind would be impossible to press beyond all refutation. But it is perhaps fair to say that he should have done a great deal more to emphasize the oddity of assimilating our everyday causal explanations to those of a highly theoretical science.

This objection is not to be confused with one often made to a theory which Mill expressly repudiated, what we may term the "familiarization" theory of explanation, where an explanation is said to be such because it assimilates unfamiliar events to familiar ones, and thus renders us able to *see how it happened.* Certainly on this view the word "cause" is central, because everyday explanations so often involve showing what —or who—*made it happen.* But Mill is quite opposed to this account: "What is called explaining one law of nature by another, is but substituting one mystery for another. . . . The explanation may substitute a mystery which has become familiar, and has grown to *seem* not mysterious, for one which is still strange. And this is the meaning of explanation, in common parlance. But the process with which we are here concerned often does the very contrary; it resolves a phenomenon with which we are familiar, into one of which we previously knew little or nothing." [30] And the example he cites is that of explaining the fall of heavy objects by the universal law that all particles of matter mutually attract one another.

Even so, Mill still commits himself to some opinions which a modern deductivist would find unattractive. One instance is his assumption that a systematic account of the universe involves the discovery of laws of a strictly universal kind, of the form "All A are B" and rules out laws of the form "Most A are B." This, of course, reflects the undefended assumption that the universe is completely deterministic, which for Mill was not an assumption that was open to serious challenge. On the need in science for strictly universal laws he is quite uncompromising; he admits that in everyday life we may know only that most A are B, and he agrees that this may nonetheless be very useful information for practical purposes. But it will not do for science. To bring such laws into science it is essential to distinguish between the nine A that are B and the one that is not, to explain the difference by a genuine law of nature. "Proportions in the form, Most A are B, are of a very different degree of importance in science, and in the practice of life. To the scientific inquirer they are valuable chiefly as materials for, and steps towards, universal truths." [31] Mill is so confident of the existence of universal laws underlying "approximate generalizations" that he expects the latter in only two instances: where we have not yet reached an accurate classification of our subject matter, and where we cannot apply our knowledge of universal laws, so that although we know what distinguishes the A which are B from those which are not, we cannot apply the distinction. But what of cases where there seems no question of further explanation producing universal laws? Mill sees the problem posed for deductivism—that first, there can be no explanation of a particular event, and second: "Independently of the inferior precision of such imperfect generalizations, and the inferior assurance with which they can be applied to individual cases, it is plain that, compared with exact generalizations they are almost useless as means of discovering ulterior truths by way of deduction." [32] That is, from an approximate generalization of the form "Most A are B" nothing follows logically about this A, and where we are dealing with laws rather than particular cases, from several laws about a proportion, little or nothing can be deduced. Mill more or less presumes the irreducibility of statistical laws out of the way; not a unique stand in the history of this problem, when Einstein's dictum that God does not play dice does much the same.

But if Mill falls short of present-day standards in these various ways—formalization, consciousness of the role of theory, ability to accept statistical as well as universal laws—can deductivism eventually do very much better? This problem has become something of an ideological battlefield, and it is not surprising to see one deductivist claiming for the theory a kind of liberal rectitude in the face of philosophical "neo-obscurantism." [33] Here I do not intend to do more than discuss three issues: the first is whether the existence of theories does not ruin the deductive model; the second, whether the deductive model can allow for statistical explanations; the third, a more general question, whether the deductive model is not too rigid a pattern into which to force all explanation.

The way in which the existence of theories might be held to compromise the deductive account of explanation is this. As Toulmin[34] points out, the sort of statement which we make in a theory, such as, for example, that light travels in a straight line, is not the sort of statement which we discover to be true or false, as we might discover that it was true that the shadow cast by a forty-foot pole on a July day in England is about fifty-five feet long at ten o'clock in the morning. It does not seem to be any kind of generalization of the facts it is used to explain, and thus cannot stand in any very simple logical relation to them. In other words, there can be no syllogistic inference from the principle that light travels in a straight line to the length of the shadow which it explains. The inference proceeds via a translation of physical phenomena into Euclidean trigonometry. The light which is said to be "traveling" is "mapped" or "translated" into a line of no width, which, passing directly from the point that is its origin to the spot on the ground that is its other end, just touches the top of the pole. The "mapping" image is particularly natural here, because such theory-governed explanations are so often given in diagramatic form. The important point, then, is this: since the nonempirical terms involved in the theory are not those used in describing the empirical phenomena which are to be explained, there can be no deductive, syllogistic relations between them. Replies given by deductivists to this objection vary. Miss Brodbeck[35] holds that the objection is a miserable pun on the word "deductive"; if it means syllogistically derivable, then indeed there are few deductive explanations. It did mean this for Mill, so that he cannot benefit from any stretching of the term. But in any case, much of the point of the deductive theory of explanation is to provide a *standard* for the relation between *explanans* and *explanandum,* and the most rigorous standard is the sort of entailment relations which hold between the premises and the conclusion of a syllogism. Miss Brodbeck should be more careful of the enemy than this. A more conciliatory reply is to suggest ways in which we may *make* the explanation deductive, where deduction is still understood in the sense of syllogistic deduction. In effect the answer is to supply a major premise to the deduction. Nagel puts this at its simplest.[36] It is true that one can regard a man using a map to discover a route as engaged in nondeductive inference, employing the rules of projection of the map as his "inference-license"; and similarly a theory will furnish inference-licenses linking premise and conclusion of a nondeductive argument. But, the argument can be made deductive if we put the rule of inference as the major premise to it; thus we make our theory explicit as a premise in our explanation, and rely only on the rules of deductive reasoning. This Nagel thinks we should do.

The second difficulty, that of statistical explanation, is one which we have seen Mill refer to. His statement of the case against "approximate generalizations" is still unanswerable. In the first place, from a statistical law no particular conclusion logically follows. That is, "All A are B; this A is not B" are formally inconsistent, so that the whole sequent "All A are B; this is an A; so this is a B" is analytic. But "Most A are B; this A is not B" is *not* formally inconsistent, so that "Most A are B; this is an A; so this is a B" is not analytic. Since an argument pattern is either analytic and thus valid or not analytic and thus not valid, it seems that no explanation can be derived from statistical laws. Miss Brodbeck again takes a bold way out, and renounces all weak-kneed notions of merely probable inference. "From a statistical law, then, nothing can be predicted about an individual event. . . . neither can we explain an individual event by reference to such a law." [37] And this does not worry her, because "From statistical generalisations, we do not deduce 'with probability' that a certain event will occur, rather we deduce exactly the relative frequency or 'probability' with which an event will occur in a certain group." [38] But although Miss Brodbeck finds these "elementary matters" and "embarrassing to rehearse," it is not clear that she has got them right. It does not seem right to equate probability and relative frequency; we make statements about what will probably happen on the evidence of relative frequencies, but the statement we make on the *basis* of the statement of relative frequency is scarcely a mere rehearsal of it. Moreover, she is wrong to deny that we infer with probability, unless she means only that we cannot give mathematical values to the strength of the inference. She may, of course, take her stand on the word "deduce"; for if deduction in the tough sense is at issue, then certainly we cannot deduce with probability. Inferences are either valid or not. But in the nonformal sense of deduce, we do deduce with probability. Thus "Virtually everyone treated with penicillin gets over this" would license the patient to expect to recover, while "Almost no one has ever got over this, whatever steps we take" might not forbid hope, but would certainly daunt expectation. Yet the inference is not syllogistically deductive. We simply do infer with probability from approximate generalizations, and as Mill remarked: "To be indecisive and reluctant to act, because we have not evidence of a perfectly conclusive character to act upon, is a defect sometimes incident to scientific minds, but which, wherever it exists, renders them unfit for practical emergencies." [39] Moreover, the assertion that probable inference is not what it appears is a strange way to try to save deductivism. For the only set about which a deductive inference can be made from a statistical law is an infinite set; and statements about such a set seem indeed less like inferences from the law than a restatement of it.

As for the final question whether the deductive mold is one into which to force all explanation, this has in some degree been answered by our statement of the apparent difficulties in doing this. It is, however, worth remarking how little like a deductive explanation most explanations are. Take the familiar example of explaining the bursting of a car radiator after a severe frost; to reply to someone who asked why it had broken, that all radiators in such circumstances do so would not be much of an explanation. The explanation wanted is that which is couched in terms of water expanding when it freezes, and how water cannot be compressed so that if it expands, its container must expand with it or else burst; and since metal contracts when it gets colder, it is not possible for a car radiator to expand with the water; so that ultimately it will burst. Most explanations are histories of how things have happened; they relate sequences of events. In the majority of cases, the sense in which it is true that explanations do not necessarily tell us of a familiar sequence is not that they tell us of an unsuspected generalization; rather, it is that they get us to visualize the situation in a new way. So much more than simply producing a law covering the case in hand is needed for a good explanation that it is open to doubt whether the attention paid to law-covered explanation has been responsible for more light than darkness being shed on the subject. So, in the first place, we may say that the deductive form is not the natural form for an explanation, whereas the narrative form is, and that the deductive elements in the narration take a good deal of bringing out. Second, it is not clear that we can do this even in principle; we have seen the obstacle presented by the existence of theories and the need for some account of how these apparent nongeneralizations are related to the empirical statements they explain. Third, we have seen the obstacle presented by statistical laws which present the deductivist with the dilemma of denying the obvious truth that we do use such laws in explanation and prediction or else of admitting some kind of probable inference; this latter course is, obviously, equivalent to abandoning the requirements of deductivism. Fourth, it might be argued that the insistence on deductivity is heuristically useless, in that it concentrates attention on the formal properties common to explanation in any of a dozen different fields, whereas the philosophy of science would be better employed in bringing out the differences between the various kinds of inquiry. Lastly, it may be said that deductivity is not a logical requirement of explanation, but a dogma of empiricist metaphysics, which regards the achievements of Newton as definitive of scientific rationality. In this way, it is tied to the theories of the last scientific revolution and quite unable to visualize what a new revolution in scientific thought would involve. It is the failing of empiricist metaphysics to have chained itself irrevocably to one kind of science and to have done its best to petrify scientific invention.[40]

But, whatever the failings and merits of Mill as a deductivist; whatever the failings of deductivism as an account of scientific explanation; the point which most needs making is that there is the utmost difficulty in classing Mill as a deductivist at all. To do so without acknowledging the problems in the way would be to miss half the interest of Mill's philosophy of science. The obstacles to placing Mill squarely in the deductivist tradition stem largely from his account of reasoning in the second book of the *System of Logic*. To introduce these, one need only give a bald catalogue of Mill's utterances which run counter to the doctrines of the deductive school. The first point to give one pause is Mill's extended use of the term "logic." It was remarked earlier that in his review of Whately, Mill seemed to make a clear distinction between *deduction* and *induction*, and to be prepared to apply the term *"reasoning"* only to the former. But in the introduction to the *System of Logic* it becomes clear that logic, the "science and art of reasoning" is not concerned with formal inference alone, but with the most general principles involved in the search for truth. Logic is still "the science of Proof, or Evidence," [41] but proof and evidence are no longer the general statements which form the major premises of syllogisms, but the singular statements about particular facts which nondeductively support prediction and explanation. And in *Hamilton*, Mill attacks the view that formal logic is the only logic, and protests energetically against "the doctrine of Sir W. Hamilton, Mr. Mansel, and many other thinkers, that this part is the whole; that there is no other Logic, or Pure Logic, at all; that whatever is more than this belongs not to a general science and art of Thinking, but (in the words of Mr. Mansel) to this or that material science." [42] Mill proposes to go on using the word "logic" to describe the whole of the investigation on which are based the rules for judging accurately of the truth, on the ground that "what the Logic of mere consistency cannot do, the Logic of the ascertainment of truth, the Philosophy of Evidence in its larger acceptation, can. It can explain the function of the Ratiocinative process as an instrument of the human intellect in the discovery of truth." [43] That he subscribed to this view twenty-one years previously, at the time of the *System of Logic,* there is no doubt. In a footnote to the eighth edition he refers the reader to *Hamilton* for a defense of the theory behind his views, but says that he remains, practically speaking, "content that the justification of the larger extension which I gave to the domain of the science should rest on the sequel of the Treatise itself." [44]

The second blow to the view that Mill's allegiances lie with deductivism is his statement that "all inference is from particulars to particulars." [45] This strikes hard at the deductive/inductive dichotomy, and is quite opposed to the view that all reasoning consists of deductive inference involving general propositions. The third point is related; it is Mill's view of the place of statistical laws. Mill certainly does not wish them to have any place in science; but he sees their place in everyday life, and where they do occur, they do not render inference impossible, but make it, rather, a matter of "probable inference" instead of "certain inference." [46] This is again closely connected with Mill's celebrated view of the role of the general premise in a syllogism, to the effect that we do not reach the conclusion by "an inference drawn *from* the formula, but an inference drawn *according to* the formula." [47] This in essence is the view that the major premise is not a premise at all, but a material rule of inference—probable or certain. To the reasons behind these views and their consequences for Mill's theory of explanation we must now turn.

NOTES

1. Hempel and Oppenheim in Feigl and Brodbeck (eds.), *Readings in the Philosophy of Science*, p. 324n.   2. *Delaware Seminar for the Philosophy of Science*, p. 42.   3. Hempel and Oppenheim, *loc. cit.*, p. 322.   4. Popper, *Logic of Scientific Discovery*, pp. 251–54.   5. Popper, *Logic of Scientific Discovery*, p. 59.   6. *Ibid.*, p. 75.   7. Braithwaite, *Scientific Explanation*, p. 12.   8. *Minnesota Studies, Series III*, p. 105.   9. *System of Logic*, III, xii, 1.   10. *Ibid.*   11. Popper, *Poverty of Historicism*, p. 122.   12. *System of Logic*, III, xii, 1.   13. *Ibid.*, III, xii, 2.   14. *Westminster Review*, Vol. 9 (1828), p. 147.   15. *Ibid.*   16. *Ibid.*, p. 150.   17. *Ibid.*   18. *Minnesota Studies, Series III*, pp. 104–105.   19. *System of Logic*, II, iii, 5.   20. *Ibid.*, III, v, 2.   21. *Ibid.*, III, i, 2.   22. *Ibid.*, II, iii, 7.   23. Nagel (ed.), *Mill's Philosophy of Scientific Method*, pp. xl–xli.   24. *System of Logic*, III, xii, 6.   25. Einstein, *The World as I See It*, p. 125.   26. Popper, *Conjectures and Refutations*, p. 221.   27. *Ibid.*, p. 221, and *System of Logic*, II, iii, 5.   28. *System of Logic*, III, xii, 4.   29. *Ibid.*, III, xii, 5.   30. *Ibid.*, III, xii, 6.   31. *Ibid.*, III, xxiii, 2.   32. *Ibid.*   33. *Minnesota Studies, Series III*, p. 272.   34. Toulmin, *The Philosophy of Science*, pp. 23–28.   35. *Minnesota Studies, Series III*, pp. 262, 240.   36. *Mind* (1954), pp. 404–408.   37. *Minnesota Studies, Series III*, p. 248.   38. *Ibid.*   39. *System of Logic*, III, xxiii, 2.   40. Feyerabend in *Minnesota Studies, Series III*, pp. 91–95.   41. *System of Logic*, Introduction, 4.   42. *Examination of Hamilton*, p. 457.   43. *Ibid.*, p. 462.   44. *System of Logic*, Introduction, 7n.   45. *Ibid.*, II, iii, 3.   46. *Ibid.*, III, xxiii, 1.   47. *Ibid.*, II, iii, 4.

"REAL" INFERENCE

The reasons behind Mill's contention that, contrary to appearances, the major premise of a deductive argument is not a premise at all are to be found in his account of syllogistic inference. His difficulties with the syllogism were by no means novel; it had long been a criticism of the syllogism in Barbara that it involved a *petitio principii*. The difficulty that was felt arises in several ways, and is not easy to meet convincingly, for all that Mill's views on this subject have aroused an almost affectionate contempt. In one guise the problem seems to be psychological. A man asserts: "All men are mortal"; he believes it to be true, and in conjunction with the singular premise that he, John Smith, is a man, infers from it that he will die. But what did he believe, when he believed that "all men are mortal"? Did he believe that he, John Smith, was mortal? If he did not, then how could he have believed that *all* men were mortal? If he did, then how could he have *inferred* that he was mortal, since it seems that he believed it in the first place? If he did believe it in the first place, then it must have been part of the premises of his inference; it must have been used in proving itself and must thus have been the occasion of a *petitio principii*. Again, aside from the question of what a man believes, there is the problem of *proving* the particular statement which forms our conclusion. The general statement "All men are mortal" can only be exhaustively proved by finding out the truth of a great many particular statements: "Socrates was a man and was mortal"; "Cicero was a man and was mortal"; and so on. When this has been done for all the men there will ever be, the general statement will be proved true. But long before the general statement can be known to be true by such a method, the particular statements which we wish to prove will have been found to be true; in proving the mortality of all men by noting the mortality of each man, we shall, for example, note the mortality of Socrates quite early in our list. How then can we use the general statement to *prove* the singular statement? We seem, rather, to have used the fact of Socrates' mortality to prove the general statement; to go on and use the general statement to prove the singular would appear to be a *petitio*.

The problem about proof has another aspect; it is the problem of the meaning of general statements. John Smith, again, asserts that "all men are mortal." Among the men who have lived and died is, let us say, a Cantonese Hsang Hsiao who died in 1640, and of whose existence John Smith is quite unaware. Was John Smith *really* talking about this unknown Cantonese? If he was not, then what did he mean when he uttered the general statement? If we suppose that the meaning of the general statement rests in any simple way on the meaning of the singular statements which its utterer would be willing to assent to, then the meaning of the general statement must change with the knowledge of its different users. And it seems an unpalatable consequence to allow the meaning of a statement to vary in this subjective fashion. Again, says Mill, we have the problem of a purely deductive science such as geometry where it is said that the conclusions, though perhaps unknown for centuries, are nonetheless contained in the axioms, or premises, of the subject. In what sense can the conclusions of geometry, or any other deductive science, be said to be "contained" in the premises?

Mill had, in passing, raised the question when reviewing Whately, but had at that time not pressed his objections. In the *System of Logic* he brings Whately more firmly to book, and puts his difficulties with extreme clarity and persuasiveness. A few sentences will serve to give the drift of the argument. "It must be granted that in every syllogism, considered as an argument to prove the conclusion, there is a *petitio principii*. . . . it is unanswerably urged by the adversaries of the syllogistic theory, that the proposition, Socrates is mortal, is presupposed in the more general assumption, All men are mortal: that we cannot be assured of the mortality of all men, unless we were previously certain of the mortality of every individual man: . . . that, in short, no reasoning from generals to particulars can, as such, prove anything, since from a general principle we cannot infer any particulars, but those which the principle itself assumes as foreknown." [1] And, again: "When Archbishop Whately, for example, says that the object of reasoning is 'merely to expand and unfold the assertions wrapt up, as it were, and implied in those with which we set out, and to bring a person to perceive and acknowledge the full force of that which he has admitted,' he does not, I think, meet the real difficulty requiring to be explained, namely, how it happens that a science, like geometry, *can* be all 'wrapt up' in a few definitions and axioms. . . . When you admitted the major premiss, you asserted the conclusion, but, says Archbishop Whately, you asserted it by implication merely: . . . you did not know you were asserting it; but, if so, the difficulty arises in this shape—Ought you not to have known?" [2] The usual response to this kind of objection is to see it as the regrettable effect of confusing psychological and logical considerations. Objections to the syllogism couched in terms of what people think they are doing are wholly misguided; the force of an assertion is not psychological but logical, so that the meaning of a general statement rests on the formal rules enshrined, for instance, in the predicate calculus. The question of whether people are startled by the conclusions of deductive inferences is wholly irrelevant to the question of whether the inference is valid. But such a response is less than satisfying, even if we have ultimately to accept it as substantially right. For there is indubitably an asymmetry between general statements and singular statements, which requires some explanation. A singular statement is readily explicable as a more or less complicated elaboration of pointing to a subject of interest and saying something about it; the pointing and describing involved in, say, "John Smith is wearing his hat" is readily understood. But where the subject is not John Smith, but "all men," the pointing and describing explanation is not available; surely there is a legitimate question to be asked of how it can be that a general statement can be said to be true or false—or even meaningful—in the face of this asymmetry.

Let us, therefore, begin by giving an account of what Mill takes to be involved in *real* inference; we can then show how this meets some of the difficulties of the deductive account of explanation; and we may ultimately draw some conclusions about which account we should say was really Mill's theory of explanation. Mill's description of real inference can scarcely be stated more lucidly than it is stated by him; the problem posed, he goes on: "From this difficulty there appears to be but one issue. The proposition, that the Duke of Wellington is mortal, is evidently an inference; it is got as a conclusion from something else; but do we, in reality, conclude it from the proposition, All men are mortal? I answer, no." [3] That is, we do not infer *from* the major premise of the syllogism, for by the time we assert the major premise we have done all the discovering and inferring that there is to be done. But here we must note a confusion implicit in Mill's view of what inference is; and this is a confusion which certainly tends to justify the belief that psychological and logical issues are muddled. Mill is not careful to distinguish between inference as a simple leap of expectation and inference as a process of proof. Thus, he says of children and animals that they infer or reason: "The child, who, having burnt his fingers, avoids to thrust them again into the fire, has reasoned or inferred, though he has never thought of the general maxim, Fire burns. . . . In the same way, also, brutes reason. . . . animals profit by experience, and avoid what they have found to cause them pain, in the same manner, though not always with the same skill, as a human creature. Not only the burnt child, but the burnt dog, dreads the fire." [4] And a similar opening for ambiguity is left by Mill's use of the word "proof." Here the problem is partly psychological in aspect, but partly also epistemological. The syllogism is only held to be circular when it is thought of as an argument to *prove* the conclusion.[5] It seems that the *real* proof has to be something which the person drawing the inference knows about already; or perhaps, only that the person could in principle have known about already. Psychologically, it appears that the process of proof can only be exercised on the existing contents of the mind; epistemologically, that only what has already happened can feature in the evidence. The reason behind this is that knowledge is assimilated to perception, so that only what has happened can in this sense be part of what is known; no future events can be known in this way, since they are manifestly not susceptible of current observation. The link between this view of proof, and Mill's account of real inference is simply that real inference must lead us from the known to the unknown.

Having asserted that we do not reason from the general premise in a syllogism, Mill explains how we do reason. The answer is that "All inference is from particulars to particulars: General propositions are merely registers of such inferences already made, and short formulae for making more: The major premiss of a syllogism, consequently, is a formula of this description; and the conclusion is not an inference drawn *from* the formula, but an inference drawn *according* to the formula; the real logical antecedent or premiss being the particular facts from which the general proposition was collected by induction." [6] In a universe which consists only of particular events, particular facts, it must be these that form our evidence; we cannot observe anything other than particular events, we cannot know anything other than particular facts, so that we cannot reason from anything but particular facts. A general statement, however, is not simply a short way of stating our evidence, not a shorthand utterance of many singular statements, although for a moment it seems that Mill is about to say that this is what it is: "for a general truth is but an aggregate of particular truths; a comprehensive expression, by which an indefinite number of individual facts are affirmed or denied at once." [7] But he at once goes on to correct any false impressions: "But a general proposition is not merely a compendious form for recording and preserving in the memory a number of particular facts, all of which have been observed. Generalization is not a process of mere naming; it is also a process of inference." [8] And a little later the recording or shorthand element in the generalization becomes even less important. "Those facts, and the particular instances which supplied them, may have been forgotten, but a record remains, not indeed descriptive of the facts themselves, but showing how those cases may be distinguished, respecting which, the facts, when known, were considered to warrant a given inference." [9] The general statement is thus a kind of warrant, allowing us, for example, rationally to expect mortality wherever we meet with human beings, whether now, or in future, or in the remote past. It is also a claim that the evidence for this warrant is adequate in various ways, in particular in that there has never been observed a case where humanity was conjoined with immortality. No information is given about the mortality of particular men; so the general statement is not in this sense decomposable into singular descriptive statements at all.

Given that this is the way to analyze general statements, the question now arises, whether general statements are in any sense indispensable to an argument or explanation. It is clear to Mill that they are not *logically* indispensable at any rate. If the real proof that the Duke of Wellington is mortal is the mortality of those who have resembled him in being human, it cannot be necessary to assert the general proposition as well as the singular ones. "The mortality of John, Thomas, and company, is, after all, the whole evidence we have for the mortality of the Duke of Wellington. Not one iota is added to the proof by interpolating a general proposition. Since the individual cases are all the evidence we can possess, evidence which no logical form into which we choose to throw it can make greater than it is: and since that evidence is either sufficient in itself, or, if insufficient for the one purpose, cannot be sufficient for the other; I am unable to see why we should be forbidden to take the shortest cut from these sufficient premisses to the conclusion." [10] But though the intermediate generalization cannot be necessary as a part of the logic of inference, there are so many advantages in using generalizations in arguments as to make them practically indispensable. Mill compares generalizations to a vantage point at the top of a hill: "There may be a resting point at the top of the hill, affording a commanding view of the surrounding country." [11] Again, they afford a useful route to travel by, if not the only one. The metaphor of the vantage point is cashed by Mill very explicitly. We use generalizations, and deductive arguments, as a *check* on our inferences. In the first place, they remind us what we are committed to; if we argue from the Duke of Wellington's humanity to his mortality, we are committed to a like inference in any like case: "whenever, from a set of particular cases, we can legitimately draw any inference, we may legitimately make our inference a general one. . . . the experience which justifies a single fact must be such as will bear out a general theorem. This theorem it is extremely important to ascertain and declare in its broadest form of generality, and thus to place before our minds, in its full extent, the whole of what our evidence must prove if it proves anything." [12] Mill does not explain why, if all inference is from particulars to particulars, we are nevertheless committed to general statements which we may never have heard of—which, of course, in the case of animals there is no possibility of their ever hearing of. It seems on the face of it to be exactly the converse of the problem of how we can be committed to singular statements we have never thought of, when we utter a general proposition. There are a number of possible explanations, though Mill never explicitly acknowledges a problem to be solved. We might argue that our statements are statements of causal connection, and that all causal statements are generalizations, if only implicitly. In the way of doing this, however, lies the fact that our grounds for saying that all causal statements were implicitly general was formerly that they were what explained particular cases, that is, were covert major premises of deductive arguments. Now that the major premise has been drastically reinterpreted, we no longer have that ground for thinking that causal statements are essentially general. A possibility canvassed by Mill is that "the general principle offers a larger object to the imagination." [13] This, though, is either a strange piece of psychology, or else is a reiteration of the point that we can only explicitly set about falsifying prospective inference rules, if we first make these rules explicit—so that, for instance, a man who concluded from the lives of the Antonines that Commodus was a good emperor, could make his inference rule explicit, perhaps "All Roman Emperors were good emperors," and see that this would allow the false conclusion that Nero was a good emperor. This, however, is a point about the *usefulness* of generalizations, and not about the problem of whether we are *logically* committed to them.

The confusion must, I think, lie in Mill's ambiguities about the nature of inference. We have seen that he asserted, and with obvious polemical intent, that brutes can reason. This needs looking at. The brute undoubtedly learns from experience, as does the as yet inarticulate child; it learns new things, and some of its expectations can no doubt be reversed by further experience. Is this sufficient to entitle the learning process to the name of *reasoning* or *inference*? It might seem to be a piece of human arrogance to insist that the possession of complex linguistic abilities is required before the ascription of reason can be meaningful; but the case for insisting on these is extremely strong. When the dog in Pavlov's experiments hears the bell ring, the animal's mouth waters; and we may say the dog expects food to arrive shortly. If the dog were to expect the food on the basis of a belief in the causal sequence bell-food, then presumably the dog would abandon this belief the first time the bell rang without food following; and manifestly the dog does not behave in any way compatible with such a thought-process taking place. The dog simply goes on salivating when the bell rings, until in the absence of reinforcement the response fades. In a case like this, we can say, we have good reason for denying that the dog has done any inferring at all, because of the way the animal reacts to what would be for a rational being a falsifying instance for the inference rule on which he had been basing his expectations. But could there be a case where we had anything resembling adequate evidence for thinking that the animal had been acting according to reasons? Short of it being able to utter some kind of general proposition, I do not think there could be. Without a language, there seems no way to distinguish between mere expectation and rational expectation; and inference is essentially a process of justifying expectation rationally. Mill sees something of the problem; in discussing the case of a man who can produce marvelous results by dying cloth with dyes mixed by the handful, he agrees that it is a great drawback that the man cannot communicate the theory he is employing; he appeals to a distinction which is almost Aristotle's distinction between *science* and *experience* to point out how indispensable are general instructions which can be framed for everyone to follow. But the defect in *experience* is still the contingent one that the rule of inference actually being followed cannot be communicated. However, we may suppose it is rather more than that. For, if no rule is framed, then the concept of *evidence* has only a very slender foothold here. If a man makes some prediction, and gives as his reason for the prediction, not a general statement, but a number of particular facts between which we can see no connection at all, how can we know that he has reasons? If neither he nor we can say what the connection is, can we say that there is a process of inference involved at all? Many writers would be inclined to say not. Mill, I think, would probably have been unmoved by this criticism. Certainly, he has no room to concede it, for it would make it essential to *produce* a rule of inference, which must be a general statement, and it is a minimum of Mill's case that we should allow as an inference a case where no rule is explicitly given. It might well be possible to save Mill's account, moreover, with an adequate theory of how people and intelligent animals can be said to recognize similar cases, on behavioral criteria, and how these behavioral reactions are the basic elements of linguistic classifying and inferring. Such an account would meet the objection that the ability to produce rules of evidence is essential for the ascription of inferential powers.

In any case, in the examples with which Mill is concerned, there is no doubt that we are dealing with a process properly described as inference; the problem is how we are to explain the process. And, for the most part, Mill's account makes perfectly good sense. Inference is both general and particular; a man may thus reason from particulars to particulars, committing himself to a rule of inference which he may have infinitely greater skill in employing than in articulating. To deny that he is inferring something would be perverse; to require him to produce his rules of inference, hopeless. A man says it will rain today, and gives as his evidence that there were such-and-such signs; the particulars he is reasoning from may be something like the fact that last Friday the rabbits were keeping close to their warren, the wind was blowing strongly from the west, and so on, and that this had happened two days before that, and again a few days earlier, and on every occasion rain followed. The prediction that it will rain is certified by the material rule of inference to the effect that we may expect rain shortly after such signs. The particularity of the explanation for the forthcoming rain lies in the particularity of the facts cited as evidence; the generality, in the fact that they are only cited as being relevant in certain respects; last Friday, for example, may have been the day the cat drowned in the milk churn; but we do not cite this as evidence. Resemblance between last Friday and today is resemblance *in some respect*, and to cite a respect is to use a universal or general name. In thus citing a universal as related to another universal, we commit ourselves, if defeasibly, to a general statement. But particulars in a sense come first, since the primitive form of citing a universal is just to indicate several individuals and say "like them." A farmer judging that there will be a good harvest is committed to making the same judgment in the same circumstances, even where he cannot *say* quite how they are the same. The commitment to a general principle is thus not a commitment to knowing a general principle; so that the psychological problem as we described it is not insuperable; and the logical problem can be solved on an adequate theory of universals. Mill, in any case, is concerned to have us make our rules of inference quite explicit; to be rational involves at least subjecting our associations of ideas to analysis, and this can be done only by making our inferential habits articulate. This is the point of the syllogism; and in view of the enormous importance Mill attached to analyzing our natural associations, he cannot be accused of having disparaged the syllogism in assigning it this role.

The "logic of consistency" is thus rescued by Mill's account; so successfully on Mill's own terms that there is no reason to wonder at the unending insistence on the virtues of deductivism which fills the *System of Logic*. Consistency is obviously of the greatest importance; if we intend to state the truth about any set of facts, we are doomed to failure if we utter two inconsistent statements about them. Yet, it is not so very easy to avoid inconsistency; if we do not take care to make explicit what we are already committed to, we may easily contradict ourselves; in arguing from particular to particular we may be forcefully struck by some fortuitous feature of a new particular and fail to see that we have a case which our rule ought to cover, which either *is* covered, or which falsifies our rule. Superstitions plainly thrive because no one recognizes counterinstances to them. Where, too, there is any complicated transition from evidence to prediction, especially where evidence and conclusion are separated by space and time, or are otherwise dissimilar, it is plainly impracticable to recall particular cases save by general principles. For all that, the important point to emphasize is that the logic of consistency is only a weapon in the armory of the logic of truth. General principles are only a support for our explanations and inferences to the extent that the particular cases we observe are such. Or as Bambrough says: "All reasoning, including all mathematical, scientific, and moral reasoning, is ultimately concerned with particular cases, and laws, rules, principles are devices for bringing particular cases to bear on other particular cases. . . . They are invaluable and indeed *practically* indispensable, but they are not *logically* indispensable. They depend on the particular cases, and the particular cases do not depend on them." [14]

After such an account of the role of the syllogism, we clearly cannot any longer assimilate Mill to the deductivist school of thought, at any rate in the confident way we first seemed able to do. When Mill argues that the "major premise" of the syllogism is not a *premise* of inference, but a *rule* of inference, his place is, rather, with Toulmin who talks of laws and theories as "techniques of inference." [15] The first question, then, which we ought to ask is how much difference Mill's "inference license" account makes to his "deductivist" account. In brief, are they completely incompatible accounts? Leaving aside what Mill says about real inference, it seems that Nagel is right when he says that any argument written

informally with a material rule of inference can be written formally, depending on formal rules of inference only. Thus, to take an argument which is used as an example by Toulmin, we argue: "Harry was born in Bermuda, so Harry is a British subject," using the material rule of inference that persons born in Bermuda are British subjects. Schematically, this appears as: "Data   →   So Conclusion" [16] But this can
Since Warrant
equally well be written out as a straightforward syllogism, with the warrant featuring as the major premise: "W, and D, so C." In other words, "All persons born in Bermuda are British subjects; Harry was born in Bermuda; so Harry is a British subject." And this is simply a rewriting of the other argument. The reason why we can rewrite in this way is simple enough; wherever the inference from data to conclusion is a certain inference, this must be because the data and the warrant together logically imply the conclusion; in other words it is because the argument can be turned into a valid syllogism. Mill saw this, as is evidenced by his account of what our evidence must be able to prove, and his emphasis on inconsistency as the enemy of inference rules. But he goes astray, through a misguided attempt to solve the problem of the syllogism twice. Had Mill been content to argue that the relation between the major premise and the conclusion of a syllogism was not the same as the relation between the actual evidence and the conclusion, he would have been in safe waters. But he will not leave well alone, even going to the length of objecting to the dictum *de omni et nullo* because it is a tautology. "We must consider it not as an axiom but as a definition; we must look upon it as intended to explain, in a circuitous and paraphrastic manner, the meaning of the word *class*." [17] He does not see, that is, that it has to be a tautology, if the syllogism is to be employed as a test of inconsistency; as he himself points out with some care, it is not between the statements about particular cases of humanity-with-mortality and the statement that the Duke of Welling-

ton is both human and immortal that inconsistency lies; it lies only between the statement that the Duke of Wellington is a man and immortal and the statement that *all* men are mortal.[18]

There are, however, some good grounds for arguing the case which Mill chiefly wants to argue, namely, that there are points about the actuality of inference which the syllogistic, linguistic clothing masks. The point of writing arguments out in the "rule of inference" mode is largely heuristic; indeed it could scarcely be anything else, given that the argument of the previous paragraphs is correct. We can by writing out arguments in this form make them *display* their important features. So, for instance, we argue: "The Duke of Wellington is a man, so he must be mortal." Having said that the Duke *must be* mortal, we presumably think that the inference is quite certain. This it can only be in virtue of a certifying rule of inference—"All men are mortal"—which necessitates the conclusion being true. But we might have argued: "Jones has been given penicillin, so he'll probably get better." Now, we have already seen that there can be no deductive probable inference, so that an argument like this cannot be turned into a valid syllogism. But we can apply the notion of a probabilifying rule of inference—"Most people treated with penicillin get better"—as Mill certainly seemed to realize. For he says: "As every certain inference respecting a particular case, implies that there is ground for a general proposition, of the form, Every A is B, so does every probable inference suppose that there is ground for a proposition of the form, Most A are B." [19] Thus we may imagine Mill as likely to have been sympathetic to the view that his account does justice to the actual force of arguments. Nonetheless, it cannot be a conclusive argument on his behalf, since on this heuristic point, someone might want to argue that the whole point of *not* admitting a "rules of inference" account is to rule out anything other than certain inference, to distinguish absolutely between certainty and probability.

The second heuristic point which might be made is that this picture allows us to distinguish clearly between the backing for our rules of inference and the rules themselves. Both of these might be expressed as "All A is B," but whereas the rule of inference is a nomological general statement, the backing statement can only be an enumerative statement, a point which emphasizes the well-known distinction between statements such as "All the balls in this box are white" and "All bodies gravitate toward each other." In Mill's epistemology, I believe this point has a good deal of significance. For Mill, propositions are in some sense pictures of the facts they describe, or mirror. It is not possible to argue that Mill held a fully explicit picture theory of meaning, but his account of meaning has a strong picture element in it, especially in the account as it appears in *Hamilton*. Now this means that nonenumerative general statements cannot be pictures in any very simple way; the world is made up of particulars, and there are no "all-" anythings to be depicted. So general statements must be something else, and much the most plausible candidate is that they are rules for making new pictures out of old ones. Even if the ascription to Mill of a picture theory is thought dubious, the standard Berkeleian account of meaning in terms of the word's capacity for arousing ideas gives ample ground for such an account. In the same way that statements about "nobody" cannot be quite what they seem, neither can statements about "all" whatever it is; they cannot be literally "about" the nonentities in question. For general propositions, an instrumentalist view is much the most appealing.[20]

Another point which gives us grounds for supposing that there were epistemological considerations behind Mill's account of the syllogism emerges when we consider his account of causation. To put it briefly, he offers one account in terms of uniformities, and a second in terms of tendencies. If propositions are to be in any sense pictures, it is reasonable to suppose that tendencies would be mirrored more readily by rules of inference than by enumerative general statements; enumerative general statements, on the other hand, would mirror uniformities. For uniformities just are lots of single events; tendencies are not. Enumeratively, general statements are conjunctions of singular statements; rules of inference are not. And this connects very closely with a third epistemological point. If causal laws state tendencies, then what scientists observe is not the nonexistent subject of nomological general statements. What scientists see is a set of particular events; what they predict is more of the same kind of thing. These are our *real* premises and our *real* conclusions, for they are the stuff of the universe. All the observables are particulars; existing at particular places and at particular times. So general statements must be something over and above these statements of particular facts. They must be rules of inference, pictures of pathways among the individual events; if they appear as premises, their point is lost.

The final point that we might make in favor of the "rule of inference" account is one made by Toulmin.[21] It focuses our attention on the differences between different sorts of inquiry. The man reading his map *travels* with its aid; the man applying moral rules *comes to a decision* on their basis. So we might argue that the way to understand a particular inquiry, the way to understand the kind of rationality which is involved in it, is to see how it actually proceeds, to see what sorts of informal inference it uses. To such an argument Mill would have been unreservedly hostile. The epistemological point about inference and generalization having once been made, Mill was thereafter anxious to see systematization, the reduction of one kind of science to another kind, the unification of science. The danger of an argument like Toulmin's would have struck Mill at once; it is an intellectually conservative position, and it is perhaps less surprising than it might have seemed at first sight that Toulmin who shares so many of Mill's views should never acknowledge the fact, should in fact disparage him in praising Whewell.[22] For

Mill's point was simple. System and formalization are the two great enemies of pseudo-science. The great merit of casting theories into a deductive shape is that without this systematization rival explanations cannot be seen to be incompatible. And if we are right in arguing that there is no logical inconsistency in Mill's stressing the importance of deductivity alongside his account of "real" inference, it is hardly to Mill's discredit that he saw clearly that the system he had to create was one which we cannot simply assign to either of the current camps. To understand Mill as an "inductivist" it is essential to see him in something other than these anachronistic terms.

NOTES

1. *System of Logic*, II, iii, 2.   2. *Ibid.*   3. *Ibid.*, II, iii, 3.   4. *Ibid.*   5. *Ibid.*, II, iii, 2.   6. *Ibid.*, II, iii, 4.   7. *Ibid.*, II, iii, 3.   8. *Ibid.*   9. *Ibid.*, II, iii, 4.   10. *Ibid.*, II, iii, 3.   11. *Ibid.*   12. *Ibid.*, II, iii, 5.   13. *Ibid.*   14. Bambrough, "Principia Metaphysica," *Philosophy* (1964), p. 100.   15. Toulmin, *The Philosophy of Science*, pp. 17–30.   16. Toulmin, *The Uses of Argument*, p. 99.   17. *System of Logic*, II, ii, 2.   18. *Ibid.*, II, iii, 4.   19. *Ibid.*, III, xxiii, 1.   20. Popper, *Conjectures and Refutations*, pp. 107–114.   21. Toulmin, *The Uses of Argument*, cf. Chap. V *passim*.   22. *Ibid.*, pp. 249, 259.

III

INDUCTION AND
ITS CANONS

The task of explaining Mill's canons of inductive logic is one which is incumbent upon us, whether we regard natural laws as the major premises of deductive arguments or as the rules of inference of nondeductive arguments. If they are viewed as premises, the question is: How are we to discover true major premises in the form of laws of nature? If they are viewed as rules of inference, the question is: How are we to discover valid rules of inference in the form of laws of nature? With the important exception of Mill's remarks about the law of universal causation, there is nothing in Mill's account of the inductive canons to make us choose between the premise and the rule-of-inference view. If we were right in arguing that the views are not contradictory, then there ought not to be. To test an inference license is to test the licensed conclusions against the facts; to test a major premise is to check the conclusions deduced from it against the facts. Mill's definition of induction is that it is the "establishment of general propositions," [1] which does not prejudge the nature of the general proposition one way or the other.

One preliminary objection should be met before we discuss Mill's account of inductive logic. It is Popper's objection that there can be no such thing, since all logic is deductive. What has led scientists and philosophers astray is that they have confused the question of how we *think of* a hypothesis with that of how we *test* it; the latter process alone is of interest to the philosopher of science, and the latter process is deductive. It may be of interest to a psychologist that a scientist produced a new hypothesis by free association rather than by a series of guesses; but the philosopher has no professional interest in the matter. And at first sight, it looks as though Mill does make precisely this error, as though he does try to give rules for inventing hypotheses. Thus he says: "Induction may be defined, the operation of discovering and proving general propositions." [2] Given the psychological flavor of much of the second book of the *System of Logic,* does it not follow that he was very probably making just this mistake? In fact, the answer is that he certainly was not and, indeed, that Popper's objection is misleading. On a falsificationist analysis—and *only* on a falsificationist analysis—natural laws are thought of as *hypotheses;* and clearly the only sense to be given to discovering a hypothesis is that of inventing it. But, of course, no one supposes that induction is a way of inventing hypotheses; for if we take the view, which Mill certainly took, that generalizations cannot merely be not known to be false, but can be known to be true, it follows that discovering general propositions is not a matter of inventing anything, but a process of finding out *true* statements about the world, or *valid* inference licenses. Mill's statement of what induction is may be a pleonasm, but is certainly not a confusion. Moreover, Mill is quite clearly forearmed against the very danger Popper sees, for when he is discussing the problem of how scientists invent hypotheses capable of accounting for the observed facts, he says: "Success is here dependent on natural or acquired sagacity, aided by knowledge of the particular subject and of subjects allied with it. Invention, though it can be cultivated, cannot be reduced to rule; there is no science which will enable a man to bethink himself of that which will suit his purpose." [3]

However, thinking in terms of hypotheses is usually far from Mill's mind. He has an almost Aristotelian tendency to identify generality and certainty;[4] and he never ceases to stress the need to arrive at certain natural laws. He certainly would not have been content with a merely undisproved hypothesis; science aims at proof. Whewell had stressed the importance of hypotheses, since Whewell's concept of induction was strikingly like Popper's, save for the crucial difference that the eventual result of falsifying hypotheses was supposed to be that one hypothesis would remain as a necessary truth, an intuition of the underlying order of the universe. Mill derived a great deal of help from Whewell's writings,[5] but was more than ready to bite the hand that fed him when it came to the question of proof. Thus he says of Whewell: "He allows of no logical process in any case of induction other than . . . guessing until a guess is found which tallies with the facts; and accordingly he rejects all canons of induction, because it is not by means of them that we guess. Dr. Whewell's account of the logic of science would be very perfect if it did not pass over altogether the question of Proof." [6] Whewell, in leaving out the stage of proof, leaves out what Mill considers to be the whole point of science: arriving at the truth; hypotheses aim at being true laws of nature, and of course Mill will not for a moment accept any sort of truth which seems to depend on the capacity of our minds, as the intuitionist theory does.

Mill's experimental methods, then, are designed to prove natural laws to be true. They do this by establishing causal connections between events, and are thus canons of causal inquiry. Thus their study contributes to the answer to the question of what Mill thought was involved in a statement like "A is the cause of a." Since Von Wright's admirable discussion[7] of the methods, his view has prevailed that they form a logic designed to test for sufficient conditions. The reasons behind this view are sound and compelling. Mill's discussion of plurality of causes, for instance, is only compatible with a cause being a sufficient condition: "Many causes may produce mechanical motion; many causes may produce some kinds of sensation; many causes may produce death. A given effect may really be produced by a certain cause, and yet be perfectly capable of being produced without it." [8] Nonetheless, it will emerge in what follows that Mill's account of the experimental methods is incompatible with an account of causes as sufficient conditions alone. We may make a number of suggestions as to what underlies this apparent confusion; but it cannot be very confidently said that the confusion is wholly eliminable.

A second point about the canons concerns Mill's manner of exposition. It has been objected that both the notation employed and the arguments used by Mill are ludicrously oversimple. Even where judgments are not so harsh, it is often said that "without guiding ideas required for working the methods, but not provided by them, the methods are helpless to advance an inquiry. On the other hand . . . once such guiding ideas have been found for analyzing the specific problems under investigation, perhaps the most essential step in the discovery of new truths has been taken." [9] This is, perhaps, not quite fair since Mill devotes quite a portion of the third and almost the whole of the fourth book of the *System of Logic* to the problem of how we are to cast our experimental situations into the atomistic form which the methods presuppose. It is, at any rate, not surprising that Mill should choose to state the methods as if they dealt with the wholly known and atomically organized world which he in many ways saw science as revealing.

A final preliminary question is that of what the methods as stated by Mill are seen as doing. The standard account of the methods is that they are eliminative and deductive; and there seems every reason for proceeding on this assumption, which has Mill's backing. For he agrees with Whately that "every induction is a syllogism with the major premiss suppressed," [10] and he certainly sets out his arguments in this way. So, I shall make no attempt to link the methods with Mill's account of inference in general until after this more orthodox exposition.

Mill heads the chapter on the inductive canons: "Of the Four Methods of Experimental Inquiry" [11] but goes on, in fact, to produce five canons and five methods; nor is it obvious which is excluded from the official count. It might be the Method of Residues, which is said to be "not independent of deduction," [12] were it not that it is explicitly included in the sentence preceding. Probably it is the Joint Method of Agreement and Difference that is omitted, since it is, after all, the Method of Agreement used twice over. At any rate, like Mill, we shall expound the four methods as five. The first of them is the Method of Agreement: "If two or more instances of the phenomenon under investigation have only one circumstance in common, the circumstance in which alone all the instances agree is the cause (or effect) of the given phenomenon." [13] Two sets of antecedents ABC and ADE have two sets of consequents *a b c* and *a d e*. Suppose we wish to know what the effect of A is. It cannot be *b, c, d, e;* for, in one or other of the instances, A was present and they were not; it must be *a*, since that one of the consequents is the one common to both sets. Now, for the purposes of this inquiry it seems that a cause is certainly a sufficient condition, since what we have eliminated is the possibility that A was sufficient to produce *b, c, d, e.*

But Mill argues rather differently, when arguing that it must be A that is the cause of *a,* because he argues: "The phenomenon *a* cannot have been the effect of B or C since it was produced where they were not; nor of D or E since it was produced where they were not." [14] What this means, however, is that they have been eliminated as necessary conditions of *a*, not as sufficient ones; as a method of eliminating sufficient conditions it is extremely weak. A believer in a plurality of causes cannot argue that any of the antecedents has been eliminated at all. For example, if the antecedent A is the fact that it is raining, while B is the administering of a dose of poison to a man, and D is the firing of a bullet into the heart of that man, then if *a* is simply described as a case of death, we are highly unlikely to say that it was the rain which killed the man in question. Both poison and gunshot are so much more plausible causes of death, that the mere coincidence of its having rained on both occasions will be dismissed as merely that. Mill, of course, saw a good deal of the force of this objection, when he criticized the Method of Agreement as a very weak method. But he does not make it at all clear why the Method of Agreement is so weak, and this, I think, is because he was not at all sure in his own mind whether a cause was no more than a sufficient condition.

The second method is the Method of Difference; and its canon states: "If an instance in which the phenomenon under investigation occurs, and an instance in which it does not occur, have every circumstance save one in common, that one occurring only in the former; the circumstance in which alone the two instances differ, is the effect, or the cause, or a necessary part of the cause, of the phenomenon." [15] We have two situations, A B C followed by *a b c,* and B C followed by *b c.* We want to know what the effect of A is; we examine our two cases and see that A cannot be the cause of *b* or *c;* for they occurred when it did not. So it must be the cause of *a.* And here we have again found out something about necessary conditions, namely that A is a necessary condition of *a.* On the other hand, if we ask for the cause of *a,* we find ourselves asking about sufficient conditions; it cannot be the case that B C are the cause of *a,* since they occurred when *a* did not; therefore it must be that A is the cause of *a.* Strangely, for someone who is always thought to be interested in sufficient conditions, Mill describes the process in such a way as to make it appear that he is interested, rather, in necessary conditions. He says that "we must select an instance, as *a b c* in which the effect occurs, and in which the antecedents were A B C, and we must look out for another instance in which the remaining circumstances, *b c,* occur without *a.* If the antecedents, in that instance, are B C, we know that the cause of *a* must be A: either A alone, or A in conjunction with some of the other circumstances present." [16] It seems as though Mill wants to know what antecedent cannot be suppressed without suppressing the effect, and this is to find out about a necessary condition. A point worth making here is that, on our reading, Mill has no reason to prefer the Method of Difference to the Method of Agreement; each is as strong or as weak as the other; and each is strong precisely where the other is weak. The rational approach would seem to be to employ them both together.

This is in effect what the third method discussed by Mill does. It is the Joint Method of Agreement and Difference. It has aroused more interest than have the other methods; but Mill himself is not so concerned with it that we need to go into it at great length.[17] Mill's strongest argument in favor of the Method of Difference had been that it was peculiarly the method of experiment; we could add or subtract a circumstance and see what the effect of our doing so might be. Now he argues that a natural equivalent to experiment can be found. But here he confuses the logical problem of what a method demonstrates with the practical problem of whether we can employ it. As a matter of logic the Joint Method is not merely eqivalent to using the Method of Difference; it is as strong as both the first two Methods together, and yields information about causes and effects where the causal bond is considered as that of necessity and sufficiency together. So it must tell us both, for example, what the effect of A is, meaning what A is necessary and sufficient to produce, and what the cause of *a* is, meaning what is both a necessary and sufficient condition of *a.* Employing the usual notation we begin with A B C followed by *a b c,* and A D E followed by *a d e;* we ask: what is the effect of A? We see A cannot be sufficient for *b, c, d, e;* for they are absent where it is present. But we now look for a chance of finding what A is the necessary

c

condition for. There are two cases possible, which Mill does not distinguish, but both depend on our looking for cases of the absence of A to acquire the negative instances on which the Method of Difference depends. In the first case, we have a straightforward case of the Method of Difference; i.e., we have A B C followed by *a b c,* and B C followed by *b c.* In the second case we have an inverse or negative case for the Method of Agreement; for we have B C followed by *b c,* and D E followed by *d e.* In the case of the Method of Difference, we argue as before that A cannot be necessary for *b c,* since they occur where A does not. In the case of the inverse Method of Agreement, we consider our instances B C and D E and *b c,* and *d e* as cases where Ā and *ā* respectively are present. Thus we have Ā B C followed by *ā b c,* and Ā D E followed by *ā d e.* Now Ā cannot be sufficient for the absence of *b, c, d, e,* for A is absent and they are present; so Ā must be sufficient for the absence of *a,* i.e., for *ā;* in other words A is a necessary condition of *a.* We have therefore arrived at the point of discovering what A is both a necessary and a sufficient condition of. And plainly the same thing will be true when we inquire what the cause of *a* is. The fact that the Method of Difference, when employed to see what the effect of a given cause is, yields necessary conditions seems to have been in Mill's mind when he wrote that the Method rested on the axiom that "whatever antecedent cannot be excluded without excluding the phenomenon is the cause, or a condition of that phenomenon." [18] And he saw the equivalence between this and the negative Method of Agreement as lying in the fact that the latter "establishes the same connection between the absence of A and the absence of *a,* which was before established between their presence. As then it had been shown that whenever A is present *a* is present, so it being now shown that when A is taken away *a* is removed along with it, we have by the one proposition A B C, *a b c,* by the other B C, *b c,* the positive and negative instances which the Method of Difference requires." [19] The whole tendency of Mill's account is toward an account of causal conjunction in terms of sufficiency and necessity; the very lettering which Mill uses seems to indicate his presupposition that the presence of an antecedent is enough to produce the consequent, and its absence the absence of the consequent.

The last two methods we need only state. Of the Method of Residues, Mill says: "Its principle is very simple." [20] If when we are faced with A B C, *a b c,* we already know that B is the cause of *b,* and that C is the cause of *c,* then we may conclude that the residual phenomena are causally related, i.e., that A is the cause of *a:* "Subduct from any phenomenon such part as is known by previous inductions to be the effect of certain antecedents, and the residue of the phenomenon is the effect of the remaining antecedents." [21] What indeed could be simpler, at least, given that we know how the phenomenon is constituted so exactly as to have no difficulty in making sense of the instruction to subtract various portions of it? The last Method, of Concomitant Variations, seems not to be on all fours with the others, in that it does not seem to establish causation in the same way as do the others, i.e., between distinct events. Its canon states: "Whatever phenomenon varies in any manner whenever some other phenomenon varies in some particular manner, is either a cause or an effect of that phenomenon, or is connected with it through some fact of causation." [22] The point of the Method is to deal with cases where we cannot entirely remove the phenomena involved; for example, where we are dealing with heat and volume, we cannot take away all the heat from a body to see if all its volume is taken away also. But this example—which is Mill's[23]—shows that there is something odd involved in his conception of a causal relation. If the picture to which his notation naturally corresponds is correct, then the phenomena to be related are not such abstract entities as Heat and Volume but, rather, events such as heating a given body by 10 degrees and its volume increasing by 15 per cent. And such a case is perfectly well managed by one or both of the first two

Methods. Again Mill suggests that the Method is to be used where we are dealing with what he calls "permanent causes," one of which is the earth. It is certainly true that we cannot dispose of the earth to see what it is the cause of; but it is dubious whether in any case we could make much sense of a law which began: "the Earth causes . . ." other than by rephrasing it in the language of particular events, such as "eclipses are caused by the earth passing between the sun and the moon." What Mill is plainly correct in saying is that many scientific laws are in fact statements of concomitant variation, as that the intensity of light varies inversely with the square of the distance it has to travel. But it is hard to see why this requires a separate canon of induction. The idea that we might annihilate distance to reach infinite intensity is nonsensical. Perhaps the most charitable view is that Mill misled himself by trying to fit all forms of scientific law into a causal pattern which they will not fit. But in so doing he was ignoring lessons which he could certainly have taught himself.

So much for Mill's statement of the experimental methods. There are several questions still to be answered. The first question is whether Mill really meant a cause to be considered as a sufficient condition, in spite of all that we have seen of the deficiencies of his account of the methods of inductive proof if that is so. This is not exactly to answer the problem of what were Mill's views on causation; but it is at least a necessary preliminary before we try to decide between causal tendencies and mere uniformities. A second problem is that of what assumptions we need to make about the world in order to employ the Methods; we have commented from time to time on the sort of picture which seems to lie behind Mill's notation, but this needs to be made explicit. Finally, there is the problem of how the Methods are to be made demonstrative proofs of causal connection, and this involves the celebrated question of the status of the law of universal causation.

That Mill was committed to the view that a cause is a sufficient condition is, as we have said, common doctrine. It explains very plausibly why Mill had reservations about the Method of Agreement. Von Wright, for example, says: "In the logic of Mill the word 'cause' means *sufficient condition* (in time). For this reason the Method of Agreement, as described by Mill, can be used as *a method of elimination* solely for the purpose of looking for the effect of a given cause and *not* for the cause of a given effect. This, however, was overlooked by Mill." [24] "On the other hand, the fact—although not clearly grasped by Mill—that the method, when applied to sufficient conditions, was not one of elimination but of enumeration, drove him to the reservation which he expressed by saying that this method can prove a characteristic to be an *invariable* but not an *unconditional* antecedent of a given characteristic." [25] The only objection we might bring to this account is that Mill sees clearly enough what it is that is wrong with the Method of Agreement, for he says: "If there are but two instances, A B C and A D E, though these instances have no antecedent in common except A, yet as the effect may possibly have been produced in the two cases by different causes, the result is at most only a slight probability in favor of A." [26] If the Method thus turns out to be enumerative rather than eliminative, the probability in favor of A depends on the improbability that there is a different cause on each occasion, which is why Mill requires our instances to be "very numerous as well as sufficiently varied." [27] We have already seen that Mill's doctrine of the plurality of causes is further supporting evidence of the correctness of Von Wright's account. Unconditionality seems to involve much the same thing as sufficiency when Mill says: "We may define, therefore, the cause of the phenomenon to be the antecedent, or the concurrence of antecedents, on which it is invariably and *unconditionally* consequent." [28] And he declares himself ready to accept the "convenient modification" [29] of the term by which we understand by "unconditionally"—"subject to no other than negative conditions." [30]

But Mill is far from unambiguous about the meaning of the

word "cause," even if it is admitted that the account in terms of sufficient conditions is both the most firmly rooted and most in accord with the everyday acceptation of the word. For Mill is not consistently willing to accept the vulgar usage according to which a cause is merely that one of the conditions which is under our control. For he is prepared to object to the distinction between causes and conditions precisely on the grounds that "All the conditions were equally indispensable to the consequent," [31] which he takes to show that all have an equally good title, philosophically speaking, to be called causes. And he cites as a case in favor of equating cause and necessary condition that where "a person eats a particular dish and dies in consequence, that is, would not have died if he had not eaten it." [32] It seems that it is not enough to establish merely that a result happened after such and such a consequent, but that we must also establish that it would not have happened without it. If we suppose that A is the cause of *a*, and we have any kind of control over the phenomena involved, then we "will not neglect, if an opportunity present itself, to exclude it from some one of these combinations" [33] to see presumably if it is necessary as well as sufficient.

What Mill sees as underlying this, I believe, is that we are not, as a matter of fact, content with everyday causal statements, and feel that for any kind of scientific inquiry something a good deal tougher is required. So we do not rest content with a statement such as: "It was enough in the circumstances to hit him on the head with a chair-leg to render him unconscious." We try to state clearly *what* the circumstances are. And in doing so we come increasingly close to stating sufficient and necessary conditions, for we both restate the effect and analyze the circumstances in order to achieve precisely this. And plainly it is laws of the high-level sciences which Mill regards as the paradigm of explanatory rigor, not our everyday causal statements. The merit of a law stating both sufficient and necessary conditions is the obvious one of allowing us to reason from cause to effect and effect to cause with equal certainty. One of the reasons why Mill was able in spite of everything to include the Method of Agreement was that he did not, ultimately, believe in plurality of causes; the plurality of causes is not a fact about the world, but a fact about our inadequate classification of phenomena. If we reclassify and reclassify, we shall find in the end that there is no such thing as plurality of causes; the universe is composed of a multitude of single facts, which follow and precede one another in an absolutely rigid order. "The whole of the present facts are the infallible result of all past facts, and more immediately of all the facts which existed at the moment previous. If the whole prior state of the entire universe could again recur, it would again be followed by the present state. Here then is a great sequence, which we know to be uniform." [34] This, however, is an underlying order, not what strikes us at first sight: "The order of nature as perceived at a first glance, presents at every instant a chaos followed by another chaos." [35] To achieve understanding of the uniform order which really does obtain, we have to sort out the chaos into simpler elements—into precisely the well-organized, clearly distinguished atomic facts, which we can label A B C, a b c. "We must decompose each chaos into single facts. We must learn to see in the chaotic antecedent a multitudè of distinct antecedents, in the chaotic consequent a multitude of distinct consequents." [36] We must depart from the classifications of ordinary speech whenever necessary, in order to achieve this decomposition of the phenomena; the failure of the Greeks to do this was one of the reasons why their science ultimately failed to make progress. The influence of atomic, Newtonian physics, the great model to which the school of Locke paid homage, is again apparent. The idea that we might decompose the world into single facts, even though as Mill admits, "it would be difficult to say where we should find them," [37] is plainly based on an analogy with the atomic structure of matter, where there is a genuine possibility of decomposition into those "minute parts," the "invisible motions" of which hold the key to reality as we see it.[38] And the laws which hold between these atomic facts are patently of such a sort as to make inferences both backward and forward in time absolutely conclusive; the most rigorous bonds link one single fact with its antecedent, and that bond must involve both sufficiency and necessity.

This, of course, does not prove Von Wright wrong; for it is possible to argue either of two things in the circumstances. The first is simply that Mill is muddled about causation, and that it is probably the case that he never noticed the contradiction between an account which admitted plurality of causes and one which ultimately did not. More charitably, we may accept that there is confusion here, but locate it differently. Mill's account of causation as involving sufficient conditions applies to everyday causal inquiry; it applies particularly to inquiry into how to bring about all sorts of results in the social and political sphere, where the practical thinker is faced with numerous alternatives in the way of policies to achieve a given goal. But his account of causation as involving both sufficient and necessary conditions applies to the sort of world which metaphysical considerations inform us must be the real world of science.

The discussion of what Mill understands by a causal connection for the purposes of the inductive methods contains implicitly the answer to our second question concerning the kind of assumption which has to be made in employing the methods. We have quoted already the criticism that the methods are useless without guiding ideas to employ them by, and redundant when these guiding ideas are supplied. What this complaint amounts to is this. If we are trying to ascertain the cause of a given effect or vice versa, it is no use employing the methods unless we can be sure that we have enumerated the phenomena to be explained as accurately as possible; and, of course, we can have no absolute guarantee that this is so. Mill, as we saw, could not say quite what the "single facts" were, into which phenomena were to be decomposed; the reason why he could not is that the notion that there are such single facts is a mistake. To describe any situation we must select some of its features rather than others; in most sciences, the description depends on what theory we accept to explain the phenomena thus described. Mill in effect assumes that there is, or might be, some theory which is ultimate and un-challengeable; some theory which would indicate what the *only* description of the phenomena had to be. At the very least this is an implausible assumption, though less so no doubt in Mill's day than in ours. Similar to the assumption that the facts have been described exactly is the assumption that the cause lies somewhere among the phenomena de-scribed. If we were to take a case such as the causation of tidal flow by the moon's orbit about the earth, we could imagine a situation where Mill's methods were inapplicable precisely because the causal sequence was not visualized in the right way. It would be no use at all decomposing the state of the tide at say 10 P.M. and the state of the tide at 9 P.M. in order to ascertain the causation of tidal phenomena; the cause we are looking for lies in the lunar orbit, and unless we have some reason to involve the moon in our description, we shall never achieve the explanation we are looking for. And, of course, we are likely to perceive the relevance of the moon to our problem, not through employing Mill's methods at all, but because of the implications of gravitational theory in general. In short, then, one major assumption on which the inductive methods rest is that we have described the facts *completely* and *relevantly;* and the objection which the as-sumption meets is that we cannot ever be sure that it is ful-filled in the absolute sense Mill appears to envisage, while in any sense short of that absolute sense, it seems that it is the success of our explanations which leads us to suppose it to have been met, and not vice versa.

In addition to the requirement of what we may call "com-pletely classified instances," there is one further assumption which the canons require, if they are to be demonstrative proofs of causal connection. This is the assumption that the noneliminated candidate for cause or effect is the cause or the effect, that it cannot be the case that there is no cause or effect in this instance. In other words, it is the assumption that every event has a cause: the law of universal causation. And our third problem is to ascertain its status. The principle has been pretty thoroughly mocked at, and the reason why is obvious. It seems that the principle is required for the proof of causal laws, and yet it seems to rest only on inductive evidence; therefore, there is a *petitio principii* involved in causal proofs. For instance, Day writes: "Mill's proof of causal laws is circular in the following sense. On the one hand, he says that the law of causation, 'Every event has a cause,' is proved true by enumerative induction from the fact of the existence of numerous true causal laws, such as 'Malaria is caused by anopheles.' On the other hand, he says that such a causal law is properly proved true by the method of difference,—that is by a deductive argument in which it is shown to follow necessarily from true premises, one of which is the law of causation." [39] This is a powerful objection, often repeated. But what is strange about it is that no one seems to have considered Mill's defense on this very point. It is certainly true that Mill's defense is not very clear. It rests on his account of inference, for in the section where he speaks of every induction as a syllogism with a suppressed major premise, he says of the law of causation that it will "stand to all inductions in the relation in which, as has been shown at so much length, the major proposition of a syllogism always stands to its conclusion; not contributing at all to prove it, but being a necessary condition of its being proved; since no conclusion is proved, for which there cannot be found a true major premiss." [40] This is elucidated at the end of the third book. Mill states the difficulty quite clearly; if in proving causal laws by means of the law of causation we also think we prove the law as well, is this not circular? "Can we prove a proposition by an argument which takes it for granted? And if not so proved, on what evidence does it rest?" [41] Mill's chief concern, as often, is to argue that the evidence is not our intuition of the principle's necessity. He rejects all arguments from the inconceivability of its contradictory on the grounds that, first, people are often unable to conceive what turns out to be true, and that, second, many people have been so far from finding it inconceivable that the principle is false that they have not thought it true at all. Mill asserts quite confidently that its truth is ascertained only through induction *per enumerationem simplicem*.[42] He says that at one point it must have been reasonable to believe in the law only as an empirical law, that is, only as the statement that events in the past had causes. But does not this at once involve circularity? How could we have known even that past events had had causes if the proof of this was the law that every event has a cause? Mill's answer is that the *proof* of particular causal statements does not rest on the law of causation; the proof consists in particular sequences observed and particular sequences successfully predicted. In this case, as always, we infer from particular facts to particular facts; it is they which are the evidence, the proof, of the rightness of our laws. Thus the picture Mill offers us is that we strengthen laws by successful predictions, and assure our predictions by resting them on successful laws; but, of course, the success of a prediction depends, not on our having deduced it in accordance with a law, but on its matching the facts. Thus, for example, the proposition that "heat causes bodies to expand" is proved by past cases of bodies expanding on being heated, and by future cases where we come across them; and in this context Mill's analogy of an inferential road is a better one than Ryle's simile of an inference ticket. For tickets are good for only a certain number of journeys; but a path which is used often, which serves its purpose well, turns with use into a decent track. So we prove particular causal laws, not by deduction *from* the law of universal causation, but by induction *according to* it; what proves the particular laws are our successes in prediction and explanation; each successful prediction gives its law and the universal law so much more support. The place of the law of universal causation is thus that we can object to particular predictions on a variety of grounds, and the weakest of these is that there might just be no cause at all. As Mill says: "Any new fact of causation inferred by induction is rightly inferred, if no other objection can be made to the inference than can be made to the general truth that every event has a cause. The utmost certainty which can be given to a conclusion stops at this point. When we have ascertained that the particular conclusion must stand or fall with the general uniformity of the laws of nature—that it is liable to no doubt except the doubt whether every event has a cause—we have done all that can be done for it." [43] It is important here again to recall the opponent against whom Mill is arguing—Whewell and his fellow intuitionists—for only so can it be appreciated that the whole point of this passage is to argue that whatever certainty we give to empirical, causal truths, they remain empirical truths; we cannot turn them into something else by deriving them from the law of universal causation. When we have made them as certain as it, we have still made them no more than empirically true. Mill is clearly right to argue in this negative-seeming way. To worry that the past does not *logically* guarantee the future is less obviously preposterous than to propose anything else for the job of providing evidence for the future; so that Mill in effect forces his opponents to say how the future can be known other than through inductive inference. And again, he is clearly right not to want to turn inductive truths into necessary truths; he is right to preserve the contingent nature of the truths arrived at by induction.

So what Mill's defense of the law of universal causation seems to amount to is this. It would be a *petitio* either to deduce the law of universal causation from some equivalent principle or to deduce particular causal laws *from* it. But we do not do this. We infer particular events—ultimately, single facts—from particular events, and in so doing establish the laws according to which we make our predictions: in our inductive logic we can test our predictions in a great variety of circumstances and these methods have been successful. What more can we do? We know that the methods are as a matter of fact successful; to turn them into demonstrative methods, we put the law of universal causation at their head as a major premise, which is, as everyone agrees, to make our result demonstrative truths at the price of circularity. But if we do not make them demonstrative we do not make them circular. And hence the apparent paradox is explained; the principle of accepting the noneliminated connection leads us to true predictions, so it is a good principle to use. But its goodness rests on the particular truths, not they on it. Each time we make a successful prediction we notch up a point in its favor, thus showing, so Mill argues, that particular facts prove both particular conclusions and the methods used to reach them. The crucial point is that Mill is *not* "justifying induction" in the usual sense of that phrase. Philosophers should have known better than to be deceived into thinking that he was doing so, since the objection which Mill brings to inductions transformed into deductions is exactly that which he brings to any syllogism, "considered as an argument to prove the conclusion." [44]

NOTES

1. *System of Logic*, III, i, 2.   2. *Ibid.*   3. *Ibid.*   4. *Ibid.*, III, xii, 4.
5. Anschutz, *The Philosophy of J. S. Mill*, pp. 81–82.   6. *System of Logic*, III, ii, 5.   7. Von Wright, *Logical Problem of Induction*, p. 73.   8. *System of Logic*, III, x, 1.   9. Nagel (ed.), *Mill's Philosophy of Scientific Method*, p. xxxix.   10. *System of Logic*, III, iii, 1.   11. *Ibid.*, III, viii.
12. *Ibid.*, III, viii, 7.   13. *Ibid.*, III, viii, 1.   14. *Ibid.*   15. *Ibid.*, III,

viii, 2. **16.** *Ibid.* **17.** Von Wright, *Treatise on Induction and Probability*, pp. 97–102, 119–126; Jackson, *Mind* (1937), pp. 417ff.; *Mind* (1938), pp. 1ff. **18.** *System of Logic*, III, viii, 2. **19.** *Ibid.*, III, viii, 4. **20.** *Ibid.*, III, viii, 5. **21.** *Ibid.* **22.** *Ibid.*, III, viii, 6. **23.** *Ibid.* **24.** Von Wright, *Logical Problem of Induction*, p. 73. **25.** *Ibid.*, p. 74. **26.** *System of Logic*, III, x, 2. **27.** *Ibid.* **28.** *Ibid.*, III, x, 6. **29.** *Ibid.*, III, v, 6. **30.** *Ibid.* **31.** *Ibid.*, III, v, 3. **32.** *Ibid.* **33.** *Ibid.*, III, x, 2. **34.** *Ibid.*, III, vii, 1. **35.** *Ibid.* **36.** *Ibid.* **37.** *Ibid.* **38.** Locke, *Essay on the Human Understanding*, II, xxiii, 8. **39.** Day, *Critical History of Western Philosophy*, pp. 349–350. **40.** *System of Logic*, III, iii, 1. **41.** *Ibid.*, III, xxi, 1. **42.** *Ibid.*, III, xxi, 2. **43.** *Ibid.*, III, xxi, 4. **44.** *Ibid.*, II, iii, 2.

TENDENCIES AND
UNIFORMITIES

So far, in this account of Mill, I have represented him as an
empiricist; as a rationalist, certainly, in that he admired system, in that he took the task of science to be the creation
of explanatory systems with deductive relations holding between the laws contained therein; but as an empiricist ultimately in his belief that the basic elements of reality are particular empirical facts, facts which can be ascertained by careful analysis of the gross phenomena distinguished by ordinary
speech. He has been presented as an empiricist, too, in opposing the intuitionists, in maintaining that the most far-reaching truths about the world are nonetheless empirical truths,
in denying that their universality involves any occult kind of
necessity; and he has been implicitly accepted as analyzing
causation in terms of uniform sequence; it is true that doubts
were raised about the strength of the sequential tie, and about
the status of the facts involved in the sequence, but the equation of causation with uniform sequence was left undisturbed.
It is now time to meet some attacks on this account. The
question we have to ask is whether Mill's criteria of rationality do not show that he was in the end not an empiricist,
not an "inductivist" at all. A powerful case in support of this
view has been made out by Anschutz, whose ultimate account

of Mill is of a Platonist, a realist in the old sense of one who believes that the ultimate constituents of the universe are not particular facts, but universals. The two areas of Mill's philosophy which Anschutz particularly appeals to are his account of causation and his views on mathematics. To the first of these we must now turn.

Anschutz's view of Mill can be shortly summarized. He says: "in order to apply the experimental methods we have, in Mill's language, to 'decompose' the universe into 'single facts.' This means that we have to suppose that we have . . . penetrated beneath the surface of experience to its underlying tendencies." [1] And he equates this belief in the possibility of decomposing facts with "a popular Newtonian view of the universe, interpreted in a Platonic sense." [2] Of course, there is no denying the popularity of the Newtonian picture; it is the Platonic interpretation which is the disputatious point. Anschutz's case rests in effect on Mill's use of the word "tendencies"; Mill held two views of causation, according to one of which causation was a matter of uniformities of succession, according to the other of which it was a matter of tendencies; a subsidiary element in the case is Mill's distinction between laws of nature and merely "empirical laws," a distinction which certainly sounds incipiently Platonic. It is to the twin threats posed by these opinions of Mill's that any account of Mill as an empiricist of whatever kind must pay heed. The usual account of Mill's views on causation is that he held a simple "constant conjunction" position. He, after all, asserts categorically that his definition of cause comes from Hume and Brown;[3] and that it is one of constant conjunction: "The invariable antecedent is termed the cause, the invariable consequent, the effect." [4] And he is scathing in his criticism of philosophers who wish to penetrate into the supposed essences of things. He refers to the "supposed necessity of ascending higher, into the essences and inherent constitution of things, to find the true cause, the cause which is not only followed by, but actually *produces* the effect. No such necessity exists for the purpose of the present inquiry, nor will any such doctrine be found in the following pages. . . . The only notion of a cause, which the theory of induction requires, is such a notion as can be gained from experience." [5] This tallies very exactly with his discussion in *Hamilton* of the view that we derive our ideas of cause and effect from the experience of our volitional action, which Hamilton thinks of as a case of efficient causation. But Mill replies that "no more in this than in any other case of causation, have we evidence of anything more than what experience informs us of; and it informs us of nothing except immediate, invariable, and unconditional sequence." [6] This looks, in short, like cut-and-dried proof that Mill equates causality with constant conjunction, with regular sequences of observable phenomena.

One point which may give us pause is that such an account of causation would naturally coexist with a view of general statements which held that they ought to be read in *denotation;* and we have seen Mill reject this view. Then, too, we find Mill's account of causation changing drastically under the impact of such problems as the composition of causes until we find him giving an account in terms of tendencies, stating the view that causal laws "require to be stated in words affirmative of tendencies only, and not of actual results." [7] What drives Mill to give an account in terms of tendencies is that uniformities are inherently prone to exceptions, where scientific laws are not. As Toulmin remarks, if we want to regard the law of the rectilinear propagation of light as a uniformity, we should have to write it as: "Light always travels in a straight line, save on the numerous occasions when it does not." [8] And in his first discussion of cause, Mill contrasts phenomenal uniformities unfavorably with the uniformities of mathematics: "Now among all those uniformities in the succession of phenomena, which common observation is sufficient to bring to light, there are very few which have any, even apparent, pretension to this rigorous indefeasibility." [9] But rigorous indefeasibility is required of a scientific law. Unfortunately, at this crucial point in his account, Mill does not explain *why* laws of nature cannot have exceptions. In the face of accusations of Platonizing, this is a distressing omission on Mill's part. For it seems that there are two obvious alternatives he can take; he can make the requirement that laws have no exceptions a requirement which *we* impose, and then explain why we do this, and what makes it a respectable practice; alternatively, he can claim that in the real world there are, ultimately, no exceptions, no irregularities. Now, even in this second case, he is not committed to a Platonic position, for he is not committed to saying that the uniform and regular connections are connections between universals; he may hold that there are uniform connections between empirically discoverable particulars, which further analysis reveals. I do not think that a conclusive case can be made out for any particular view as being Mill's; but I do think that the balance of evidence can be shown to point away from the kind of account favored by Anschutz.

That scientific laws cannot, properly speaking, have exceptions, Mill maintained in the essay on the *Definition and Method of Political Economy*; and he quoted himself *verbatim* in the *System of Logic*. He says: "Doubtless, a man often asserts of an entire class what is only true of a part of it; but his error generally consists not in making too wide an assertion, but in making the wrong *kind* of assertion; he predicated an actual result, when he should only have predicated a *tendency* to that result—a power acting with a certain intensity in that direction. With regard to *exceptions;* in any tolerably advanced science there is properly no such thing as an exception." [10] Thus, of a collection of heavy objects such as bricks, balloons etc., we cannot say they *will* fall to the ground; the balloon when released will fly upward; the brick if placed on the table will stay there and will not burrow remorselessly toward the earth. Or, as Geach says: "Mill is, in fact, pushed by the facts (*quasi ab ipsa veritate coactus*) into saying 'All laws of causation, in consequence of their liability to be counteracted, require to be stated in words affirmative of tendencies only.' " [11] Thus the law concerning heavy bodies is "that all heavy bodies *tend* to fall; and to this there is no exception, not even the sun and moon; for even they, as every astronomer knows, tend towards the earth, with a force exactly equal to that with which the earth tends towards them." [12] Since the idea of an exception to a natural law is absurd, Mill regards highly those sciences which have developed a terminology to deal with the situation: "In those sciences of causation which have an accurate nomenclature, there are special words which signify a tendency to the particular effect with which the science is conversant; thus *pressure,* in mechanics, is synonymous with tendency to motion, and forces are not reasoned on as causing actual motion, but as exerting pressure. A similar improvement in terminology would be very salutary in many other branches of science." [13] One that Mill has in mind is what he called Ethology, or social psychology, whose laws "must not assert that something will always or certainly happen, but only that such and such will be the effect of a given cause, so far as it operates uncounteracted. It is a scientific proposition, that cowardice tends to make men cruel; not that it always makes them so: that an interest on one side of a question tends to bias the judgment; not that it invariably does so." [14] Thus, it looks as if Mill wants to argue that causal laws are not about uniformities at all, but about powers, tendencies, forces, and the like.

But do these tendencies, or forces, *underlie* phenomena in the way that Anschutz maintains? There is only one passage where Mill directly faces this question, but it is in itself conclusive if Mill's position on this point remained constant. To suppose that Mill holds a Platonic position is to hold that he supposes statements of tendencies and the like to picture occult, nonempirical properties in things; and, of course, I have been arguing that Mill does at least tend to think of propositions as pictures. But there is an alternative to thinking that what statements about tendencies depict is an invisible real world behind the phenomena of experience. The alternative is to suppose that we do not depict a world of tendencies and forces, and then reason concerning the phenomena which they underlie, but that we reason concerning a phenomenal world, and that words like "tendency" or "force" depict only our ability to do this. In other words, what general statements depict is our habits of successful inference. And what Mill says in this connection strongly argues that this is what he thought: "This capacity is not a real thing existing in the objects; it is but a name for our conviction that they will act in a particular manner when certain new circumstances arise. We may invest this assurance of future events with a fictitious objective existence, by calling it a *state* of the object. But unless the state consists, as in the case of the gunpowder it does, in a collocation of particles, it expresses no present fact; it is but the contingent future fact brought back under another name." [15] The merits of this account in averting Platonism are obvious; if they need stressing, we need only compare what Mill says with a statement of Ryle's about dispositional statements; they "are neither reports of observed or unobserved states of affairs, nor yet reports of observable or unobservable states of affairs[16] . . . they apply to, or are satisfied by, the actions, reactions and states of the object; they are inference-tickets which license us to predict, retrodict, explain and modify the actions, reactions and states." [17] And it might be felt that there is no need further to defend Mill against charges of Platonism until such charges are leveled at Ryle.

However, though I think we have certainly shown that Mill *need* not have succumbed to Platonism, and that he took care to avoid it, there are still some alarming statements to explain. The most alarming of these are Mill's views on the subject of the mechanical composition of causes. And because these provide what is in some ways the most plausible attempt to reconcile the uniformity account of causation with the tendency account, it is convenient here to discuss the problem of whether these two accounts can be reconciled. One of the few writers to have seen that there are two accounts is Geach; he has no doubt that the accounts are quite inconsistent, and that it is the tendency account which is the right one. "The laws that scientists aim at establishing are not *de facto* uniformities, either necessary or contingent. For any alleged uniformity is defeasible by something's interfering and preventing the effect; to assert the uniformity as a fact is to commit oneself to a rash judgment that such interference has never taken place and never will. Scientists do not try to describe natural events in terms of what always happens. Rather certain natural agents—bodies of certain natures—are brought into the description and we are told what behaviour is proper to these sets of bodies in these circumstances." [18] And he says that to talk of "what would failing interference happen . . . is to abandon the Humian position." [19] Mill's apparent reconciliation of the two positions by way of the composition of causes is extremely vulnerable, and lends a certain credibility to Anschutz's suspicions. It looks as though Mill thinks that because laws of nature do not admit of exceptions, and causes are sufficient conditions of their effects, then causes *must* produce effects, even if they do not appear to.

Thus we have Mill's statement of what happens in the case of the mechanical composition of causes where all the effects of the separate causes "still take place, but are intermingled with, and disguised by, the homogeneous and closely-allied effects of other causes. . . . although two or more laws interfere with one another, and apparently frustrate or modify one another's operation, yet in reality all are fulfilled, the collective effect being the exact sum of the effects of the causes taken separately." [20] He says of the case where two forces acting on a body have kept that body at rest: "It is evident . . . that each force has had, during each instant, all the effect which belonged to it." [21] Manifestly on any uniformity theory of causation this is not true; if effects are supposed to be observable phenomena, then the idea of a sum of effects in this situation is absurd. The correct statement of the situation is that neither force had any effect because of the opposing force. To argue that, because a body acted on by two forces remains where it would have arrived had both acted separately, the effects *really did* occur is absurd. All sorts of things which would have been true if the body had moved are not in fact true. In terms of what visibly happened, the answer is that nothing visibly happened. Mill's difficulty here, I suspect, is partly his hanging onto the word "cause" where there are no effects; it seems as though the fact that a cause is an unconditional antecedent means that it must produce an effect even where the effect is invisible.

Is it, then, the case that Mill tries to reconcile the uniformity and the tendency accounts by retreating into a position of holding that there are uniformities, only that they are uniformities among underlying forces and tendencies? The account of the mechanical composition of causes does not in the end support such a view. One reason why it does not is that it is a case which is important largely because of the contrast it offers to the chemical admixt re of effects. In the case of the chemical mixture of effects, Mill is prepared to say that the effects are annihilated, in other words that they cannot be inferred from the effects which would have been produced by each agent separately. So we cannot ascribe to Mill such a view of causation as would imply that the effect of each cause was always produced *really;* the point of tendencies is not to save uniformity after all. The explanation seems somewhat different. Geach points out quite rightly that there is a great deal of difference between the statement "It always happens unless it does not" and the statement "It always happens unless something prevents." The latter is not vacuous, where the former certainly is. At least part of the difference is the heuristic one that the latter statement invites us to look for interfering causes wherever the uniformity is defeated; and it is this latter statement which Mill equates with the statement of causal necessity.[22] And this is what lies behind Mill's insistence that we should decompose phenomena until we come to single facts. For if this is done, we may hope to arrive at actual phenomenal uniformities hidden beneath phenomenal disorder. Thus the ordinary causal statement that a given drug cures a given disease may be defeasible. It can be rendered indefeasible by saying that it tends to cure that disease. But we can do more than this. We can tighten the causal links between the administration of the drug and the cure of the disease by redescribing the initial conditions and the later ones in chemical terms, so that we get increasingly close to phenomenal uniformities which really are indefeasible, to causal chains in which every link is indefeasibly linked to its neighbors. The sense in which uniformities of this kind underlie phenomena is not a Platonic one; it is the sense in which we might say that, for example, physical uniformities underlay what at a chemical level did not look at all like uniformities. There is no conclusive evidence to show either that Mill did or did not think that we could find uniformities of this sort underlying tendencies; the only passage which seems to bear on it at all is that in which he says that the explosive nature of gunpowder *consists in* its atomic or molecular structure (the "collocation of particles"). But, though not conclusive, this does seem to show that Mill thought that talk of tendencies was related in two ways to the gross and defeasible uniformities we observe ordinarily. First, the descriptions of the gross phenomenal uniformities could be broken down into more accurate descriptions, and the finer and more accurate the descriptions become, then the more indefeasible become the statements of uniformity. This obviously fits the scientific analysis of rule-of-thumb causal laws. And the metaphysics which underlies it is not Platonic in the sense of holding the real world to be composed of universals; it is an empiricist a priorism, like Locke's, to the effect that the world ultimately consists of distinguishable particulars which are logically and epistemologically simple. It is certainly a Newtonian metaphysics, for it assumes a logical atomism to match the atomic structure of matter; but it is not Platonism. In the second place, tendencies may be related to phenomenal results by the language of "as-if." When we say that the body of one ton has a tendency to move the body of three tons, although, of course, it does not actually move it at all, we may say that it is *as if* the three-ton body were composed of three bodies of one ton each, one of which had been raised by the body weighing one ton. This, of course, is the language of forces, where we talk in terms of foot/pounds. To the question, What is a foot/pound? we cannot return an answer in terms of describing the nontangible entity of a force; all we can do is give a lesson in elementary mechanics. To offer Mill these alternatives to Platonism is not to argue that Mill was clear and unconfused about tendencies, forces, and causes. It is only to answer the question of what Mill's metaphysics were, not that of what they should have been.

The second large threat to our account of Mill as an empiricist is his distinction between laws of nature and empirical laws. Besides the interest of the contrast in the connection of Mill's alleged Platonist tendencies, it is an interesting aspect of his preoccupation with law-governed explanations, and his emphasis on the place of *certainty* in science. It also becomes relevant later on in the *System of Logic* when Mill discusses the kind of laws which historical inquiry can hope to establish. Mill's distinction between empirical laws and laws of nature is not as precise as it might be; and it is certainly not as precise as that which Anschutz credits him with. Anschutz finds the distinction between empirical laws and laws of nature to be the same as the distinction between description and explanation, which again is the distinction between an answer to the question "How?" and an answer to the question "Why?": "as for Plato, the distinction between description and explanation is based upon the distinction between a phenomenal world of 'actual results' and a real world of 'tendencies.' True statements about the former (like Kepler's laws of planetary motion) are called empirical laws, while true statements about the latter (like Newton's laws of motion) are laws of nature. But according to Mill there is an important difference between the kind of truth, claimed by these statements, which qualifies one of them to answer the question how? and the other the question why?" [23] But this is plain misreporting; apart from the fact that Mill is, as we have seen, not inclined to exalt tendencies over phenomena, Mill never drew a distinction between laws which answered how-questions and laws which answered why-questions. Explanation is "but substituting one mystery for another; and does nothing to render the general course of nature other than mysterious: we can no more assign a *why* for the more extensive laws than for the partial ones." [24] Again, the solid empiricism of Mill's position emerges when he discusses what, to him, is the only sense to be given to the idea of an ultimate explanation of the universe: it would be to deduce from the state of the universe at its inception and the laws governing its behavior, the state it is in currently. Beyond this, there is no explanation to be had; and in particular there would be no explanation concerning its primeval elements and their distribution: "collocations cannot be reduced to any law." [25] As for the laws, if they really were the ultimate ones then all we could say is that that was how things were, without any further reason being assigned. It is important to recall, at this point, the intuitionist view that phenomenal causation was nonexplanatory in the last resort, so that the universe could only be finally understood as the pattern of events willed by an intelligent being. So little did Mill think of this doctrine that even after he has forsworn all intention of discussing it, he is quite unable to resist the temptation to argue that in any case volitional action is but another example of physical causation: "to my apprehension, a volition is not an efficient, but simply a physical cause. Our will causes our bodily actions, in the same sense, and in no other, in which cold causes ice, or a spark causes an explosion of gunpowder." [26] This makes it as certain as could well be that Mill's distinction between empirical laws and laws of nature is not a distinction between levels of understanding or types of explanation. But what, then, is the distinction between?

The most explicit of Mill's declarations is his first: "It is implied . . . in the notion of an empirical law, that it is not an ultimate law; that if true at all, its truth is capable of being, and requires to be accounted for. It is a derivative law, the derivation of which is not yet known." [27] The trouble with this is that Mill's conception of what it is to derive a law is not notably clear. In particular, there is a clash between one account on the strength of which empirical laws are not really laws at all, but compressed descriptions of our observations and another account on the strength of which they are genuine laws, but low-level ones. Thus he sometimes refers to empirical laws as colligations,[28] to which the derogatory title of "description" is perhaps to be strictly applied. A science has to order its materials to begin to explain them: "This preparatory treatment consists in finding general propositions which express concisely what is common to large numbers of observed facts; and these are called the empirical laws of the phenomena." [29] These, however, are not laws at all, by Mill's usual account; they are the conclusions to which "concrete deductions" lead. They are the result of two things, some causal laws and a particular antecedent organization of the natural agents in question, and we can pursue their derivation further back until "the different series of effects meet in a point, and the whole is shown to have depended ultimately on some common cause; or, until, instead of converging to one point, they terminate in different points, and the order of the effects is proved to have arisen from the collocation of some of the primeval causes, or natural agents." [30] But there are in this three possibilities, which Mill does not clearly separate and to all of which the title of empirical, or derivative, law can be applied. The first is the case of the *summary:* "all observed positions of Mars lie on an ellipse" where nothing is done other than to summarize what we have

seen. The second is the case of the *low-level law,* as for example: "all positions of the planets of the solar system (observed and unobserved) lie on an ellipse." Here there has been
an induction, but the law is still empirical, in the sense that
an observer could in principle *watch* the planets moving in
elliptical orbits. The third is the *derivative law* to the effect
that any body acted on by the appropriate gravitational
forces and with the appropriate momentum, will describe an
elliptical orbit. Here there is no question of observing what
"any body" will do, even though we may observe lots of particular bodies behaving in the manner predicted. In other
words, this is a derivative causal law. Mill's real interest, I
believe, lies in the second kind of case, rather than the first
or third. It lies in the fact that "From a limited number of
ultimate laws of causation, there are necessarily generated a
vast number of derivative uniformities, both of succession and
of coexistence." [31] What interests him is the way in which a
small number of laws, together with the arrangement of the
initial constituents of the universe, can generate the whole
subsequent history of the universe. It is certainly true that
Mill draws the distinction between empirical laws and ultimate laws because he wishes to get to the bottom of the order
of things; but it is quite false that this is in any sense a Platonic move.

This can be seen the more readily from what Mill says
about the methods by which we can find out whether "if an
observed uniformity be a law of causation, it is not an ultimate but a derivative law." [32] His answer, roughly, is that a
law of the form "A causes *a*" is not ultimate if we can break
down the A $\rightarrow$ *a* sequence into smaller elements; if, that is,
the real law is that A causes *x* and *x* causes *a*. The goal all the
while is certainty; if A causes *a* via *x*, then there are two places
where counteraction might occur; so we may expect a more
nearly perfect uniformity of sequence between A and *x* and
x and *a*, than between A and *a*. The second test for deriva-
tiveness is, as we might guess, complexity of antecedent. It is

hard not to feel that this is a test which begs the question, for it is difficult to see what it is to know that the antecedent is complex besides being able to distinguish numerous causal elements within it. But it does bring out Mill's underlying view of the universe as composed of strings of perfectly uniform causal chains, with single fact entailing single fact, instant by instant from the dawn of time. All cases other than mechanical composition of causes are played down, while his atomism appears in such remarks as: "All true propositions, therefore, which can be made concerning gravity are derivative laws; the ultimate law into which they are all resolvable being that every particle of matter attracts every other." [33] And, typical of the faith of Newton is his statement that "ultimate laws are in all cases relatively simple." [34] It is nothing if not an empiricist picture of the world which Mill provides us with; the world is a collection of discrete facts, which can ultimately be seen to be simple; each fact is linked with its predecessors and successors by an unbroken causal bond; each fact's relations with its neighbors in time and space are determined by the twin factors of its position in the causal chain, and the wholly inexplicable coincidence of facts at the beginning of the whole process. The model is that of astronomy, with its emphases on the two elements of regularity in recurrent states of affairs, and the possibility of building up a history of the entire process by pure deduction. Mill recognized this affinity when he praised the sciences of "concrete deduction," of which "celestial mechanics" was the supreme example. Mill's certainty that the methods of induction could yield us absolutely accurate information about the universe was in the end founded on just such a metaphysical enthusiasm for a science which it is not clear he more than imperfectly understood.

NOTES

1. Anschutz, *The Philosophy of J. S. Mill*, p. 109.   2. *Ibid.*, p. 112.   3. *System of Logic*, VI, ii, 2.   4. *Ibid.*, III, v, 2.   5. *Ibid.*   6. *Examination of Hamilton*, p. 362.   7. *System of Logic*, III, x, 5.   8. Toulmin, *The Philosophy of Science*, p. 30.   9. *System of Logic*, III, v, 1.   10. *Essays on Some Unsettled Questions*, pp. 161–162.   11. Geach, *Three Philosophers*, p. 103, quoting Mill, *System of Logic*, III, x, 5.   12. *System of Logic*, III, x, 5.   13. *Ibid.*   14. *Ibid.*, VI, v, 4.   15. *Ibid.*, III, v, 5.   16. Ryle, *Concept of Mind*, p. 125.   17. *Ibid.*, p. 124.   18. Geach, *Three Philosophers*, p. 102.   19. *Ibid.*, p. 103.   20. *System of Logic*, III, x, 5.   21. *Ibid.*   22. *Ibid.*, VI, ii, 3.   23. Anschutz, *The Philosophy of J. S. Mill*, p. 167.   24. *System of Logic*, III, xii, 6.   25. *Ibid.*, III, xvi, 4.   26. *Ibid.*, III, v, 11.   27. *Ibid.*, III, xvi, 2.   28. *Ibid.*, III, ii, 4.   29. *Ibid.*, VI, ix, 5.   30. *Ibid.*, III, xvi, 2.   31. *Ibid.*   32. *Ibid.*, III, xvi, 6.   33. *Ibid.*   34. *Ibid.*

V

MATHEMATICS AS
AN INDUCTIVE SCIENCE

It is for more than the sake of completeness only that we have
to devote some attention to Mill's account of mathematical
truth. In the first place, it is important as an illustration of
how far Mill was prepared to go in his attacks on intuitionism, and how far reaching his empiricism was. In the second
place, it is on the basis, in part, of Mill's account of mathematics that Mill has been said to be anything but an empiricist at heart. But as a contribution to the philosophy of mathematics, Mill's views have always enjoyed an extreme unpopularity: to quote Day: "Mill's philosophy of mathematics is
generally considered to be the least acceptable part of his
logic, and indeed he enjoys on this account a certain succès
de scandale." [1]

I think it is important to point out in Mill's defense that
he did not invent the problems he faced in explaining mathematical truth. We are too apt to assume that every thinker
might have posed himself our own problems in our own
terms; but for Mill to ask, for example, whether mathematics
might be reduced to formal logic would have been ludicrous
when the only logic as yet in existence was that of the syllogism. The terms of the problem as it came to Mill were essentially Kantian. Mathematical truths were said to be true of

the world, and were said by Whewell to be intuitively perceived synthetic *a priori* truths. Whewell, no less than Mill,
thought that mathematical truths were true of the world, that
they embodied laws of nature. And this intuitionist view was
not even as sophisticated as was Kant's modification that
mathematics was about the *form* rather than the *content* of
intuition. In other words, the problem for Mill is that of
what sort of laws of nature we find in mathematics; the alternatives are that we find inductive ones or intuitive ones; that
we find no laws of nature at all is not an alternative to be
considered.

Mill's problem, then, is to account in inductive terms for
the apparent necessity possessed by such propositions as 7 +
2 = 9; but the necessity involved is obscured by the examples
chosen by Mill. For he supposes that what we must prove to
be necessarily true are propositions such as: "Six cows and
four cows make ten cows." Thus he says: "That half of four
is two, must be true whatever the word four represents,
whether four men, four miles, or four pounds weight." [2] In
contending against Whewell that the test of these truths is not
the inconceivability of their falsity, Mill produces what he
takes to be his opponent's definition of necessity: "what he
means by a necessary truth, would be sufficiently defined, a
proposition the negation of which is not only false but inconceivable." [3] But Mill will not accept any such test: "I
cannot but wonder that so much stress should be laid on the
circumstance of inconceivableness, when there is such ample
evidence to show that our capacity or incapacity of conceiv-
ing a thing has very little to do with the possibility of the
thing in itself, but is in truth very much an affair of accident, . . ." [4] Mill appeals to the law of association to explain
how people very often cannot imagine apart what they have
never seen separated in reality; and this he takes to dispose
of the question. Of course, Mill assumes that to *conceive* of
something is rather like having a mental image of it; if this
were so, then naturally we should not normally be any more

prepared to believe that something could not happen because we could not form a picture of it than to believe that our next-door neighbor did not exist because we had never happened to meet him. Moreover, it must be said in Mill's favor that the modern willingness to equate inconceivability with analytic falsity would not have been accepted by Whewell; he in effect did demand that our minds should mirror, in some almost literal way, the course of nature: what could not be mirrored in the one could not happen in the other.

Mill considers whether mathematical truths might be analytic only to reject the possibility. He sees that it is implausible to say that algebra, for example, is "about" anything more substantial than "modes of formation" [5] of numbers, and says that "the extreme generality, and remoteness not so much from sense as from the visual and tactual imagination, of the law of number, renders it a somewhat difficult effort of abstraction to conceive these laws as being in reality physical truths obtained by observation. . . ." [6] He agrees with Berkeley that we do not have images in mind while we do algebra, and comes up with the almost Fregean suggestion that "Each number is considered as formed by the addition of an unit to the number next below it in magnitude, and this mode of formation is conveyed by the place which it occupies in the series." [7] But, as Frege himself said of this passage: "this spark of sound sense is no sooner lit than extinguished, thanks to his presupposition that all knowledge is empirical." [8] Mill's trouble is twofold. He does not want to admit the existence of numbers as real entities, and yet he cannot see how anything informative is to be derived from mere definitions. In not wanting to admit the real existence of numbers, he follows a traditional empiricist position; numbers must be numbers of something, they cannot be allowed to exist in some Platonic heaven. We must perform a process of *reduction* on them, so that we are still left with a world of things rather than of abstract entities.

Thus Mill is driven inescapably to argue that mathematics is

D

an inductive science. Mathematics is founded on what are termed "definitions" and axioms; but these so-called definitions are not definitions at all. They are factual statements. The sort of propositions which they assert is, for example, "that collections of objects exist, which while they impress the senses thus ooo, may be separated into two parts, thus oo o." [9] This is not an identity statement; for though it is true that a parcel of three stones and a parcel of two stones and one stone are one and the same parcel, yet they represent very different physical facts. "Three pebbles in two separate parcels, and three pebbles in one parcel, do not make the same impression on our senses; and the assertion that the very same pebbles may by an alteration of place and arrangement be made to produce either the one set of sensations or the other, though a very familiar proposition is not an identical one." [10] But to this account of the meaning of $2 + 1 = 3$, there are innumerable objections; Frege asks simply whether mathematics would be made false if everything were nailed down.[11] We can think readily of countable objects which cannot be rearranged, as, for example, the successive chimes of a clock. And finally, Mill has done away with the demonstrative character of mathematics and replaced it by a dubiously true empirical statement about the possibility of rearranging certain sorts of object.

As with definitions, so with axioms. The only one he cites is the axiom that "The sums of equals are equals; the differences of equals are equals," [12] which again he thinks is the result of induction. Unlike the axioms of geometry which are only hypothetical statements, the axioms are "exactly true, without the hypothetical assumption of unqualified truth where an approximation to it is all that exists." [13] Though, even here, he admits that we need to make the qualification that what are being added or subtracted are really equals— troy pounds with troy pounds and avoirdupois pounds with avoirdupois pounds. But the implausibility of arguing that the axiom of equals is an inductive truth is made painfully clear when Mill says that it is certain "that 1 is always equal in *number* to 1," [14] and emphasizes that we must be sure we are talking of "equal units." [15] In the light of the qualifications it seems that the axiom is to read: "Equals added to equals are equals if and only if equals really are added to equals." How this could be thought to be other than an analytic truth it is difficult to imagine.

Nonetheless, it was Mill's views on geometry rather than his account of mathematics which drew the first fire from his critics. It was Jevons who first launched the attack,[16] as part of his attempt to show how completely illogical Mill essentially was. That Jevons was thoroughly unfair in many ways is evident;[17] what is less evident is that Mill can be saved in any better sense than getting him into the frying pan out of the fire. Jevons takes the problem as Mill finds it. Geometry is thought to be a body of demonstrative truths; yet it is also thought to be about the world we see around us. Mill, with Whewell always in mind, cannot accept that there are necessary truths about the world. How then to account for the apparent necessity of geometry? Mill takes the way out which all empiricists since have taken; geometry is derived from definitions and these are neither true nor false. So that the necessity of geometry would be only that it was deduced from its definitions; and the applied geometry of everyday life would not be necessarily true at all. But Mill's views on definition again cause him difficulty: "It is acknowledged that the conclusions of geometry are deduced, partly at least, from the so-called Definitions, and that those definitions are assumed to be correct representations so far as they go, of the objects with which geometry is conversant. Now we have pointed out that from a definition as such, no proposition, unless it be one concerning the meaning of a word, can ever follow; . . ." [18] The effect of this is fatal; nothing can be deduced about the world from a definition, and Mill refuses to contemplate the possibility that there is a sense in which geometry is not about the world. He says that "science cannot be supposed to be conversant with non-entities";[19] and since he is unenthusiastic about admitting a special class of entities for geometry to be conversant with, he concludes that "nothing remains but to consider geometry as conversant with such lines, angles, and figures which really exist." [20] But this lands Mill in another problem; if the lines, etc., which do exist do not correspond to the "definitions" (which are not really definitions at all), then geometry is not exactly true; in fact it is at best an approximation to the truth, and seemingly the Exact Sciences are no more. It is in explaining how we may meet this objection that Mill gives hostages, not to fortune but to Jevons. For Mill rashly says that we gain our experience of straight lines, right angles, and the rest from imagination; we can perform our inductions and experiments on the contents of our minds. And this, Jevons says, is a straightforward contradiction of what Mill admits concerning the fact that there are *no* perfectly straight lines, perfectly right angles, and the rest. "Although straight lines do not exist, we can experiment in our minds upon straight lines as if they did exist. . . . Moreover these mental experiments are just as good as real experiments, because we know that the imaginary lines exactly resemble real ones," [21] an attack which Jevons sums up by saying that in the space of one chapter Mill both admits and denies that genuine straight lines exist.

Mill, in fact, does not verbally contradict himself in this fashion; though what he does say is not very plausible. To the problem of what geometry is about, he returns the answer that it is about real or imaginary lines; neither of them can be perfectly straight, but either will do for experimentation. The only reason why Mill discusses experimentation with mental straight lines at all is his anxiety to be proof against Whewell. For Whewell made much of the fact that the experience from which we generalized to the miscalled "definitions" could include looking at mental images; or rather, Whewell wanted to count *imaginary looking* as something other than experience, and the truth of geometry therefore as something other than empirical truth. As Mill puts the objection: "Intuition is 'imaginary looking'; but experience must be real looking: if we see a property of straight lines to be true by merely fancying ourselves to be looking at them, the ground of our belief cannot be the senses, or experience; it must be something mental." [22] So far from Mill being concerned to support imagining as superior to experience, what he is doing is admitting grudgingly that in mathematics and geometry the experiences of imagination are as good evidence as the experiences of sensation; and this is a concession which applies to no causal situation. And Mill is willing to make even this concession only because he does not see intuition, as does Whewell, as some kind of superexperiential activity, but as a form of sensation—as emerges from his characterization of imaginary lines as "diagrams in our minds." [23]

All the same, Mill proceeds to make his account look really implausible by his description of geometry as a hypothetical science. Geometrical properties are ascribed to hypothetical entities (which seem for the moment to have escaped the ban on nonentities) and we infer further truths from these hypotheses. And in this lies the necessity of geometry: "The necessity consists in reality only in this, that they follow correctly from the suppositions from which they are deduced." [24] If the matter were left there, no trouble would follow. But now Mill insists on pointing out that the suppositions are false: "These suppositions are so far from being necessary that they are not even true; they purposely depart more or less widely from the truth." [25] It is a strange account of the necessity of geometry which has it consist in the falsity of its premises. Mill's trouble springs in part from the impossibility here, as with mathematics, of distinguishing between pure and applied sciences, where the pure sciences are necessary, and analytic, while the applied sciences are approximate and synthetic. The reason Mill gives for our ignoring the falsity of the premises of geometry is that they are so nearly true as to allow us to feign them to be exactly so. We can, moreover,

reason about a line *as if* it had no breadth, *as if* it were perfectly straight: "we have a power of *attending* to a part only
of that perception or conception," [26] a remark which leads
one to sympathize with Jevons' complaint that if we can "reason about lines without breadth, but can only experiment upon
thick lines" it would be "much better to stick to the reasoning process whatever it may be, and drop the mental experimentation altogether." [27]

In all this, the obvious defect which Mill's doctrines suffer
from is his belief that all knowledge is empirical knowledge,
knowledge which can be acquired through the senses. His insistence on this is not unreasonable in face of the alternative
offered by intuitionism; but it is perhaps so thoroughgoing
an empiricism as to be quite implausible here. However, it
has been argued that Mill did not subscribe to an empiricist
position with anything like the firmness which I have all along
been suggesting. This argument is Anschutz's, who holds that
Mill eventually subscribes to a "realist" or Platonist theory of
mathematical truth. "What Mill really requires, it would
seem, is a theory which somehow combines the positive truth
which he sees in the experiential theory with the negative
truth which he sees in the hypothetical theory. It seems plain
enough, moreover, that the only theory capable of satisfying
both these conditions is the realist theory to which he subscribed in his later years." [28] But did Mill subscribe to a
realist theory in his later years? It seems on the face of it very
unlikely. The greatest blows to Mill's empiricism came in his
youth; and it is one of the obvious weaknesses of *Hamilton*
that it fails to notice the lacunae in empiricist views that Mill
saw in his youth. Anschutz's case rests on two short passages
from *Hamilton* and Mill's *St. Andrew's Address*. It would be
going too far to say that Anschutz places much weight on
them; in fact, he is careful to point out their inconclusiveness.
But since, even so, he is able to assert confidently that Mill
accounts for the role of mathematics in science in terms of a

"thoroughly Platonic conception," [29] I do not think it is going too far to try to upset this case altogether.

The only real ground for supposing that Mill held a Platonic position is that no other is satisfactory. That Mill's doctrines are *not* satisfactory is certain; but that Mill felt them to be unsatisfactory is not. The evidence for Mill's "realism" comes when Mill is attacking Hamilton for regarding mathematics as no part of an education. Mill says that this is the wildest obscurantism because mathematics is vital in science; no science can be systematic without the greatest possible use of mathematics. And he says of the place of mathematics in Newton's cosmology: "While the laws of number underlie the laws of extension, and these two underlie the law of force, so do the laws of force underlie all the other laws of the material universe." [30] This indeed shows an enthusiasm for mathematical physics as the key to all truth; but it is not Platonic unless we can give great weight to the metaphors of *underlie,* and to Anschutz's *surface of experience.* Anschutz certainly does: "At the base, supporting the rest of the laws of nature, are the laws of number; above them are the laws of extension; above them are the laws of motion; finally, on top, immediately underlying the surface of experience, are the other laws of the universe." [31] The impression we are given is that Mill finally says that phenomena are the appearances of numbers; and it is hard to believe that he does. The sense in which numerical laws underlie all others is simply that everything is subject to these laws, whereas some things are not subject to laws of motion, and so on. Mill's own gloss on what he says is hardly Platonic: "As an extension is not a number, though a numerical fact may be a mark of an extension, so a force is neither a number nor an extension. But a force is only cognisable through its effects, and the effects by which forces are best known are effects in extension. The measure of a force is the space through which it will carry a body of given magnitude in a given time. . . . All

questions of force, therefore, can be reduced to questions of
direction and magnitude: and as all questions of direction
and magnitude are capable of being reduced to equations between numbers, every question which can be raised respecting
Force, abstractedly from its origin, can be resolved if the corresponding algebraical equation can." [32] We cannot say very
much more about this than that Mill is pointing out how
useful mathematics is in science, and how mathematized mechanics is one of the great scientific successes. And this is
substantially the tone of the *St. Andrew's Address*. There in
fact Mill makes one statement which Anschutz fails to cite,
which looks much more like a piece of Platonism. He says:
"It is chiefly from mathematics that we realise that there
actually is a road to truth by means of reasoning; that anything real, and which will be found true when tried, can be
arrived at by a mere operation of the mind." [33] It is hard to
see quite what Mill means; but easy to see that he does not
mean that we can have *a priori* knowledge of reality, for he
at once goes on to account for the mistrust of deductive reasoning by citing "The flagrant abuse of mere reasoning in the
days of the schoolmen, when men argued confidently to supposed facts of outward nature without establishing their
premises or checking their conclusions by observation." [34] The
panegyric to which Anschutz draws our notice is one in favor
of mathematical physics, and it is closely followed by the un-
Platonic advice to study chemistry along with it as the needed
reminder that ultimately what matters is the care with which
we make our observations and obtain the premises which we
shall use in our deductive arguments. It would, in any case,
be hard to infer much from an address in which Mill is doing nothing more intellectually demanding or philosophically
significant than explaining the virtues of the several university
disciplines. But we may conclude on a thoroughly anti-Pla-
tonist note by recalling what Mill says of the dangers of
mathematics in *Hamilton*: "It leads men to place their ideal
of science in deriving all knowledge from a small number of

axiomatic premises, accepted as self-evident, and taken for the immediate intuitions of reason." [35] It is hard to envisage a convinced Platonist making such a complaint. We have argued often enough that Mill was a convinced admirer of system in science; it is necessary to add to this that he was quite aware that the furthest perfection to which scientific systems were brought would not make them one whit less empirical sciences. The school of Mill is the school of Locke.

NOTES

1. Day, *Critical History of Western Philosophy*, p. 347. 2. *System of Logic*, II, vi, 2. 3. *Ibid.*, II, v, 6. 4. *Ibid.* 5. *Ibid.*, III, xxiv, 6. 6. *Ibid.*, III, xxiv, 7. 7. *Ibid.*, III, xxiv, 5. 8. Frege, *Foundations of Arithmetic*, p. 9. 9. *System of Logic*, II, vi, 2. 10. *Ibid.* 11. Frege, *Foundations of Arithmetic*, p. 11. 12. *System of Logic*, II, vi, 3. 13. *Ibid.* 14. *Ibid.* 15. *Ibid.* 16. Jevons, *Pure Logic and Other Minor Works*, pp. 199–221. 17. Jackson, "Mill on Geometry," *Mind* (1941), pp. 1–18. 18. *System of Logic*, II, v, 1. 19. *Ibid.* 20. *Ibid.* 21. Jevons, *Pure Logic and Other Minor Works*, p. 205. 22. *System of Logic*, II, v, 5. 23. *Ibid.* 24. *Ibid.*, II, v, 1. 25. *Ibid.* 26. *Ibid.* 27. Jevons, *Pure Logic and Other Minor Works*, p. 217. 28. Anschutz, *The Philosophy of J. S. Mill*, p. 157. 29. *Ibid.*, p. 158. 30. *Examination of Hamilton*, p. 603. 31. Anschutz, *The Philosophy of J. S. Mill*, p. 158. 32. *Examination of Hamilton*, p. 603. 33. *St. Andrew's Address*, p. 46. 34. *Ibid.* 35. *Examination of Hamilton*, p. 611.

VI

MIND AND MATTER

Until now, the account I have given of Mill's philosophy of
science has rested on, and sometimes referred to, a more or
less implicit view of his metaphysics. As a running com-
mentary on the problems he faces concerning the status of
natural laws, the nature of causal connection, the place of
suspect entities such as "forces," it has been suggested that
Mill's philosophy embodies a reductionist, atomist drive. In
discussing Mill's views on mathematical and geometrical truth,
I have tried to link this to his belief that all knowledge is
ultimately of empirical particulars, that in consequence it
must be possible to show that apparently necessary truths
about the physical world are not necessary at all, but well-
attested empirical truths of a wider than ordinary scope. But
in coming to Mill's account of our belief in the external world
and his account of our belief in our own identity, we come to
the metaphysical heart of Mill's system, where at last the
assumptions appear clearly, and where the difficulties they
create are most strikingly obvious.

But first let us briefly recapitulate the process by which we
come to this core of Mill's philosophy. It will be recalled that
the problem Mill faced over laws of nature was, to put it
crudely, that of what laws of nature are *about*, in the sense

that we can readily agree that particular statements are about particular facts, or particular things, but find it hard to believe that there are "general facts" for generalizations to be about. Mill's way out of the dilemma is to agree that everything which exists is particular. But the percipients of these particular states of affairs form expectations in accordance with the laws of association, and when they make these expectations explicit they do so by enunciating rules of inference which license them to expect certain particulars on the strength of their knowledge of others. In short, Mill reduces laws of nature to the rules which we consciously or unconsciously follow in linking one particular to another, one atomic state of affairs to another atomic state of affairs. Again with troublesome concepts like "force," Mill is clear that they are not the names of occult entities but, rather, are our names for inference-rules, for our belief that such-and-such a result would follow from such-and-such a cause. In other words, suspect entities are reduced to nonsuspect ones, and the mode of reduction is to refer them back to the operations of the mind of the percipient upon the raw material of experience. Similarly, when we turn to mathematical truth, Mill defends two vital aspects of his doctrine, one that there are only the objects of empirical experience for mathematics to be conversant with, and the other that there can be no intuitive knowledge of empirical truth. So mathematics is accounted for by the mind's habit of thinking that what is always perceived together always exists together, and its habit of imagining that what is nearly so, is exactly so. Again, the emphasis falls on the way the percipient deals with the atoms of experience by the conscious or unconscious employment of rules of inference.

In the light of this, we can also look ahead to Mill's views on the explanation of human action and its consequences for an ethics of calculated utilities. If the possibility of natural science is so closely linked to the presupposition of atomic events, whose causal connections are mapped by natural laws, it would seem that a similar presupposition must lie behind any attempt at human psychology, the natural science of the perceiving subject. It seems, that is, as if the percipient must also be explicable as a series of psychological events of which he is the locus, causally linked and mapped by the laws of mind. This, indeed, is the assumption which we shall see underlying Mill's explanation of how man is subject to necessity and nonetheless free. As we have argued all along, Mill's belief in a "scientific" ethics rests on the assumption that the feelings and actions of men are amenable to scientific explanation, so that it looks as if he must be committed to an atomistic account of personal identity to preserve the unity of scientific method in which he so firmly believed. But, even though Mill's psychology is atomistic, even though his account of justice, both retributive and distributive, is permeated by psychological atomism, and even though the sociology on which utilitarian ethics is based is explicitly said to rest on psychological atomism, when Mill comes to face the question whether persons are susceptible of the same reductive analysis as things, he is unable to reply confidently that they are.

Mill's account of the analysis of mind, such as it is, is a brief and hesitant conclusion to the two confident chapters in which he criticizes Hamilton's misunderstandings of the Berkeleian and related accounts of the external world and gives his own account. These two chapters, and especially that on the psychological theory of our belief in an external world, set the standards to which the theory of our belief in the identity of mind has to conform. The account of our belief in matter is important for this reason, but it is also important in showing how far Mill was prepared to push his reductionist program—not merely to the elimination of forces, but even to the elimination of things.

Mill's problem, in contending with Hamilton's account of our belief in the existence of an external, material world is, as ever, to find some way other than that of ascribing it to the "deliverances of consciousness" to explain our belief in

the continuing existence of material objects, external to ourselves and not necessarily perceived by us.[1] Hamilton had
argued in terms reminiscent of Kant that in all our acts of
perception we are immediately aware of an ego and a non-
ego, ourselves and the external world. Mill quotes him as saying: "We are immediately conscious in perception of an ego
and a non-ego, known together, and known in contrast to
each other. . . . When I concentrate my attention on the
simplest act of perception, I return from my observation with
the most irresistible conviction of two facts, or rather two
branches of the same fact; that I am, and that something
different from me exists. . . . Such is the fact of perception
revealed in consciousness, and it determines mankind in general in their almost equal assurance of the reality of an external world, as of the existence of our own minds."[2] Mill, as
ever, objects to such an account of the deliverances of consciousness on the grounds that even if it reports what we now
think whenever we perceive anything, it is not an account of
what we *must* think—which is what it purports to be—nor
yet an account of what must be the case.

It is not easy to discover what exactly Hamilton's doctrines
amounted to; more even than in the case of Kant, he ob-
scures metaphysics with transcendental psychology. Yet, to the
extent that this is equally true of Mill, we have to see the
argument between them as in some sense both psychological
and metaphysical. As to the psychological issue between them,
we can best express it by saying that Hamilton ascribed to us
a faculty of intuition (in a non-Kantian sense) with which we
just did perceive an external world of persisting things at the
same time as perceiving ourselves as persisting subjects of this
perceptual experience. Mill, by contrast, denies the existence
of a faculty of intuition, and argues that what the intuitionist
school saw as a belief whose validity was certified by its being
the result of intuition could quite well be explained as a
belief which had grown up on the basis of a long experience
of fulfilled expectation. Or, rather, we should say that this

is what Mill argues for the belief in an external world; in the case of the belief in our own identity he is not such an uncompromising enemy of intuition. The metaphysical issue, on the other hand, can be phrased as: Does matter, or does mind, exist?[3] Plainly these are strange questions, not on the same level as asking whether there are chairs in the next room, or asking whether Mr. Pickwick really existed. For this reason, Hume, with whom Mill inevitably challenges comparison on this issue, denied that there was a legitimate problem about whether there was an external world, allowing sense only to the question of how we come to think that there is and what this belief amounts to.[4] But, of course it may be said with equal justice that to answer the question of how we come to believe in an external world is very like answering the question of whether there is an external world, for it requires at any rate an answer to the question of what we suppose an external world to consist in, and this seems an irretrievably metaphysical question. In other words, the psychological and the metaphysical problems are much the same problem.

Mill's discussion of "Sir William Hamilton's Review of Theories on the Belief in an External World"[5] is not so labored as its title, but is hard reading nonetheless. But three significant points in it are worth mentioning. In the first place, Mill does not rule out the possibility of our perceptions being *caused* by objects which in themselves are nothing like the perceptions which they cause; but he does show himself well aware of all the usual objections made to Locke's doctrine of representative perception, and it is a charge against Hamilton that he both allows and condemns representative perception. Whatever we can say, we certainly cannot claim that our perceptions are good likenesses of in principle unperceivable objects. In the second place, it emerges clearly that the reasons behind Mill's espousal of a phenomenalist position are not connected with philosophical skepticism; that is, he does not retreat to sense data as better known, or less likely to delude us, than material objects, and the point of the reduction is not that our judgments about sense data are in principle less likely to be wrong than our judgments about things, but simply that in investigating the items of our knowledge, it appears that judgments about things can be accounted for in terms of judgments about perception and the possibilities of perception. The drive is to account for our present beliefs and knowledge in terms of the minimum possible mental equipment which would suffice to generate it. Hence it is not so much epistemological anxiety as psychological curiosity which leads to his account of our belief in matter. In the third place, Mill shows himself willing to admit *some* near-intuitive elements in the mind's make-up, that is, some elements in the fully developed modes of thought which we all possess which are not susceptible of analysis into simpler modes of consciousness. In particular, he does not hold an evidential account of memory to be plausible, in that he thinks that all such accounts suffer from a *petitio;* neither does he reduce memory to part of the present stream of consciousness, but holds instead that we give an intuitive assent to certain occurrent memories as true representations of past experience. And he does not confine our knowledge to present perception and memories of perception; there is something like an intuitive awareness of some relations which does not fit this picture. Thus he says: "I do admit other sources of knowledge than sensation and the memory of sensation, though not than consciousness and the memory of consciousness. I have distinctly declared that the elementary relations of our sensations to one another, viz. their resemblances, and their successions and coexistences, are subjects of direct apprehension. And I have avowedly left the question undecided whether our perception of ourselves—of our own personality —is not a case of the same kind." [6] In other words, while Mill is anxious to reduce the elementary attributes of mind as far as possible, he has a keen sense of the limits to which this process can be pushed.

Having cleared the way by disposing of Hamilton's attacks

on various phenomenalist positions, Mill now moves to his
own account. The mental equipment which he supposes necessary to generate our belief in the reality of an external world
of persisting material things is our ability to form expectations
on the basis of the ordinary workings of the mind in accordance with the law of the association of ideas. Thus "after
having had actual sensations, we are capable of forming the
conception of Possible sensations; sensations which we are not
feeling at the present moment, but which we might feel, and
should feel if certain conditions were present, the nature of
which conditions we have, in many cases, learnt by experience." [7] The laws of association provide that impressions
which have been received in close spatial and temporal prox-
imity will be remembered together, and that what has been
experienced together will, in the absence of evidence to the
contrary, be ascribed to the concurrence of phenomena in nature. These laws, then, are enough to generate a belief in the
external world; but the question we are faced with is that
of what such a belief amounts to. Mill argues that two qualities distinguish our concept of physical objects from our concept of particular sensations. In the first place, actual sensations exist only so long as we are having them, they do not
exist unfelt, unperceived; their *esse* is *percipi*. But material
objects exist unperceived, and are in this sense permanent.
Hence we have to account for the belief in "Perdurability" [8]
as Mill calls it, echoing Kant. Permanence is one of the marks
of externality, at least in the sense of externality to our present
train of thought; thus Mill asks: "What is it we mean, or
what is it which leads us to say, that the objects we perceive
are external to us, and not a part of our own thoughts?" and
his answer is clear enough: "We mean, that there is concerned
in our perceptions something which exists when we are not
thinking of it; which existed before we had ever thought of
it, and would exist if we were annihilated; and further, that
there exist things which we never saw, touched, or otherwise
perceived, and things which have never been perceived by

man." [9] He adds to this that we believe also in the permanence of the characteristics of the object, in distinction to the fleeting nature of its appearances, so that, for example, it remains square and white whether it appears so, or appears round and yellow.[10] The other major characteristic of objects is that they are public, while particular sensations are private; the same object can be perceived by a multitude of different persons, while the occurrent sensation is different for each perceiver. By the time Mill comes to this distinction, he has already adopted the terminology of "permanent possibilities," and is anxious to show that the distinction between the public and the private remains intact: ". . . though the sensations cease, the possibilities remain in existence; they are independent of our will, our presence, and everything which belongs to us. We find, too, that they belong as much to other human or sentient beings as to ourselves. We find other people grounding their expectations and conduct upon the same permanent possibilities on which we ground ours. But we do not find them experiencing the same actual sensations." [11]

Mill, therefore, is accounting for our belief in a permanent and public source or origin of our subjective, transitory impressions. And as appears from the foregoing, he does so in terms of a belief in the "permanent possibility" of sensation. Mill's case is this: we perceive sensations which bear various relations to each other and to ourselves, and according to the laws of association we form expectations about ideas which we do *not* have, but which under certain circumstances we could and would have. In the light of our earlier discussion of natural laws, it is worth stressing that this is not a process which begins by being conscious, but is one which we can *make* explicit. As Day puts it: "inferences by association are not inferences *from* a general rule and some other premiss, but unconscious inferences from particulars to particulars *in accordance with* a rule. Hence, when I infer from the existence of a group of simultaneous possibilities of sensation the existence of a permanent, public, etc. object (say a mountain), I am doing the same kind of thing as I do when I infer from its faintness that the mountain is several miles distant, and say (what is strictly speaking false) that I see that it is so." [12] In other words, what Mill is saying is that to say, for instance, that we see a chair is to express our conviction that the sensations we are having are related to a complex set of sensations which we might, if we chose to, experience under various conditions. We infer from sensations present to sensations past but remembered, and to sensations absent and perhaps never experienced by anyone but nonetheless possible. As Mill points out, the process of inference is so habitual and rapid that we are not conscious of there being any such process, except when we come to analyze the situation. But the logic—or the psychology—of the case is that we are actually performing an inference, and not directly experiencing external objects. Chairs, tables, and the rest of the furniture of the material world are thus inference rules for linking sensations.

The problem is: In what sense and to what extent does this account for our belief in the existence of a material world? Mill, following Berkeley, holds that it is adequate to account for all our actual experience, and is thus an adequate account. Dr. Johnson is dismissed as beneath the level of argument, and Mill repeatedly declares that the behavior of Berkeleians will be no different from that of anti-Berkeleians.[13] But Mill's position is not as clear as the certainty with which he gives it leads us to expect it to be. At one point he seems to think that he believes in matter as emphatically as does the plain man, at another he strongly hints that the plain man is under an illusion about the existence of matter. As to permanence and publicity, however, he is clear that permanent possibilities meet these requirements: "We believe that we perceive a something closely related to all our sensations, but different from those which we are feeling at any particular minute; and distinguished from sensations altogether, by being permanent and always the same, where these are fugitive, variable, and alternately displace one another. But these attributes of the object of perception are properties belonging to all the possibilities of sensation which experience guarantees. The belief in such permanent possibilities seems to me to include all that is essential or characteristic in the belief in substance." [14] But this does not solve the problem. Roughly, it is this: what the plain man believes is that objects *cause* sensations, in that sensations are part of his private psychological life, caused in him because he comes into one and another kind of causal relationship with physical objects. It is not clear that a possibility of sensation is the sort of thing —indeed not clear that it is a thing at all—which would cause a particular sensory experience. In other words, Mill's account at its toughest reduces things to rules for linking sensations; the popular view at its weakest is that things cause sensations, and that they are able to do so because human percipients are corporeal objects standing in definable physical relations to objects in the (spatially) external world. These views do not seem to be identical by any means. Further, Mill himself at least suggests that there is something dubious in the plain man's views, for he explains the belief in matter as the outcome of long experience of causal relations holding between the several parts of our sensory experience; inevitably, he says, we are led to extrapolate from these relations to the idea of a causal relation holding between *all* our experience and something beyond it which is its cause. Mill does not say that this process is invalid; but it is plainly in his mind that it is, for he has certainly absorbed enough Kant to accept that where our understanding of a relation is essentially based on its application within experience, we cannot apply it intelligibly beyond that experience. [15]

Ultimately, indeed, ambiguity about such terms as "experience" is fatal to Mill's phenomenalism. This is demonstrated clearly enough by the expression to which he attaches such store—the "permanent possibility of sensation." For this expression suggests both that there are external things, waiting to be sensed, and also that there are not, that there is only the sensory stream in the mind and the possibility of different streams. If permanent possibilities are things which can permanently be sensed, this is all very well, but this is a non-Berkeleian, realist view; if things are merely the possibility that we can have experiences, this is an immaterialist, almost Berkeleian view. (The chief difference being that for Berkeley objects are occurrent ideas, not possible ones, which of course is the reason why they have to be thought by God when they are not thought by man, a complication which Mill's account avoids.[16]) Moreover, the identification of objects with *possible* sensations seems almost more shocking than their identification with actual sensations. The view that the metaphysical or epistemological "solidity" of a potential but not actual idea is equal to that of an actual object is a difficult one to swallow.

However, flawed though it is, Mill's account of matter is put forward with great confidence, and this confidence is important, for it accounts, if the thesis of this book is correct, for Mill's convictions on topics not obviously closely related to the analysis of matter. The analysis of matter is, so to speak, the occasion when the phenomenalist and reductionist has to put all his cards on the table; it is the point at which he has to state what he supposes the basic constituents of our experience and our understanding of the world to be. To Mill it is clear that the answer is that we build the external world out of internal sensation; we bind the atoms of sensation with the mortar of inference rules. Philosophical analysis is required to bring this process to light, to show the rules we unconsciously use, the basic elements which we usually do not examine. But, having gone so far, it is impossible to rest. Part of the natural order—and it was very important in Mill's eyes to insist that they *are* part of the natural order—are people and their behavior. Among the stream of events in the universe a significant element consists of the actions of human beings. Since for Mill it is imperative to apply the methods of the physical sciences to human beings and their behavior, it is an inescapable question whether the analysis which he gives of matter can be given of persons as well.

In the next chapter, when we come to look at Mill's reconciliation of free will and determinism, we shall see the extent to which Mill assumed in general that the same atomistic analysis was applicable. But when he is actually trying to answer the question he is quite unable to persuade himself that the phenomenalist account is the correct one. In this he is unlike Bain, and unlike Grote, but resembles Hume, when the latter found that he had chased himself into a blind alley from which no escape was possible.[17] In many ways, it seems obvious that the reductionist program is bound to collapse at this point. All along, the assumption has been that philosophical analysis will reveal the world as the construction of an essentially disembodied spectator. Natural laws, forces, even material objects, are the rules of inference according to which the spectator links his sensations. But then we must ask: What of his own identity, how can he identify himself? How is this disembodied spectator to account for the existence of this disembodied spectator, to distinguish himself from the flow of experience? Or, more maliciously yet, we may inquire how he is to "construct" himself, analogously to the way he "constructs" the physical world. One could almost leave the matter there, knowing that Mill has no answer to these questions, but there is something to be said for not treating the case so cursorily. For Mill thinks that the phenomenalist analysis can go a long way even in dealing with personal identity, and of course he must think this if he is to give as much credence as he does to traditional empiricist psychology. And, equally, no nonphenomenalist account of the mind will satisfy him; for the events which go to make up a person's— or a mind's, since the terms are here interchangeable—history will be susceptible of the usual atomistic analysis, and if we say that the self is something over and above these psychological events, we have the embarrassing task of characterizing the bare self, as hard a task as characterizing matter without its sensible qualities. Moreover, it is distressing to admit to such an asymmetry between mind and matter as this introduces; if, like Mill, we hold that the world is one unitary order, such an asymmetry is more than merely untidy.

Mill is quick to point out that all we know of Mind is "as represented by the succession of manifold feelings which metaphysicians call by the name of States or Modifications of Mind." [18] But we have, just as in the case of matter, a belief in something permanent and distinct from these feelings. And this permanence is amenable to precisely the same analysis as is permanence in the case of matter: "The belief I entertain that my mind exists, when it is not feeling, nor thinking, nor conscious of its own existence, resolves itself into a belief of a Permanent Possibility of those states." [19] Mill digresses to attack the charge that such a doctrine amounts to solipsism, by giving an account of our knowledge of other minds as essentially inferential, resting on the assumption that the physical phenomena which precede and follow mental activity in our own case do so in other cases also. But he admits that even though the phenomenalist theory can withstand the usual objections, it "has intrinsic difficulties . . . which it seems to me beyond the power of metaphysical analysis to remove." [20] The phenomena which make for difficulties are memory and expectation. Mill regards both of these as in part consisting of present feelings, and in this respect on a par with sensation; but the fatal difference is that "each of them involves a belief in more than its own present existence." [21] That is, a memory involves the extra belief that it resembles some past experience, and an expectation the belief that it resembles some future experience. But not this only, for the important point, and fatal to the theory, is that the experience in either case has to be *ours* and not someone else's, that a memory essentially refers back to the experiences of an owner of these experiences, that not any past experiences will be remembered, but only those of the person doing the remembering. Or, as Mill puts it, the belief is "that I myself formerly had, or that I myself, and no other, shall hereafter have the sensations remembered or expected." [22] In other words, the fatal flaw of the phenomenalist account of personal identity is that in order to construct the series of thoughts which constitute a given person, the principle of selection which we must employ to construct the *correct* series already involves reference to the person whose thoughts they are. To construct *my* mind, I must employ only *my* thoughts, *my* memories, *my* expectations. But to suppose that this can be done already implies that we have some criteria for identifying the person who is the owner of the appropriate thoughts. If this is so, it cannot be the case that we have to construct persons out of their thoughts; the owner, as it were, is prior to the property. The stumbling block in Mill's account, both of mind and of matter, is that our existing criteria for identifying both persons and things plainly rest on the fact that persons are embodied, i.e., are spatially distinct from each other and from other physical objects, and will not readily survive transplantation into a metaphysics which involves an insubstantial view of the self.

Mill, however, accounts for the breakdown in terms of the ultimately inscrutable nature of the universe. "The truth is, that we are here face to face with that final inexplicability, at which, as Sir W. Hamilton observes, we inevitably arrive when we reach ultimate facts." [23] There are less charitable accounts of Mill's failure than this; one of them was given by Bradley, who first dismissed the "bag theory" of the self with his mocking *mot:* "Mr Bain collects that the mind is a collection. Has he ever thought who collects Mr Bain?" [24] and then went on to say of Mill that "With the . . . fact before him, which gave the lie to his whole psychological theory, he could not ignore it, he could not recognise it, he would not call it a fiction; so he put it aside as a 'final inexplicability,' and thought, I suppose, that by covering it with a phrase he got rid of its existence." [25] This, if brutal, is not unfair, for it is undeniable that Mill goes on to discuss free will and related problems as if there were no difficulties involved in his phenomenalism. Mill felt that this was justified by the facts; I am much less certain, for it seems to me that the primacy of persons over their feelings and their actions raises problems for Mill's attempt to reconcile free will and determinism, and again, later, for his attempt to reconcile utility and justice. This latter will not concern us until we discuss Mill's attempts to "prove" utilitarian ethics, but the former rests at the heart of Mill's belief in a natural science of man and society, and to it we must turn at once.

NOTES

1. *Examination of Hamilton*, XII, pp. 234–243.   2. *Ibid.*, pp. 183–184. 3. Day, "Mill on Matter," *Philosophy* (1964), pp. 59–60.   4. Hume, *Treatise of Human Nature*, II, iv, 2.   5. *Examination of Hamilton*, X, pp. 182–218.   6. *Ibid.*, p. 210n.   7. *Ibid.*, p. 219.   8. *Ibid.*, p. 221.   9. *Ibid.* 10. *Ibid.*   11. *Ibid.*, pp. 226–227.   12. Day, "Mill on Matter," *Philosophy* (1964), p. 53.   13. *Examination of Hamilton*, p. 228.   14. *Ibid.*, p. 229. 15. *Ibid.*, pp. 229–232.   16. Berkeley, *A New Theory of Vision*, etc., pp. 266, 271; cf. Mill, *Dissertations*, Vol. IV, p. 174.   17. Hume, *Treatise*, Appendix, pp. 633–636.   18. *Examination of Hamilton*, p. 235.   19. *Ibid.* 20. *Ibid.*, p. 241.   21. *Ibid.*   22. *Ibid.*, pp. 241–242.   23. *Ibid.*, p. 242. 24. Bradley, *Ethical Studies*, p. 39n.   25. *Ibid.*

VII

FREEDOM IN
A DETERMINED WORLD

Mill's discussion of "liberty and necessity" is appropriately placed at the beginning of the final book of the *System of Logic.* The final book is concerned with the way in which a natural science of social life can be created and with the problems which such an attempt will meet. To reveal one of our conclusions from the outset, we can say that Mill's picture of social science was that the science of society should be constructed from the science of the individual member of society; the laws which govern the behavior of men in the aggregate must be the result of inference from the laws which govern the behavior of individual men, just as the laws governing the behavior of a complete physical system can be inferred from those which govern the behavior of its components. This at once raises two questions; the first, whether the actions of individuals form a subject for science in the way that Mill supposed, and the second, whether if they do we must revise our current beliefs about human nature, and particularly about what is involved in our making choices or taking decisions. And it is this second question which Mill believed to be the important one, since he thought it was almost indisputable that the only obstacle to everyone accepting the validity of a mechanistic psychology was the common prejudice that the existence of choice is incompatible with such a psychology. Mill, of course, had very strong reasons for wishing to persuade his readers that they could accept a deterministic framework for human behavior without loss to their ordinary ideas about free will and choice; as we saw in the Introduction, Mill believed the establishment of a science of society to be an essential step toward implementing rational policies of social change. If determinism took away our freedom of choice, so it seemed to him, there could be no place for science as a guide to choice; we should simply be helpless spectators of a future which we knew to be inevitably ours. But if the reality of choice eliminates determinism—and this for Mill was as much as to say that it eliminates science— then it seemed that choice could not be guided by science. So Mill was forced to show that a scientific sociology and psychology could in no way impair our freedom of choice.

Mill was, in fact, more pleased with his discussion of this problem than with any other part of the *System of Logic*.[1] He never lost his belief that his argument did reconcile freedom and necessity, by showing that our actions are both freely chosen and causally determined.[2] By the time that he came to write the essay *On Liberty,* he was satisfied that the problem was no more than a pseudo-problem, generated by miscalling determinism by the name of necessity.[3] The essentials of the case which he made in the *System of Logic* were reiterated twenty years afterward in *Hamilton.* The interests involved in the two accounts are rather different; in *Hamilton* Mill addresses himself directly to the problem of whether a determinist account of human action is compatible with moral responsibility, while in the *System of Logic* he puts forward the problem as more obviously methodological: "we are met by an objection, which, if not removed, would be fatal to the attempt to treat human conduct as a subject of science. Are the actions of man, like all other natural events, subject to invariable laws? . . . This is often denied; . . ."[4] But, of course, the argument is fundamentally the same, since the case against Mill's psychology is precisely that this psychology is wrecked by the existence of free choice, and the argument in both books is to the effect that a determinist psychology can accommodate our usual conception of choice, and therefore moral responsibility and allied concepts.

Mill's first argument in defense of his case that free will and determinism are compatible is the familiar argument that causes do not constrain, that necessity is not the same thing as coercion. In both the *System of Logic* and *Hamilton,* Mill complains that it is a mistake to apply the term "necessity" to what he preferred to call "moral causation." [5] Mill maintained that the erroneous belief that free will must imply the absence of causation was largely the result of "the associations with a word; and that it would be prevented by forbearing to employ, for the expression of the simple fact of causation, so extremely inappropriate a term as Necessity." [6] The word "necessity" implies not merely the fact of uniform sequence but the fiction of irresistibleness; it implies that it is not we who govern our actions but some power outside ourselves against which there is no point in struggling. Mill therefore identifies two fatalist positions from which he dissociates the determinist; he labeled these "Asiatic" and "Modified" fatalism respectively.[7] The former view is that none of our desires, wishes, choices, and so on have any effect on the outcome of events; events are governed by fate, by the unpredictable and unintelligible will of some power beyond our control: "A Fatalist believes, or half believes (for nobody is a consistent Fatalist) not only that whatever is about to happen will be the infallible result of the causes which produce it (which is the true Necessarian doctrine) but, moreover, that there is no use in struggling against it; that it will happen however we may strive to prevent it." [8] But it is the modified fatalist view which is the more dangerous, because it is much more credible; it is the Owenite view which had so distressed Mill in the period of his nervous collapse when the doctrine of necessity had hung over him like a cloud. The Owenites were agreed that our actions were the result of our wishes and choices, and as reformers they were more than willing to agree that our actions did have effects on the course of events; but they believed that our choices and hence our actions were the inevitable results of our characters, characters which we did not produce, for which we were not responsible, so that ultimately we were not really responsible for our actions—"our character having been made for us, and not by us, we are not responsible for it, nor for the actions it leads to, and should in vain attempt to alter them." [9] Believing as he did that this was to confuse the fact that our characters cause our actions with the fiction that our characters force our behavior on us, and vulnerable as he was to the charge that his own character had been made for him by Bentham and James Mill, Mill energetically sets out to combat this "grand error."

It is, he says, quite plainly false to argue that a man cannot alter his character. It is true that our characters do not change just for the wishing; but our characters are what they are as the result of various influences and can therefore become what we should prefer them to be if we are able to place ourselves under other influences to achieve this. *We* can influence our characters, just as other persons have influenced them in the past: "If they could place us under the influence of certain circumstances, we, in like manner can place ourselves under the influence of other circumstances. We are exactly as capable of making our own character, *if we will,* as others are of making it for us." [10] To the Owenite, then, one's character appeared as a straitjacket constraining one's actions; to Mill it was a suit, to be altered and reshaped should it not fit what we wanted to look like. And Mill is plainly more right about the facts than the Owenite; it simply is not the case that we are forced to act in the ways we do by our characters. Indeed it is nearer the mark to say that to talk about our characters is to talk of how we behave when no one forces us to behave in one way rather than another. But Mill allows the Owenite a struggle; he envisages him retorting that the words "if we will" give Mill's case away, for, says the Owenite, the will to change must come from somewhere other than the agent's existing character, i.e., from outside him and hence from a source beyond his control: "it comes to us either from external causes, or not at all." [11]

Mill's reply is that this distorts the facts. The Owenite case is that we *cannot* alter our characters, while the evidence he has produced shows only that we *shall not unless* we wish to. The crux, for Mill, is the case of the man who does wish to change. The gloomy message of the Owenite is that he will be doomed to failure; his wish is bound to be frustrated. Mill agrees that a man may try to change his character and nonetheless fail; but he denies that this is in any way inevitable. If the man takes the appropriate steps in "self-culture," then he will find that "the work is not so irrevocably done as to be incapable of being altered." [12] And Mill backs up this argument with an appeal to the distinction between causation and constraint. Of course human actions are the inevitable result of whatever causes produce them; and of course if a man's present character does not alter then he will go on performing those actions which the set of causes that we call his character will inevitably produce. But this is not to say that the present set of causes cannot be modified or obstructed. It is certainly not to say that the actions which are the inevitable result of the present causes will still occur regardless of all efforts to change those causes—efforts which may take the form of deciding that these causes shall no longer operate unhindered. To agree that actions are the inevitable result of their causes is not to say that we are forced to perform them, not to say that they will happen whatever we do about it. Mill sums up his case in the well-known dictum, "when we say that human actions will take place of necessity, we only mean that they will certainly happen if nothing prevents." [13] To believe that causation is a form of compulsion is a mistake; if we say that a person of a given character *must* behave in a certain way, we do not mean that he would behave in that way, regardless of his own wants, wishes, and intentions; all we mean is that so long as *these* causes alone operate, then *these* effects will always follow. No more than this is ever asserted; as Mill says: "Any *must* in the case, other than the unconditional universality of the fact, we know nothing of." [14] And on the facts of the case, Mill is surely right; people do decide to change their characters and they do sometimes succeed in so doing. It may, as Mill was more than ready to agree, take time and patience, it might always be a matter of more and less. But for all that, it is foolish to suppose that a rational agent is imprisoned in his character, and that his relations to his character are a matter of passive acceptance of how he happens to be.

If causation does not involve compulsion, what does it involve? The most important element seems to be that of predictability. To say that human actions are subject to necessity amounts to saying that they are causally predictable: "given the motives which are present to an individual's mind, and given likewise the character and disposition of the individual, the manner in which he will act may be unerringly inferred; . . . if we knew the individual thoroughly, and knew all the inducements which are acting upon him, we could foretell his conduct with as much certainty as we can predict any physical event." [15] And so far is predictability from being incompatible with our freedom of choice that, according to Mill, our notion of what constitutes free and responsible action positively requires predictability. We should not think it a mark of our freedom, but a reflection on our rationality and intelligence if we were not to a great extent predictable in our behavior. If our friends were not certain until after the event whether we should refuse a bribe, we should not think they held a high opinion of our integrity; as Mill says, "We do not feel the less free because those to whom we are intimately known are well assured how we shall will to act in a particular case. We often, on the contrary, regard the doubt what our conduct will be as a mark of ignorance of our character, and sometimes even resent it as an imputation." [16] The argument that causal predictability constitutes a large part of our concept of responsible action is brought up by Mill when he considers the problem of how we are to distinguish between those people on whom punishment is rightly inflicted for offenses and those whom we do not wish to hold responsible. An essential part of the distinction depends on our ascertaining which persons will be predictably affected by punishment. We only want to punish responsible people, and the paradigm of a person who is *not* responsible is a person whose behavior is either quite unaffected or quite unpredictably affected by the threat or the infliction of punishment. Therefore, the justification of punishment rests on the fact that most people will be moved in a predictable way by the threat of pain, or the promise of reward. Without such an assumption punishment would be gratuitous, even if we were strongly moved to inflict suffering on those who had made us suffer, without inquiring into their responsibility for what they were doing. "Punishment proceeds on the assumption that the will is governed by motives. If punishment had no power of acting on the will, it would be illegitimate, however natural might be the inclination to inflict it." [17] Thus, Mill's position ultimately seems to be that causal regularity in human behavior is implied by our ordinary notions of responsibility; that necessity is not merely far removed from constraint but is part of freedom.

It is within the framework of causal predictability that Mill explains what we mean when we say that a man could have acted otherwise than he did. Plainly, any account of responsible action must explain what we mean by this, since we do *not* hold a person responsible for his actions if we do *not* think he could have done anything else but what he did do. Mill's account of the matter is rendered slightly obscure by the fact that it is couched in the terms of an analysis of our *feeling* that we could have acted otherwise; this is a consequence of the fact that he was attacking Hamilton's account of free will, according to which our possession of a freedom which was incompatible with causation was a truth certified to us by consciousness. Mill, of course, wanted to redescribe the deliverances of consciousness on this matter in a way which would make them compatible with the constancy of causation. Thus in *Hamilton* he writes: "I am told that whether I decide to do or to abstain, I feel that I could have decided the other way. I ask my consciousness what I do feel, and I find indeed, that I feel (or am convinced) that I could, and even should have chosen the other course, if I had preferred it, that is, if I had liked it better; but not that I could have chosen one course while I preferred the other." [18]

To this account there is one obvious objection which must seem so overwhelming that it must be stated at once. And it is somewhat surprising that Mill says little or nothing to meet it, save by implication. The objection is that Mill's account implies that we never do anything except what we want to do, that we never do what we do not want to do. For the analysis above is explicit that we always follow the preferred line of conduct, that is, the line of conduct we like best, and that to be aware of the possibility of having chosen otherwise is only to be aware that if we had liked something better we should have chosen that. On the face of it, any analysis which entails that we always do what we want to do (assuming of course that what happens can be described as something we do at all), must be wrong. And yet Mill is insistent that this is what he is saying; for he goes on to argue that when we talk of the object of our choice we must include in it all the foreseeable consequences of our bare action. Thus I may say that I wanted to go to the opera but felt that I had to stay by the bedside of a sick relative which is, after all, a perfectly normal thing to say. But when we follow Mill's instructions we see how much more plausible is Mill's case; for had I chosen to go to the opera I should thereby also have chosen to disappoint my relative and to incur the hostility and disapproval of the rest of my family. And, of course, these were not things I wanted to choose for myself. So, it is more arguable that I really did choose the line of conduct I liked the most. But this forces on us the task of explaining how it is that our analysis comes up with a result so apparently at odds with ordinary speech; and this can be simply done. To say that we did something which we did not want to do is only to say that there was some factor in the situation besides the bare action itself which determined our choice. A man who is known to enjoy going to the opera and who has a chance to do so has to explain himself if he does not go; to say that he did not want to conveys the impression that his wants have changed, while to say that he did want to but could not draws attention to the other wants which would have been frustrated by his going—giving pleasure to sick relatives and so on. Visiting people in the hospital is not a thing which gives most people pleasure for its own sake, while going to the opera is precisely one of those things which in many cases does. This is the kind of background information which ordinary speech conveys so economically. And Mill's point is simply to insist that none of this involves our believing that we could have really chosen what we did not (all qualifications made) prefer, and hence that no such belief can be involved in our feeling that we could have chosen to do what we did not do. So Mill's account of the matter is that we believe that a different want, or preference, or choice—for he is not careful to distinguish among them—would have been sufficient in the circumstances to produce a different action. It does not seem seriously disputable that such an account is compatible with what we have described as Mill's determinism; in fact, it looks very much like a logical consequence of it.

The view of the nature of wants and choices which this analysis implies is wholly consistent with the abbreviated account of the psychology of action which Mill sets out in *Hamilton*. The main purpose of this account, as also of Mill's remarks on the same subject in the *System of Logic*, is to insist that the psychological antecedents of action are straightforward causal antecedents, related to their effects exactly as any physical cause is related to its effects. Thus in the *System of Logic* he argued that "a volition is not an efficient, but a physical cause. Our will causes our bodily actions in the same sense, and in no other, in which cold causes ice or a spark causes an explosion of gunpowder. The volition, a state of our mind, is the antecedent; the motion of our limbs in conformity to the volition is the consequent." [19] Since the relation is this straightforward causal relation, Mill rejects the intuitionist view that we can foretell before experiencing them what the effects of our volitions will be; as with any causal relation, the idea of the cause can only bring up the idea of the effect after experience of the succession of the latter to the former. And Mill pushes his argument to its limit when he argues that there is no special relation between the self and its volitions. A feature of the intuitionist case was the view that the self brought about volitions in a noncausal way, that it had some form of "direct power" over its volitions. Mill rejects this out of hand: "I am wholly ignorant of possessing any such power. I can indeed influence my volitions, but only as other people can influence my volitions, by the employment of appropriate means. Direct power over my volitions, I am conscious of none." [20] Actions thus appear as the outward effect of a causal chain, where some of the links are interior psychological events, but which can be traced back beyond these to their causes, which will include other psychological events and nonpsychological events alike.

We have already seen how Mill, in discussing causal predictability, gave an account of the implications of human predictability for our everyday notions of responsibility and our belief that we could have performed many actions that we did not in fact perform. To conclude Mill's case for the compatibility of determinism and free will, we must revert to his discussion of responsibility, in terms this time of his defense of the concept against the attacks of the Owenites. It is essential for Mill to be able to justify punishment, with its attendant notions of blame, guilt, and responsibility, since Utilitarian ethics depend very closely on the idea that moral rules, like laws, are essentially backed by sanctions. These sanctions may be the physical sanctions behind the criminal law, or they may be the sanctions of public approval and disapproval, or they may be the internal sanctions of the agent's own conscience. If the notion of guilt is abandoned, then these sanctions would seem to have no justification. The Owenites had taken the heroic extreme course of abandoning the concept of responsibility as a muddle. They rested their case on the account of character which Mill attacked in the *System of Logic*, and to which he returned in *Hamilton*. Men do not make their own characters, but their actions are the inevitable result of whatever characters they happen to have been given, so that men cannot be blamed for the actions they perform. "A man's actions, they said, are the result of his character, and he is not the author of his own character. It is made *for* him, not by him. There is no justice in punishing him for what he cannot help." [21] Mill goes to great lengths to save the concept of responsibility from this attack. He begins by distinguishing two aspects of the feeling of responsibility; in the first place, it may simply be the expectation that harm in the shape of punishment is going to befall us. But this is obviously not the important aspect of the feeling, since we can plainly expect to *be* punished without feeling in the least that we deserve to be. In cases of strict liability in law, such as the law concerning dangerous driving, it is clear enough that a person may agree that he falls within the scope of the law threatening punishment to him, but yet feel that the crime is in no sense his fault. It is, therefore, the second aspect of the feeling, the belief that whether we are punished or not we deserve to be so that creates the difficulty for Mill. And this belief Mill accounts for entirely in genetic terms, in terms, that is, of our internalizing the hostility of others. It is, he says, obvious that people will resent actions which they fear will do them harm, or which they suspect to be intended to do them harm; since this is so, it is more than probable that they will band together to express this resentment and to deter those whom they fear. Most of us will be deterred, therefore, from actions which might cause us to be the targets of hostility; but the effects go deeper. Most of us do not merely fear the hostility of others, but also fear to be at odds with others in any way at all. The bare knowledge that we are out of sympathy with our fellows is distressing; hence the bare thought of the actions which will put us out of sympathy with them is itself distressing. And Mill equates feeling guilty with feeling pain at the *thought* of the projected action. To this, of course, there are also objections—though more subtle ones than to the first part of the analysis. The obvious objection is that an agent who feels pain at the thought of an action may ask himself whether he is *right* to feel this, and it is no answer to this question merely to tell him that he feels it because of a complicated process of internalization. It is, moreover, not much help toward answering the problems of remorse, i.e., of guilt feelings about some past action. A man may very well feel pain at the thought of an action he has performed, and yet not agree that he was either wholly or partially responsible; merely feeling pain does not draw a line between regret that something should have happened, where we do not assume responsibility for it, and remorse at having done whatever it was, where we do. In other words, guilt requires both that we should think that what was done was in some sense deplorable—not merely something we had come to feel averse to—and that we should think we had some choice about what happened.

Perhaps because he felt the weakness of his remarks about the feeling of responsibility, Mill takes another tack, reverting to the relation between responsibility, punishment, and our insistence that no one can be responsible unless he could help what he did. Now Mill places no stress at all on the feeling which may or may not be present in someone's mind; rather, he argues that the place of responsibility is within the causal framework whereby the threat or the infliction of punishment affects the behavior of those to whom it is threatened or on whom it is inflicted. On this account, punishment is a prop to the better motives of the criminally inclined; a man who may not be able to help what he does without the threat becomes able to help what he does when the threat is present to his mind. Thus Mill says of the criminal: "To say that he cannot help it, is true or false, according to the qualification with which the assertion is accompanied. Supposing him to be of a vicious disposition, he cannot help doing the criminal act, if he is allowed to believe that he will be able to commit it unpunished. If, on the contrary, the impression is strong in his mind that a heavy punishment will follow, he can, and in most cases does, help it." [22] As we have already seen, Mill tends to justify punishment on the grounds of its effectiveness in altering the environment within which choices are made by the potential criminal, and this passage is wholly consistent with that tendency. Mill backs up this case with an appeal to what we ordinarily have in mind when we say that someone could *not* help doing what he did; usually we mean that he was coerced or deluded or acting under so violent an impulse that the threat of punishment would have made no difference to his behavior; and it is obviously true that most people are not in this condition for most of the time.

This more or less concludes Mill's case. It is remarkable how popular the case has been with English philosophers, beginning in essentials with Hobbes, receiving its classical statement from Hume, and at times gaining the status of near orthodoxy since then. But I wish to argue that in spite of this, it is a weak case; not in the sense that it is impossible that much of what is argued is true, but in the sense that the argument certainly does not establish that everything that we ordinarily want to say about human choice could survive intact in a determinist universe. None of my criticisms of Mill implies that I believe the determinist case to be false; all I wish to argue—and it is quite enough—is that Mill has not shown, and cannot show since it is not true, that our ordinary ideas about free will are quite compatible with the mechanical determinism he envisages. In other words, though it is important to distinguish between causation and coercion, this is irrelevant to the main issue; though it is important to insist that rationality involves some kind of predictability, this does not establish that causal prediction is no threat; and that Mill's account of how human actions are caused makes his claims to have achieved a reconciliation between the claims of science and freedom quite implausible.

It is obviously important to distinguish between causation and coercion. Whatever view we take of human nature, it is plain that human beings dislike being coerced into doing things they do not wish to do; and it is equally plain that even if all our actions are causally determined, there are many among them which cause us pleasure and many which at any rate cause us no pain. But this is irrelevant to the problem of free will. The confusion which makes it possible to think it relevant arises out of calling the problem one of *freedom;* for, of course, the primary contrast is between freedom and constraint or coercion, while the problem here is essentially one of *ability,* that of whether we are in fact able to do anything other than the things which we actually do. It is not enough to say that the crucial question is that of whether a man *can* do something he does not do, because part at any rate of our notion of what a man cannot do is that he cannot do what he is not free to do. What we must ask is whether a man who is free to do something he does not do—i.e., is not coerced or constrained not to do it—is necessarily in a position to do it, is able to do it. And, in raising this question, let us again confront Mill with the Owenite.

The Owenite, it will be recalled, objected to Mill's claim that we have a more or less free choice about our future characters, because, he said, even if it is true that we are able to change our character *if we want,* the want or the will to change is not something which we can choose to have. Either we happen to have that want or we happen not to. When the point was first raised we followed Mill's own response which was, in effect, to concentrate on a rather different point, namely, to insist that a man who *does* want to change *can* do so. This, however, is only an argument against the first, overbold Owen-ite argument that we *cannot* change (even if we want to). Is it an argument against the second position that *we* cannot change ourselves (because it is not up to *us* to have the want to do so)? On the view which Mill shares with the Owenite, that a man's character is the sum total of his wants, beliefs, dispositions, and so on, it seems the wish to change either already is part of his character or it is not. If it is not, then there either is something in his existing character which will lead to his having the want, or there is not, and if there is not, then the want will simply have to happen to him. In other words, it is not something he can reasonably be expected to choose to have, and can be reproached with not having chosen. Or to put the point another way, if the agent does not want to change, then, as Mill and the Owenite agree, he will not be able to do so. We then ask, supposing he does not want to change, whether he *can* want to change; on the analysis given by Mill, this seems an intelligible question, since if we take the want in question to be one of the means to his making the change, it is reasonable to inquire whether he can acquire the means. The answer, however, is not very clear, since it seems to be the case on this account that either the want merely happens to the agent, or else that he *can* have the want if he wants to have the want; and what this means is not obvious. However, there is no great need to try to give a clearer account of the matter, since the consequences are plain already. They are that either there is already in the agent some element which will lead to his wanting to change and thus being able to change, or else there is nothing *he* can do about it. And in either case, the picture we get is of the agent sitting watching his character's behavior—not the picture which Mill intended to give us. And, of course, while it may be true that this is how some people feel about their actions for much of the time, and perhaps how most people feel about their actions for some of the time, it is certainly not a picture of what we usually think of as rational and free activity. The crux I think is this.

E*

Mill and the Owenite both share the view that a man does not choose to be the way he comes to be at the hands of those who bring him up. This initial character is simply the result of their choices and the resulting environment in which he has been placed. For none of this is he responsible, but at a certain point we want to say he becomes responsible, since he can modify at any rate the ways in which his character is expressed. But when the point is pressed of how this modification is to be effected, Mill is in difficulties; for it seems that whether or not the agent can change his character is something decided by the environment. His actions are the inevitable result of his character, according to Mill, and that character is the inevitable result of the set of causes consisting of his former character and his environment; whenever Mill talks of the agent choosing he is anxious to point out that the choice itself is the inevitable outcome of antecedent causes.[23] Where in this chain of rigidly determined actions is there room for freedom of choice? The Owenite may not be right about the control which people actually have over their choices and actions; but what he does seem to have shown is that the truth of mechanical determinism would wreak havoc with our usual conception of how responsible we are for what we do.

Before considering further the problems posed by a causal analysis of choice, let us consider the argument from the innocuousness of predictability. If causation involved nothing more than the certainty that every choice and every action could be accurately foretold, would this mean that we could accept without qualms the fact that human behavior is causally determined? In other words, would it matter that our actions might be predicted, perhaps years before we were born? Mill's view that it would not matter, that I should be able to tell myself that I had acted freely and predictably, has been echoed by many writers, among the most recent being Hare and Nowell-Smith.[24] But I think it does not require too much thought to see that this is another case where truisms have been taken as answers to nontruistic problems. A fierce attack on Mill's case was launched by F. H. Bradley in his essay on the "Vulgar Notion of Responsibility." [25] Bradley agreed with the truism that we need to be able to count on people being to some extent predictable if we are to call them responsible agents: "We saw that his (*viz.* the plain man's) notion of responsibility implied, together with rationality, a capacity for acting rationally, and further that this means to act with some regularity, to act so that your actions may be counted on, and if counted on, then with more or less certainty predicted." [26]

But Bradley sees that there may be a difference in the kinds of prediction which we make, such that some sorts of prediction will seem startling and alarming. It is all very well our agreeing that we do not mind someone else knowing what we shall do when we ourselves have stated what we shall do, or where their evidence for their prediction is some clear expression of our own intention. Suppose, on the other hand, we confronted the plain man with a detailed prediction of every event in his life up to his present age of, say, forty, and told him that this list had been compiled before his birth—as on Mill's account of the matter it is quite conceivable it should have been. Then, says Bradley, "I believe that he would be most seriously perplexed and in a manner outraged." [27] It is not clear how the issue between Mill and his allies and Bradley and his allies is to be resolved; certainly the question of whether we should be perplexed and outraged is not to be settled merely by counting heads. Nor, unfortunately, is it easy to see why Bradley thought the plain man's shock justifiable. But there is one strand in the argument which ties in closely with what was said in the previous chapter concerning Mill's attempt at a phenomenalist analysis of the self. There it was argued that the rock on which Mill's account founders is our belief that the series of psychological states out of which Mill wishes to construct the self has an "owner" by reference to whom we identify the psychological states in the first place. The psychological states are the transitory condition of a persisting person, so that we cannot construct a person out of them but, rather, abstract the notion of a psychological state from our notion of a person. As with identity, so with intention; among the "possessions" of a person are his wishes, intentions, purposes, and the like. If, following Mill's line of thought, we see these as phenomena which are causally linked and somehow identifiable independently of the person whose intentions, purposes, etc., they are, then once again we seem to be dissolving the owner into his possessions. The trouble with the account of identity was that it seemed to analyze away the whole idea of the self; and similarly with this account of action also. There is certainly room for chains of cause and effect in this picture, but it is dubious whether there is room for agents and actions. Plainly, to follow this argument in the depth it requires is the task of a book rather than a paragraph; for our limited purposes it is enough to establish that it is at any rate clear that Mill's analysis of action is not felt to be so innocuous as he claimed it to be.

Of course, prediction and the problems it creates may be a matter of more and less. For example, a man who had suffered brain injury and was told that he would not now be able to be Prime Minister might suffer various forms of anguish, but hardly the metaphysical horror suggested by Bradley. His brain is in a sense one of the necessary instruments in performing the job, and without its perfect functioning, say in remembering long strings of statistics, he would be unable to do the job at all. But this is no more alarming than learning that we cannot run for the bus when our ankle is broken. But suppose, to follow Mill's determinism through to the very end, that detailed examination revealed that only one set of possibilities could be realized; what sort of reaction might one make to prediction of this sort? It seems plain that a natural reply might be to ask whether one could do anything about it; if we were told that we could not, then surely we should be like the Owenite faced with a literally unalterable character, and we should be in the position of Modified Fatalism. If we were told

that we could, then the difficulty is to see what is left of the prediction; the whole point of prediction is to say what *will* happen, but here we seem to retreat to saying what would happen
if unpredictable things did not intervene to upset the prediction. And it is not obvious that this is a tough enough case to
be called determinist at all. If this is so, then it reinforces our
doubts whether there is room for Mill's determinism between
a fatalist Scylla, which excludes freedom of choice, and an in-
determinist Charybdis, which allows for it. At the very least
Mill must be said to have failed to show that the kind of causal
predictability which he envisaged leaves room for freedom of
choice as ordinarily conceived.

These doubts are reinforced even more strongly when we
turn to Mill's account of what it means to say of a man that
he could have done something he did not do. Mill's account,
as we saw, equates "he *could* have done otherwise" with "he
would have done otherwise *if* he had chosen to do so." The
reasons behind this equation were the same for Mill as for
G. E. Moore, but it is the latter who states them most clearly.[28]
Moore points out that if determinism is true, then it must *in
some sense* be the case that a man could not have done otherwise than he did; yet if we are to believe in the reality of choice
then it must *in some sense* be true that a man could have acted
otherwise than he did, on those occasions when he performed
freely chosen actions. Moore's way out of the dilemma is to
argue that the sense of "could have" is different in the two
cases, that it is true in one sense of "could have" that the man
who has performed a given action could *not* have done anything else, and that it is true in the other sense of "could have"
that he *could* have done something else.[29] And this he eluci-
dates along the lines laid down by Mill. To say that someone
could not have done anything else is in this context simply to
emphasize the truth of determinism, namely, that given the
causes which actually did operate, no other outcome was possible; while to say that someone could have done otherwise is
to assert the possibility of the countercausal state of affairs,

that is, that other causes would have had other effects—had the choice been different, then so would the action have been. Moore also adds a sense of "could have" which amounts to saying that "for all we know" the man might have chosen differently—but this sense is not one which Mill makes any use of, and is not relevant to our discussion therefore. On the account given above, the point of saying of a man that he could have acted differently is to maintain that there was no fatalistic determination of his actions. The "could not" to which Mill opposes his sense of "could have" is the fatalist "could not" which amounts to saying that no possible change in the antecedents would have made any difference, that the event was fated to happen and there would have been no use in struggling against it. So, in effect, Mill is fighting to distinguish causation from blind fatality, and this means that his account does not distinguish human actions from other natural events; the sense of "could have" in "he could have acted otherwise" is the same sense as that of the "could have" in "the moon could have been two hundred and eighty thousand miles away"—namely, that other causes would have had other effects.

It seems to me that the only merit which this account of what we mean by saying "he could have acted otherwise" possesses is that it is compatible with, is indeed a logical consequence of, mechanical determinism. In terms of its tendency to save our ordinary beliefs about our actions in a determinist universe it seems to have two great defects. In the first place, it seriously misrepresents what we usually mean when we say a man could not have acted otherwise. Take the case where a man is threatened by gunmen and is forced to hand over the contents of the safe for which he is responsible. We should ordinarily say that he had no choice but to hand over the money in question, that he could not have done anything else. Now, to this statement it seems quite obviously irrelevant to ask whether he *would* have done something else *if* he had chosen to do something else—say, press the alarm button. It may be true that if he had chosen to press the alarm button he would have done it, that his choice would have been perfectly effective, even if it had resulted in his being shot. But this is quite compatible with our saying that he *could not* do anything else. For generally what we mean when we say that a person could not have done anything else is not that no matter what choices he made the result would have been the same but, rather, that the consequences to him of other choices would have been quite intolerable. It is true that there is an important line to be drawn between things that we can choose to do or not do *at all* and things which simply happen to us; so, for example, it is important to distinguish between walking down stairs where I may choose to stop half way and if I do choose to I shall stop, and falling down stairs where whether I stop halfway down is not a matter of my choices at all, but a matter of my momentum, the state of the stairs, and so on. But this is a different issue, for the distinction here is not between actions, of which my choices are necessary conditions, and events, of which they are not, but between actions where I chose freely and could have chosen otherwise and actions where I did not choose freely and could not have chosen otherwise. A modified version of Mill's sense of "could have," which specified what sort of antecedents—namely choices—were to be taken into account, would draw the line between those events which we call actions and those which we do not; but the crucial point surely is that to argue that a different choice would have resulted in a different action does not show and cannot show that the agent in question could have made that different choice.

And this brings us to the second objection, which is that once we accept Mill's translation of "he could have done otherwise" into "he would have done otherwise if he had chosen otherwise," we are bound now to ask whether he could have chosen otherwise. Once we are told that the action would have been different if the antecedents of a certain kind had been different, we surely tend to ask how these antecedents could have been different. As we have seen already in the argument between Mill and the Owenite, this is a question which in these terms favors the Owenite very considerably. So long as answers to the question "Could he . . . ?" are given in terms of "He would have . . . if . . ." the only conclusion we can come to is that as the agent was situated at the time, with the desires, knowledge, and the rest that he actually had, then he *could not* do anything but what he did. To turn all statements about what a man could do into statements about what he would have done under other conditions is a tacit admission of defeat. Of course, even in a determinist universe the distinction between actions and events is going to matter to us, and the distinction between coerced and uncoerced actions is going to matter to us. But this is a good deal less than to argue that determinism would leave all or most of our everyday beliefs about human actions and all or most of our attitudes to human agents intact. And I cannot too much stress that our object here is not to decide upon the truth or falsity of the determinist case but only to decide whether Mill's attempt to reconcile determinism with our ordinary notions about our actions is successful. The evidence so far is that it certainly is not.

Why, then, did Mill embark on the unrewarding sort of analysis which we have just discussed? It seems that what happened was that Mill inherited the obvious post-Newtonian assumption that the universe was fully determined. And Mill perceived clearly enough the consequence that all our actions are inevitable in the limited sense that they are the necessary outcome of whatever causes determine them. Thus the only question we can sensibly ask is what would have led to a different outcome—and the only answer must be, different causes. Thus the question of whether a man was able to act otherwise is transformed into the question of what would have made a man able to act otherwise, and we are offered the equivalent of Moore's analysis, that we both could and in fact would have acted otherwise had we chosen differently. But, of course, one sinister implication of this must be noted, that it equates what we would have been able to do with what we would have done, and leaves the suspicion that we do all those things which we are able to do, so that what we do not actually do, we cannot or could not do either. The causal account, however, is bolstered by a perfectly respectable argument about freedom. It is said that freedom is not the absence of causation, but the absence of coercion; the paradigm case argument is invoked to show that we learn the meaning of terms such as "of his own free will" in situations where what is at issue is the nonoccurrence of certain kinds of possible coercive sanction. Hence, it is argued that *of course* we have freedom of choice because these situations define what we mean by talking of freedom.[30] But there are two drawbacks to this approach. In the first place, it is not clear that this kind of paradigm case argument is going to work for so complex a concept as that of freedom. Crudely, we might say that it is at least plausible to argue that what supplies us with the complex set of criteria that we use in distinguishing cases of free choice from other cases is a primitive conviction that when a person is not suffering from these constraints, then he simply can choose between different courses of action. Second, we can go on to ask whether, even were we to agree that the paradigm gives us our conception of freedom, this would show that a man who was free to do whatever he did or its alternatives actually could do anything else. Certainly we can think of cases where a man may be free to do something but lack the necessary abilities to do it—a man may be free to vote for any of three candidates in an election, but be illiterate and so not able to cast a vote. Normally, we think of whether a man can act otherwise than he does in terms of whether he possesses the appropriate abilities, and this is largely a matter of believing that he would or would not do whatever it is if he tried. But in the causal world inhabited by Mill we always have another question, that of whether, even given abilities, no coercion, and all the rest of it, a man who did not make a given choice could *at that point* have done so. In a determinist universe, the answer seems plainly to be that he could not have done so, since a different choice would have necessitated different antecedents, which *ex hypothesi* had not occurred. It looks very much as though freedom does not entail ability in this limited sense.

What underlies Mill's preconceptions about human actions is his mechanical psychology, according to which the laws of mind are laws such as govern the behavior of any mechanical system. The aspect of this belief relevant here is the contention that volitions are ordinary mechanical causes, and Mill's associated contention that we have nothing which he wishes to call direct power over our volitions. Since he holds these views Mill has to represent learning how to perform actions as a process of learning the connections between inner causes and outer events; and here he makes an understandable but incontestable confusion. For he takes the perfectly sensible point that children take time to learn how to perform complicated actions to be a proof of the fact that they are busy learning causal connections. But this is surely not a process of learning Humian causal connections.[31] It may be a process of learning causal connections in some remote sense, but scarcely one which would be well characterized by such an image as the child's possessing a set of mental levers, but no chart, and experimentally pulling levers to see what actions come up in the outside world.[32] For apart from any other problem this would lead us straight to that raised by Mill's disclaimer of direct power over volitions, namely, how do we bring about volitions in the first place?[33]

Mill ensures that he will run into trouble by stating categorically that we have no direct power over volitions. He has good reasons for saying this, chiefly that to say otherwise would be to surrender to the intuitionists with their belief that volitions were directly produced by the self in some manner forever inaccessible to inquiry. But Mill failed to see that the whole point of a theory of volitions was to stop the causal chain, at any rate in such a place as would give some account of how my control over my own actions differs from whatever kind of control someone else may have over my actions. If we ask how I cause my own actions, the answer that I just have volitions to do them is not unduly complicated, even if it is not very helpful either. But if we then learn that we do not have any direct power over our volitions, the whole matter becomes very difficult. For we must at once wonder how on earth we are to bring about volitions. If to get an action going I have to bring about a volition, that is one problem; but if to get a volition going I have to wait about until a desire or an aversion happens along, that is altogether another. In this case, surely, I am no longer performing my own actions even, but simply sitting about waiting for them to happen. To get a volition going I have to put myself under the appropriate influences; but to put myself anywhere at all I have presumably to have the volition to be wherever it is; but to have this volition in turn requires that I should put myself under the appropriate influences—and already we are trudging down an infinite regress.

The question arises whether this failure to reconcile determinism with what we take to be the claims of our ideas about human choice has any practical consequences. My contention is that it does, and that one place where this can be seen most clearly is Mill's account of the justification of punishment. It will be recalled that Mill agrees that the idea of guilt is an essential element in the justification of punishment, but that he drops out of this idea the notion that a man should feel that other people are justified in thinking ill of him and merely leaves the residual fact that so accustomed is he to thinking ill of the action in question along with them that the thought of the action now causes him pain. But, of course, such a man might overcome his feelings of pain without thereby leading us to think him any less culpable in what he did; and no doubt he could admit that he was guilty of an offense about which he felt more or less nothing. And in fact Mill hardly makes use of the idea of guilt at all. His view is essentially that punishment is a deterrent, either in threatening a criminal with punishment for a future action, by the example of the infliction, or by putting a criminal off a repetition of an offense. But this plausible account wreaks havoc with talk of fairness and with Mill's account of what are the facts behind our saying a man could or could not help doing what he did. It will be remembered that Mill says of a man who has a criminal disposition that he can or cannot help committing a crime, according to how we qualify the words. He can help himself, and usually does, if he perceives that heavy punishment will follow the offense. What Mill does not see about this explanation of what we mean when we say the criminal could help himself is that it is fatal to the whole idea of justified punishment. For, supposing the criminal does commit the crime, what must be supposed about his mental state? Apparently that he could not help himself, for given his criminal disposition, the crime was inevitable unless the punishment was a sufficiently good threat to deter him; but he has committed the crime, so that it clearly was not enough to deter him; in the absence of the counterbalancing force of a powerful enough threat, his nature was bound to win. Once again we can see how Mill's determinism leads to a situation where what a man can do and what he does are exactly coterminous. If the criminal *did not* refrain from crime then he *could not;* if he *could* then he *did.* Normally, of course, we believe that men can do more actions than they in fact do, that they have genuine alternatives, and it is only on the strength of this belief that we think punishment is justified. Mill never sees the full implications of his position, because as we have seen he does not take seriously the requirement that punishment be fair in the ordinary sense. What he demands instead is that punishment be effective; and although fairness and efficacy tend to coincide over large areas of social life, they are not the same consideration. The ideas of guilt and responsibility can be dispensed with altogether, or else reinterpreted in a forward-looking sense, so that the only questions we have to ask when we ask whether a man committed a crime is whether it is really *him* we wish to deter from recidivism and whether it is worth punishing him to deter him, since it may be that he did whatever it was under such odd circumstances that he will not do it again in any case. Mill in advancing along this path was coming to meet the revised views about punishment which have been put forward by such writers as Barbara Wootton.[34] The perils and merits of this revision cannot occupy us. All that can reasonably be asserted here is that while it may be true that we should abandon the concept of responsibility and blur considerably the border lines between punishment and medicine, between blame and cure, it is essentially a matter of making a change. The one thing Mill cannot pretend is that he is simply explaining or justifying beliefs which we ordinarily hold about punishment and responsibility.

To summarize briefly what I hope that this chapter has shown, and to explain briefly what it has not been intended to show, it is necessary to point out the relation of this problem to Mill's general metaphysical preconceptions. All along, we have been exploring the consequences for Mill's thought of his belief in a kind of logical atomism, in the theory that the universe, scientifically understood, consists of chains of simple facts, events which are causally connected to each other according to laws of causal sequence, and the chance of initial simultaneity. We saw in the preceding chapter that when this picture and the attendant explanations of law and inference rule are applied to explaining personal identity, they break down; the ideas we have about what it is to be a person experiencing the world around one will not survive the transplantation to the universe of the phenomenalist. Yet Mill continued to believe in his picture; he remained a determinist and in spite of its admitted failure with persons he continued to accept the atomistic analysis according to which actions and their causes are seen as causally determined events, mechanically linked. And again the truth emerges that this destroys our concept of personal identity; the agent disappears, to be replaced by a spectator of events occurring at a location which we somehow continue to call "him." And we have seen how this picture makes us unable to use any longer our former ideas about guilt and responsibility. Looking forward, we can also see that the way in which the forward-looking concept of deterrence swallows up the backward-looking concept of guilt foreshadows the way in which the forward-looking concept of utility swallows up the backward-looking concept of justice.

But to say all this is not to come up with any kind of answer. Worse, it is not even to identify any kind of problem to which an answer is in sight. All we can claim is that one statement about how to reconcile determinism and free will is wrong; we certainly cannot claim to have shown that determinism, whatever it may be, is false, or alternatively that we do after all possess free will or not. More philosophers than formerly are willing now to deny that any kind of determinist thesis is true[35] and many more have shown how complicated are the issues involved in prediction, causal explanation, and the rest. Yet, simultaneously we are nearer than ever to finding acceptable mechanical models of human behavior in the processes of information-sorting and feed-back in computers or homeostatic mechanisms. The simple-seeming "problem of free will" has become open-ended and terribly complicated. Yet one central doubt still remains; we do seem to continue to organize our knowledge about the external world and about ourselves, and we still seem not to be sure whether the knowledge we obtain will force us radically to revise our view of ourselves, possibly in ways which at present we cannot even envisage conceptually, geared as our language is to the beliefs we presently have. Mill, however, thought he had an answer, and in this confident frame of mind turned next to apply science not in individual cases but to men in social wholes. To guarantee the successful application of scientific method to sociological inquiry, it was necessary first to decide what natural science provided the appropriate model. The answer Mill finally gave was physics; but before giving this answer he eliminated two competitors—chemistry and geometry, in the form of Macaulay's empiricist historical approach, and his father's and Bentham's attempts to extrapolate the method of political economy to sociology. To this attack on his teachers and on his teachers' critic we can now turn our attention.

NOTES

1. *Early Letters*, p. 569.   2. *Letters* (ed. Elliot), II, p. 375.   3. *Utilitarianism*, etc., p. 65.   4. *System of Logic*, VI, i, 2.   5. *Examination of Hamilton*, p. 586n.   6. *System of Logic*, VI, ii, 3.   7. *Examination of Hamilton*, p. 585.   8. *System of Logic*, VI, ii, 3.   9. *Examination of Hamilton*, p. 585.   10. *System of Logic*, VI, ii, 3.   11. *Ibid.*   12. *Ibid.* 13. *Ibid.*   14. *Examination of Hamilton*, p. 560.   15. *System of Logic*, VI, ii, 3.   16. *Ibid.*, VI, ii, 2.   17. *Examination of Hamilton*, p. 576. 18. *Ibid.*, pp. 565–566.   19. *System of Logic*, III, v, 11.   20. *Examination of Hamilton*, p. 361.   21. *Ibid.*, p. 570.   22. *Ibid.*, pp. 575–576.   23. *System of Logic*, VI, ii, 3.   24. Hare in *Aristotelian Society Proceedings, Supplementary Volume* (1951), pp. 201–216; Nowell-Smith, *Ethics*, pp. 236–273.   25. Bradley, *Ethical Studies*, pp. 1–41.   26. *Ibid.*, p. 15.   27. *Ibid.* 28. G. E. Moore, *Ethics*, pp. 122–137.   29. *Ibid.*, pp. 129–130.   30. Flew, *New Essays in Philosophical Theology*, Chap. 8.   31. Melden, *Free Action*, pp. 47–55.   32. Ryle, *Concept of Mind*, pp. 61–67.   33. *Examination of Hamilton*, p. 361.   34. Wootton, *Social Science and Social Pathology*, Chap. 8.   35. E.g., Austin, *Philosophical Papers*, p. 166n.

VIII

FALSE STEPS
IN SOCIAL SCIENCE

So far as Mill was concerned, the methods of the social sciences could only be those of some portion or other of the natural sciences. As he remarks at the beginning of the sixth book of the *System of Logic*: "the methods of investigation applicable to moral and social science must already have been described, if I have succeeded in enumerating and characterizing those of science in general." [1] This belief in the uniformity of scientific procedure rests, as is perhaps obvious enough, on Mill's assumption that there is one and one only pattern into which all explanation must fit. Any science, to be a science at all, must aim at producing general laws, inductively established, which can be employed as the backing for causal explanation of particular events or sets of events. But it was as noticeable in Mill's day as it is in ours that the social sciences have not progressed very far toward establishing general laws of a reliable kind; it was noticeable, too, that there was no general agreement on how to establish such laws. Mill, therefore, raises a further question: "how far the unsatisfactory state of those inquiries is owing to a wrong choice of methods," [2] and in two later chapters he criticizes two wrongly chosen methods, which he names the Chemical Method and the Geometrical Method.[3] These methods are represented by

Macaulay and James Mill respectively, and Mill performs acts of filial piety and impiety in turn by first attacking his father's most effective critic, and then turning his weapons on his father.

There is both an overt and a covert aspect to Mill's attack on the chemical method. The covert aspect is the political one. Chemistry as a science of specific experiment proceeds by a multitude of experiments to establish low-level generalizations. If this is to be the model for a social science, then each social situation will have to be examined in isolation, looked at cautiously, and conclusions drawn with extreme diffidence—Macaulay's attitude, in many ways. Mill saw the espousal of such an attitude as conservative and unprogressive; and, of course, in the shadow of this attitude lurks the intuitionist view of history. If we cannot find out large generalizations by comparing one historical event with another, is not the answer to understand the inner meaning of the historical process by intuitive means, perhaps an empathetic feeling for the workings of God's mind as revealed in social processes? The overt reason behind Mill's attack is simply that he did not think that social phenomena as revealed in history were of the same kind of complexity as chemical phenomena. So our first task is to characterize the problems which Mill thought turned chemistry into a science of experiment to such an extent.

The oddity of chemistry is the prevalence of changes of kind, in contrast with, say, mechanics, where such changes are totally absent. We have already seen how Mill argued that in the case of the triangle of forces, all the effects really occurred and the final observable effect was a mathematical product of these effects.[4] With this he contrasts the case of chemistry, where the effects of the individual elements brought into chemical combination are genuinely annihilated, and the result is some quite different substance with causal properties not in any sense deducible from the properties of the constituents. In Mill's own words: "There is, then, one mode of the mutual interference of laws of nature in which, even when the concurrent causes annihilate each other's effects, each exerts its full efficacy according to its own law, its law as a separate agent. But in the other description of cases, the two agencies which are brought together cease entirely, and a totally different set of phenomena arise." [5] So, if we bring together two gases and ignite them, the result is water, a medium in which a spark is not made to glow more brightly, but is, rather, extinguished.[6] We do not need to go deeply into what Mill means by changes of kind; it amounts to the view that we cannot deduce from properties belonging to one natural kind properties of another natural kind; and experimentally what this means is that if in creating a compound, we create something whose properties belong to a different natural kind from those of the constituents of the compound, then we cannot infer from the properties of the constituents what will be the properties of the compound. ". . . no experimentation on hydrogen and oxygen separately, no knowledge of their laws, could have enabled us deductively to infer that they would produce water." [7] Certain properties stay constant through this change of kind; the weight of the resulting water is the same as the weight of the hydrogen and oxygen, but weight is a physical rather than a chemical property, so the exception is apparent rather than real.[8] The important consequence of this so-to-speak logical hiatus between the beginning and the end of the experiment is that chemistry must be a science of specific experiment. Mechanics can proceed by deducing lower-level laws governing the behavior of a number of bodies interacting on each other from the high-level laws concerning the behavior of individual bodies, but chemistry can do no such thing. And Mill plausibly accounted for the relatively backward state of chemistry in his time by the demand for constant experiment; and he rightly foresaw that the discovery of the physical underpinnings of chemical action was the beginning of much more rapid progress in the science.[9] But he could scarcely wish to model his new science of society on one of the more backward of the physical sciences.

With this brief picture of the peculiarities of chemistry we can now see why the science of society is not a chemical science. Of course, we may well think that Mill has already begged the question in favor of some kind of analogy to mechanics, when we think of the mechanical psychology we examined in the last chapter. So it is not surprising to find Mill beginning his attack on the chemical method by simply denying that we need to use it. There are no changes of kind in social life: "Men," he says, ". . . in a state of society, are still men; their actions and passions are obedient to the laws of individual human nature. Men are not, when brought together, converted into another kind of substance, with different properties; . . ."[10] For this view he produces no argument, and this is an oversight. For Macaulay, against whom Mill is arguing, had raised a considerable problem about basing social science on human nature. He asked how the utilitarian knew the properties of human nature on which he intended to found a new political science; the utilitarian answers: "By experience. But what is the extent of this experience? Is it an experience which includes experience of the conduct of men intrusted with the powers of government; or is it exclusive of that experience? If it includes experience of the manner in which men act when intrusted with the powers of government, then those principles of human nature from which the science of government is to be deduced . . . instead of being prior in order to our knowledge of the science of government will be posterior to it."[11] In other words, how do we know what human nature outside political society is like? It seems that at any rate we know less about it than we do about politics, and that it is the height of foolishness to try to found our more certain knowledge on our less certain inferences from it. For the other horn of the dilemma is Macaulay's question of how we know—given that we *do* know what human nature outside political society is like—that our knowledge is adequate to generate a political science. "We are reasoning from what a man does in one situation to what he will do in another. Sometimes we may be quite justified in reasoning thus . . . but the most satisfactory course is to obtain information about the particular case; and, whenever this can be obtained, it ought to be obtained." [12] That is, Macaulay's objection to the derivation of political science from the principles of human nature is that either these principles are a shaky inference from political science, or they are not known to be enough to generate such a science.

Mill has nothing much to say against this; and it is hard to escape the feeling that the objections to the chemical method which he goes on to make are attacks on positions that Macaulay never held. Anschutz argues that "it was Macaulay's errors rather than his father's which Mill was more concerned to stress in his own contribution to the controversy. . . . Macaulay was much more mistaken in objecting to political reasoning which was grounded on principles of human nature and demanding instead that it be based on the observation of political facts. . . ." [13] This is undoubtedly true; but it is nevertheless misleading. Mill plainly did want to attack the attitude which regarded economics, for example, as a valueless abstraction, and he wanted to attack the view that history could be no more than a narrative of past events, innocent of general implications.[14] But in attacking these views he was scarcely attacking Macaulay. And when he complains, for example, that it is an error to try to derive certain generalizations from history, he is in agreement with Macaulay.

Having argued that the chemical method is not necessary, Mill goes on to show that it is not possible to apply it either. His account opens with an obvious hit at Macaulay when he refers to those who think themselves true Baconians and believe themselves to be "proving their adversaries to be mere syllogizers and schoolmen" [15]—a rather less than effective retort to Macaulay's characterization of James Mill as "an Aristotelian of the fifteenth century born out of due season." [16] Mill accuses such writers of being ready to argue from two cases of agreement to a general law—a charge quite inapplicable to Macaulay who had argued against this very error.[17] But he is enthusiastic about showing that none of the methods of inductive inquiry whose canons he had set out are applicable to social inquiry. Taking a typical causal problem to be that of the effects of "the operation of restrictive and prohibitory commercial legislation upon national wealth," [18] he at once rules out the method of difference. This would require two countries, exactly alike in all features save their tariff legislation—"alike in all natural advantages and disadvantages; whose people resemble each other in every quality, physical and moral, innate and acquired; whose habits, usages, opinions, laws, and institutions are the same in all respects, except that one of them has a more protective tariff, . . ." [19] As Mill says, the supposition that we should find two countries with just this difference is absurd. But, the retort is surely that if we tried to find two cases of almost anything on which we wished to experiment which fulfilled rigid requirements like this we should certainly fail. What Mill ought to try to show is that we cannot rule out enough of the differences between countries as irrelevant to the comparison to allow us to proceed by experiment. And in this he would be arguing a plausible case which looked a good deal less like mere obstructionism than does the present one. The joint method, the next best thing to the method of difference, is next ruled out. This is because of the composition of causes; if we find one rich nation with protection, and two poor nations with free trade, which between them have all the properties of the rich nation, we can still not infer that protection causes wealth, because it may be the case that wealth is the result of a compound cause, half the elements of which belong to one of the poor nations, the other half of which belong to the other, and to which protection is not relevant or is even a hindrance. The methods of agreement and of concomitant variations are both defeated by the plurality of causes. "That some one ante-cedent is the cause of a given effect, because all other ante-cedents have been found capable of being eliminated, is a just inference, only if the effect can have but one cause. . . . in the case of political phenomena, the supposition of unity of cause is not only wide of the truth, but at an immeasurable distance from it." [20] Prosperity may be due to energy, or good legislation, or natural advantages of soil, climate, raw ma-terials, and the like. The method of concomitant variations suffers less from plurality of causes than plurality of effects: "such is the mutual action of the coexisting elements of soci-ety, that whatever affects any one of the more important of them, will by that alone, if it does not affect the others di-rectly, affect them indirectly." [21] This has a slightly *ad hoc* look about it as an objection, when we remember that Mill regards physics as the sociological model; this adherence to a Comtian view about the consensus of all the phenomena of a social system would, if adhered to strictly, render all causal inquiry impossible. For it would assign as cause only the entire preceding state of the universe and assign as effect only the entire subsequent state. Elsewhere Mill sees the danger of this and gives some account of the difference between causes and conditions,[22] but all too often the difference is lost. The final method, that of residues, is ruled out very reasonably on the ground that it presupposes already that we know the causal links between all the other phenomena involved and are wait-ing only to solve the last causal clue. Given the impossibility of finding causes under the conditions Mill imposes, it is cer-tainly not going to be possible to apply the method of residues.

But Mill's victory over the extreme empiricists is gained much too easily to be convincing. We have already had cause to remark that the methods of causal inquiry as Mill outlines them are extraordinarily remote and artificial when viewed as aids to experimental science. We have said already that they seem to presuppose what they do not supply, such rules as will help us to discern relevant and irrelevant points of contrast, guiding concepts which will organize our experience for us and make it amenable to causal explanation. Now Mill himself draws attention to this by pointing out that they cannot work in the absence of such concepts and guides, though he does this by showing how they would not work in a complex sociological or economic inquest. But strictly speaking, what he should have done was explain why he takes for granted the presence of guiding principles in the sciences such as mechanics or chemistry to which he does think the methods apply, and why he thinks it impossible to take these as much for granted in the social sciences.

But if the attack on the *a posteriori* method is not one of Mill's more attractive intellectual feats, the criticism of his father and Bentham is. He is helped, of course, by the fact that he thinks their errors were less harmful than their opponents', for he is clear that some kind of *a priori* approach to sociology is necessary. The problem is whether the a prioristic science of geometry, the model for economics, is also the model for sociology. In the essay on which the last book of the *System of Logic* rests, Mill declares his faith in the *a priori* method: "we go farther than to affirm that the method *à priori* is a legitimate mode of philosophical investigation in the moral sciences: we contend that it is the only mode." [23] We know that the *a posteriori* approach will not work, and we also know that we have a great body of knowledge about human nature from which we can argue "with as much certainty as in the most demonstrative parts of physics." [24] Yet Mill takes care to point out that *a priori* does not mean altogether independent of experience; the principles of human nature from which we reason are obtained by inductive inquiry. In the light of Macaulay's jibes at James Mill, this is an essential point to make. Whether it is made successfully is another matter.

Mill then proceeds to distinguish between the cases of geometry and physics as *a priori* or deductive sciences. In the *System of Logic* Mill makes the difference turn on the presence and absence of the composition of causes. "Among the differences between geometry . . . and those physical Sciences of Causation which have been rendered deductive, the following is one of the most conspicuous: That geometry affords no room for what so constantly occurs in mechanics and its applications, the case of conflicting forces; . . ." [25] But in the essay already referred to, the difference is that geometry is a hypothetical science, drawing inferences from premises which are only supposed true for the purposes of argument, and which are known to be an abstraction from the actual circumstances of the world. It thus arrives at hypothetical conclusions, which would be true if the premises were.[26] This second account is clearly the better of the two, since the notion of conflicting forces even possibly occurring in geometry is one it is difficult to give much meaning to; moreover, economics, which Mill takes to be a geometrical science, *is* concerned with conflicting forces; principles such as that of the diminishing marginal utility of income rest on the fact of conflict between income and leisure as motives for a rational man's actions. Abstraction is clearly the point on which to base the resemblance of geometry and economics.

And it is on this theme that the whole of the essay on definition and method in political economy is hung. We make certain limited assumptions about human nature, and then "the conclusions which are correctly deduced from the assumption constitute *abstract* truth." [27] And these conclusions, if correctly deduced, "would be as true in the abstract as those of mathematics; and would be as near an approximation as abstract truth can ever be, to truth in the concrete." [28] This, of course, is very similar to his account of geometry; its truths are hypothetically true, and they are more or less nearly true in fact, according to the nearness of the hypotheses to the facts. Mill sticks to this view in defending economics as a separate social science against Comte's criticisms.[29] Some causes of behavior can be dealt with as if they operated on men independently of all the other causes which operate on them:

F

"different species of social facts are in the main dependent, immediately and in the first resort, upon different kinds of causes; and therefore not only may with advantage, but must, be studied apart: . . ." [30] Mill agrees that it is not true of anyone that he is motivated only by desire for profit and aversion to effort; it is quite untrue of many people and much less true of persons outside northern Europe and North America. But the influence of these motives is strong in economic situations; it is the only motive common to all men in market situations, and is often the most important influence on individuals and even more often on a mass of individuals.[31] " 'Political Economy' is not the science of speculative politics, but a branch of that science. It does not treat of the whole of man's nature as modified by the social state, nor of the whole conduct of man in society. It is concerned with him solely as a being who desires to possess wealth, and who is Able of judging of the comparative efficacy of means for obtaining that end. . . . It makes entire abstraction of every other human passion or motive; except those which may be regarded as perpetually antagonizing principles to the desire of wealth, namely, aversion to labour, and desire of the present enjoyment of costly indulgences." [32] This in essence is the classical account of what classical economics is about, and it is notably lucid and sensible. But what is almost equally notable is that his account of geometry rests on, and is much inferior to, his account of economics—it is not so much that economics employs the methods of geometry as that geometry employs the methods of economics. But Mill would have been led, I think rightly, to place greater rather than less reliance on his account of economics by its progress since his day.

The account of economics thus given, which is fundamentally an account of why Mill is impressed with the results of *a priori* approaches to social science, and which is also an explanation of why economics has such a hold over sociologists and political scientists today, forms also Mill's defense of the utility of economics against Comte's attacks. Comte

took an all-or-nothing stand on the topic of sociology; anything less than his positive science of society was an anachro-
nism. Mill was swayed by Comte, but never to the extent of
being willing to abandon the one tolerably advanced social
science created thus far. Their differences are amusingly illus-
trated by the different meanings they attached to the Comtian
view that economics had a *fonction provisoire,* a provisional
utility.[33] Comte understood this to mean that political economy was a useful, though unscientific, forge for the weapons
of the positivists; but already it was outmoded as a social
science. Mill, however, accepts Comte's phrase when writing
to him about the *Principles of Political Economy,* but means
it to indicate that although economics is only a contribution
to the full understanding of society, it will serve at any rate
as a contribution. Its conclusions cannot be applied straightforwardly to predicting what will happen in society, but they
serve as first approximations to be corrected. Thus, in the
System of Logic Mill calls "political ethology" to his aid to
explain that the ferocity of competition typical of England is
not native to all mankind;[34] in the *Principles,* he goes on to
suggest that it could reasonably be restrained.[35] The methods
of political economy can be used to show us what would happen if men behaved according to the economic hypothesis—
we should eventually reach a stationary state of misery at
mere subsistence level, our excess population culled by famine
and war. But, says Mill, we can avoid this gloomy result if
we have the sense to modify our social habits earlier on. Again,
the laws of the distribution of wealth are said by Mill to be
modified by our decisions, and he reproaches economists for
discussing them "on a supposition which is scarcely realized
anywhere outside England and Scotland." [36] Thus, the conclusions of economics need to be controlled and supplemented
by sociology, but on their own terms they are true and important.

It is from this position, that economics is only abstractly
true of the world, that Mill attacks the errors of his father

and Bentham. The elder Mill is charged with having admitted
as the only motive in human conduct that of self-interest.
". . . it seems to be supposed that this is really the case with
the social phenomena; that each of them results always from
only one force, one single property of human nature." [37]
There are two sorts of thinker who have made this mistake.
The first sort cannot even distinguish between theories and
precepts, and their mistake is to try to apply to all cases some
one simple rule. This error is so gross that thinkers of this
sort can be left out of the reckoning altogether. It has been
said that James Mill is the target here, for Mill writes in an
earlier chapter: "A large proportion of those who have laid
claim to the character of philosophic politicians have attempted, not to ascertain universal sequences, but to frame
universal precepts. They have imagined some one form of
government or system of laws, to fit all cases; a pretension
well meriting the ridicule with which it is treated by prac-
titioners." [38] Anschutz assumes that this refers to James Mill:
"He was also mistaken in supposing that there is some one
form of government which would fit all societies, and this
was indeed a pretension meriting the ridicule with which it
had been treated by Macaulay." [39] But there are many reasons
why this cannot be true. First, Mill was clear that his father
did not argue that one form of government suited all cases:
"nor is it true in point of fact, that these philosophers [viz.
James Mill and Bentham] regarded the few premises of their
theory as including all that is required . . . for determining
the choice of forms of government and measures of legislation
and administration." [40] Moreover, they knew very well that
there is a "distinction between Science and Art; . . . knew
that rules of conduct must follow, not precede, the ascertainment of laws of nature, and that the latter, not the former, is
the legitimate field for the application of the deductive
method." [41] Mill, in fact, says revealingly of his father and
his friends that they were "of too sober and practical a character for such an error," [42] so that their advice would have

brought their abstractions firmly to earth. This is all too true; as Macaulay pointed out, James Mill failed to draw the absurd conclusions which his absurd theories should have forced him to draw. Moreover, he sometimes failed to draw the sensible conclusions which they licensed, as when he chose to include the interest of women in that "of their fathers, or in that of their husbands" [43] and so ruled out their having a voice of their own in political life. One cannot imagine Mill dissenting when Macaulay wrote: "Without adducing one fact, without taking the trouble to perplex the question by one sophism, he placidly dogmatises away the interests of one half of the human race." [44] Obviously, one reason why a hypothetical science of society is not enough is that we cannot trust most people to make the right allowances in practice.

Thus the error of the geometrical radicals is exposed. But to show just how inadequate were their efforts Mill devotes himself to the central proposition of their creed, that men are always motivated by self-interest. Mill makes what have become the standard objections to it; if it is true it can be so only because it is tautologous—"the proposition may be understood to mean only this, that men's actions are always determined by their wishes." [45] This lacks the force of Macaulay on the same topic: "One man cuts his father's throat to get possession of his old clothes; another hazards his own life to save that of an enemy. One man volunteers on a forlorn hope; another is drummed out of a regiment for cowardice. Each of these men has no doubt acted from self-interest. But we gain nothing by knowing this, except the pleasure, if it be one, of multiplying useless words." [46] If the proposition is not tautologous, but is understood as saying that all men pursue their selfish or worldly interest to the exclusion of all other ends, "an objection presents itself *in limine* which might be deemed a fatal one, namely, that so sweeping a proposition is far from being universally true." [47] Or, as Macaulay put it: "the proposition ceases to be identical; but at the same time it ceases to be true." [48]

Unlike Macaulay, whose intention was only to destroy, Mill attempts to shore up the theory by showing how it can be made to indicate that we should at any rate beware of our governors, since they may very well be tempted to act against our interests. But, for all that, Mill is not far from agreeing with Macaulay's final verdict. Mill excuses the geometers as having presented "in a systematic shape, and as the scientific treatment of a great philosophical question, what should have passed for that which it really was, the mere polemics of the day." [49] Macaulay's gloss on the same theme is that the sort of principles to which the first utilitarians appealed "resemble those forms which are sold by law-stationers with blanks for the names of parties, and for the special circumstances of every case—mere customary headings and conclusions, which are equally at the command of the most honest and the most unrighteous claimant." [50]

This has been a very negative chapter, largely devoted to explaining what Mill thought was wrong with two approaches to social science, and insofar as it has been critical in intention, explaining where Mill's criticisms are ill-founded. But the purpose it has served is important. Mill was convinced that social science had to be deductive, systematic—in his terms *a priori;* yet it had to mirror history, the flow of particular, empirically observable events. This obviously imposes a strain in his account of sociology as it was to be created. The strain is between a highly theoretical, deductive, axiomatized science, which possibly lacks all empirical content, and a detailed empirical account of the facts as they can be observed, with no theoretical content at all. This tension is obviously one which infects sociology today, with its divisions into extreme *a priori* theorists and empirical field workers charting anything from the incidence of second marriages among the aristocracy to the contents of the larders of the impoverished. To this tension, there is in Mill's work added another, which is that between the predictive scope of the developed sciences like astronomy and the miserably inadequate explanations produced by the traditional kind of historian. To make sense of what Mill thought a social science ought to be and what it ought to do, it is first necessary to see clearly what he thought it had to avoid.

NOTES

1. *System of Logic*, VI, i, 2.   2. *Ibid.*   3. *Ibid.*, VI, vii; viii.   4. *Ibid.*, III, vi, 1–2.   5. *Ibid.*, III, vi, 1.   6. *Ibid.*, III, x, 4.   7. *Ibid.*   8. *Ibid.*, III, vi, 2.   9. *Ibid.*   10. *Ibid.*, VI, vii, 1.   11. Macaulay, *Miscellaneous Writings*, p. 345.   12. *Ibid.*, p. 346.   13. Anschutz, *The Philosophy of J. S. Mill*, p. 84.   14. *Dissertations and Discussions*, Vol. II, pp. 121–136.   15. *System of Logic*, VI, vii, 1.   16. Macaulay, *Miscellaneous Writings*, p. 285.   17. *Ibid.*, p. 347.   18. *System of Logic*, VI, vii, 2.   19. *Ibid.*, VI, vii, 3.   20. *Ibid.*, VI, vii, 4.   21. *Ibid.*   22. *Ibid.*, III, v, 3.   23. *Essays on Some Unsettled Questions*, p. 146.   24. *Ibid.*, p. 149.   25. *System of Logic*, VI, viii, 1.   26. *Essays on Some Unsettled Questions*, pp. 137–141, 143–144.   27. *Ibid.*, p. 149.   28. *Ibid.*, p. 150.   29. *Early Letters*, p. 626.   30. *System of Logic*, VI, ix, 3.   31. *Ibid.*, VI, ix, 4.   32. *Essays on Some Unsettled Questions*, pp. 137–138.   33. *Early Letters*, p. 626.   34. *System of Logic*, VI, ix, 4.   35. *Principles of Political Economy*, IV, vi, 2.   36. *System of Logic*, VI, ix, 3.   37. *Ibid.*, VI, viii, 1.   38. *Ibid.*, VI, vi, 1.   39. Anschutz, *The Philosophy of J. S. Mill*, p. 84.   40. *System of Logic*, VI, viii, 3.   41. *Ibid.*   42. *Ibid.*   43. James Mill, *Essay on Government*, p. 45.   44. Macaulay, *Miscellaneous Writings*, p. 307.   45. *System of Logic*, VI, viii, 3.   46. Macaulay, *Miscellaneous Writings*, p. 317.   47. *System of Logic*, VI, viii, 3.   48. Macaulay, *Miscellaneous Writings*, p. 318.   49. *System of Logic*, VI, viii, 3.   50. Macaulay, *Miscellaneous Writings*, p. 355.

MECHANICS AS A MODEL
FOR SOCIOLOGY

Now that we have seen the methods which the social sciences are *not* to emulate, the way forward is clear enough. Mill, it is clear, wants to see a sociology which can mirror for social life the achievements of Newtonian mechanics; the ultimate aim of using this for the prediction and control of social change will occupy our attention in the next chapter. This chapter is concerned with the foundations of that hopeful ambition. In the search for laws of social behavior, differences between social phenomena and those studied by mechanics become apparent, and this leads Mill to modify the deductive simplicity of physics, in favor of an approach which he, following Comte, calls the method of inverse deduction.[1] So one question that we must answer is how far the qualifications which Mill makes leave intact the over-all claim that we can produce some kind of "social physics." The claim that there can be a science of society similar in its methodological structure to physics, rests on Mill's assumptions that the laws governing the behavior of people in social interaction can be inferred mechanically from the laws governing individual people in isolation from society. This is a thesis which closely resembles "methodological individualism,"[2] and an insight into the atomism which Mill took to be the basis of a de-

F*

ductive social science can be gained by considering some of the ambiguities inherent in this theory of social methodology. Lastly, we can ask more directly than we have done up till now whether Mill's belief in the uniformity of scientific method is well founded, by considering the claim that is sometimes made to the effect that historical explanation at any rate does not involve deductive inference of *explanandum* from *explanans*. If rationality does not necessarily involve backing all explanations with general laws, then Mill's assumptions about rationality are wrong; and the consequences he draws for the explanation of human behavior must also be wrong.

Mill arrives at the conclusion that physics supplies the model for social science by a process—appropriately—of elimination. The two candidates of chemistry and geometry having been rejected, we are left with the method of physics, the method of "concrete deduction." [3] As he says, "After what has been said to illustrate the nature of the inquiry into the social phenomena, the general character of the method proper to that inquiry is sufficiently evident, and needs only to be recapitulated, not proved." [4] The distinguishing mark of physics, in contrast to chemistry, is the possibility of long deductive sequences, and the impossibility of frequent experiment; its distinguishing mark in contrast to geometry is that there is composition of forces, but also that the deductions are concrete, that is, nonhypothetical, allowing positive prediction. The most perfect example of such a science is "celestial mechanics," [5] but Mill does not in fact spend a great deal of time comparing sociology and celestial mechanics, for it is as clear to him as to his opponents that if we were to wait until we had a sociology of the elegance and power of celestial mechanics we should do so at the cost of not developing the sociology we have already. Indeed, what Mill does do is explain why, for example, it is necessary to develop partial sciences such as economics and "ethology" first. The purpose of this in beating off Comte's criticisms of political economy and all other sciences antedating his own sociology has already been explained. But it does mean that we have to do some of Mill's work for him in explaining what a concrete deduction in social science ought to look like.

We begin, says Mill, with generalizations about psychological phenomena, the elementary laws of mind. Of these, he thinks, there are probably not many, the complexity of predicting human behavior arising rather from "the extraordinary number and variety of the data or elements—of the agents which in obedience to that small number of laws, cooperate towards the effect." [6] It is not quite clear what these "agents," "data," or "elements" are supposed to be; most plausibly, they are human feelings, desires, aversions, and the rest, as they conflict with and modify each other. Such conflicts are explained by Mill in terms of the composition of forces; and this, it appears, boils down to such facts as that two people who both want the same thing but are unable both to obtain it, and cannot rely, for either side, on the successful use of force, will modify their wishes in favor of sharing the good in question in some way or other. But, when we are faced with a situation of even ordinary complexity, it seems that calculation of the outcome is impossible: ". . . by attempting to predict what will actually occur in a given case, we incur the obligation of estimating and compounding together the influences of all the causes which happen to exist in that case; we attempt a task, to proceed far in which, surpasses the compass of the human faculties." [7] In reply to the obvious complaint that this renders the hoped-for social science unobtainable, Mill replies that it does not, since we can check the results of our deductions: "The ground of confidence in any concrete deductive science is not the à priori reasoning, but the consilience between its results and those of observation à posteriori." [8] While this is true, it is not a solution, since the problem is not that of checking deductions once they are made, but that of making the deductions in the first place. It is certainly true that one would want to check the results of any inference against the facts; but it is also true that one would want to be assured that the inference itself was possible in the first place. What is here at the back of Mill's mind is a rather different defense of his position, to the effect that we can limit the calculation to a few significant items, and thus make the calculation feasible, and subsequently see how accurately our inferences fit the facts; but this is, in essence, to defend the hypothetical and abstracting science of economics.

Because of the abstraction required to render calculation possible, social science cannot, after all, "be a science of positive predictions, but only of tendencies." [9] Thus we cannot say how people *will* behave in certain circumstances, only how they *would* behave in the absence of (unforeseen) modifying factors. Thus we might infer from our knowledge of human nature and the fact that there was hunger due to unemployment in Britain in 1933 that the unemployed tended to go about robbing farms and foodstores. Of course, there was actually very little theft, because there were enough counteracting tendencies—aversion to dishonesty, fear of social disorder, effectiveness of the police—to stop it occurring. But, says Mill, the knowledge of tendencies, if inadequate for prediction, will suffice for explanation of the past. But this reply is open to the previous objection that too many tendencies will produce the same inferential blockage as too many facts. Mill, surprisingly, accepts this objection as a valid one. He argues, following Comte, that social facts are so interlinked that we cannot expect tendencies visible in one society to appear unchanged in another, nor that the tendencies obtaining in a given society will remain unchanged for very long.[10] The only way to make our inferences more reliable would be to introduce more complications, and this would soon make them impossible to perform. So soon enough we appear to reach once again the conclusion that concrete deduction, the method of physics, fails to produce any result. But this is not wholly true, for there are some types of social fact which are relatively distinct from the rest of the fabric of social fact, which are thus influenced to a lesser extent by the *consensus* of social phenomena—in other words, economics is not impossible.[11] Economics no longer appears as the geometry of the social sciences but, rather, as the geometrical physics; the obvious reasons for studying economics separately from the rest of social science are connected with the similarity of economic phenomena in all societies, and with the fact that the particular modifications which we may have to make in our predictions to deal with an actual case are very varied while the laws on which we base our predictions are stable. Thus it is sound policy to work out the laws first and apply them with an eye to particular situations, rather than wait to establish universally valid laws.

But defending economics does not really bring us nearer to establishing social mechanics. And Mill adds to the methodological gloom by explaining in great detail why the verification of concrete deductions is all but impossible in social matters. The pattern of verification should be that we deduce testable conclusions, either in the shape of low-level empirical laws or in the shape of particular conclusions from our causal laws and our knowledge of events. But it is almost impossible to isolate the effects of particular causes in social affairs. Suppose we wanted to know what the effects were of the protectionist legislation of the Napoleonic Wars; it is not just a matter of working out the pure economic theory of the effects which restriction of trade tends to produce, but of applying this theory. And the trouble is that it is only after the events have actually occurred that we can be sure that they match the model situation. Mill is absolutely right about this; indeed, most economists are careful still to point out how little *predictive* value economic theory as such possesses. And this means that, for the moment at any rate, we must renounce prediction and content ourselves with explanation of what has already happened. The event which "comes too late to verify the particular proposition to which it refers, is not too late to help towards verifying the general sufficiency of the theory. The test of the degree in which the science affords safe ground for predicting (and consequently for practically dealing with) what has not yet happened, is the degree in which it would have enabled us to predict what has actually occurred." [12] That is, the complexity of the facts is such that a specific prediction about what will happen at any remote time or place is quite out of the question; but we can, after the event, explain the event in the light of the facts which we now possess. The more adequately our theory accounts for these, the better is the theory, and the better it can be relied on for such limited predictions as our factual information will allow.

Still, this is little enough. It seems that for the most part we cannot verify the deductions we make, and that if we could it would not profit us much since we should find ourselves unable to make them. But the dark prospect is in part the result of Mill's stage management of his account; for it is his thesis that by a fortunate chance it is precisely in the sciences where direct deduction is impossible that we have available the resource of "inverse deduction," [13] the characteristic of historical science, or general sociology. Mill derives this suggestion from Comte, but in the form in which Mill presents it, it comes to represent a considerable concession to the views of the empiricists such as Macaulay, whom we saw Mill decrying such a short time before. The basic thought behind the principle of "inverse deduction" is that where it is not possible to deduce truths about the actual course of history from the laws of human nature, we may nonetheless be able to guess at "axiomata media," middle-level propositions which we verify, not by testing against the facts of history, but by seeing whether they are derivable from the laws of human nature, or whether at any rate they are compatible with those laws. My chief concern with this account is to show how it concedes more than Mill supposes to the empiricist position; it has more general significance than this for the philosophy of science, but this I shall ignore.

We saw Mill criticizing the empiricists for a misunderstanding of Bacon's views on induction; at that point he maintained that experiment in social matters was impossible and that observations adequate for the applications of the inductive canons were also impossible. Now it seems that this was an exaggeration; history shows us similar trends or empirical laws which obtain in several societies. These empirical laws suggest to us the middle-level, derivative laws which govern the way in which one state of society succeeds to another; and these derivative laws are verified by deduction from the laws of human nature. If this were possible, Mill would have made good his claim that the science of society was a concrete deductive science; for, even if the method of discovery of the laws governing social change had been shown to be somewhat unusual, in that it reversed the usual method of verification in the first instance, once the discovery had been made, it would presumably be possible to infer from the principles of human nature, via axiomata media, to trends of social phenomena. But Mill's claim is not nearly so strong as this. Initially he says that the aim is to connect axiomata media "with the laws of human nature by deductions showing that such were the derivative laws naturally to be expected as the consequences of those ultimate ones." [14] We must pause a little at the phrase "naturally to be expected," which hardly suggests a rigorous logical tie, such as that of deductive inference; and indeed it seems that such a tie is not expected: "It is . . . hardly ever possible . . . to demonstrate à priori that such was the only order of succession or of coexistence in which the effects could, consistently with the laws of human nature, have been produced." [15] But having opened the gate a little, Mill now leaves it to swing wide; not merely can we not deduce the axiomata media with any great rigor, "we can at most make out that there were strong à priori reasons for expecting it, . . . Often we cannot even do this; we cannot even show that what did take place was probable à priori, but only that it was possible." [16] This means that there has been no verification, no question of competing hypotheses being falsified by testing against the laws of human nature. Indeed the laws of human nature are rapidly ceasing to matter to social science. If we take a skeptical view of inverse deduction, as I think we must be allowed to do, in conjunction with Mill's own assertion that there are in any case very few principles of human nature which can be relied on universally, it is difficult to see what beyond the assertion of faith in deduction has been preserved from Macaulay's criticisms.

In fact this overstates the case, for it is unwise to concentrate too shortsightedly on the problems of performing deductions in one or another area of social science; for part of Mill's emphasis on deduction comes from his feeling for a hierarchy of sciences. And this is analogous to the underlying feeling in the case of his account of the physical sciences that he sees them also as forming a hierarchy, with, as we saw, the mathematical sciences underlying the physical sciences, and these underlying other scientific investigation. Mill hangs onto the name of deduction, where he admits that there can actually be no deductive inferences, because he thinks of the various moral sciences as being "deduced" from each other. Mill's picture of the hierarchy is roughly this: basic to everything else is psychology, because all the moral sciences are concerned with the behavior of human beings. This makes psychology basic in several senses; in the first instance because, if there were no human beings, there would be no moral sciences at all; but also in the way in which the most general laws of physics are basic to, for example, astronomy as well as atomic physics, that all laws are in some sense special cases of these general laws. In the same way as we accept the Newtonian principle concerning the uniform motion of bodies uninfluenced by disturbing forces, even though there may well have been no bodies uninfluenced by disturbing forces, so we can accept the basic laws of psychology even if no one has ever acted exactly in accordance with them alone. Closest to psychology comes what Mill calls "ethology," the study of the development of character, which is the science of how circumstances modify the basic dispositions of men.[17] Thus, to take an example of Mill's own, we can break down the everyday generalization that old men are cautious and young men are rash into the basic law of association and the generalization that old men will usually have seen a good many evils befall the incautious while young men will not. Old men who have not formed the association between lack of caution and disaster will be as rash as the young.[18] Thus ethology can correct exaggerated generalizations and explain where they will break down and why they will do so. Ethology, again, stands in a controlling relationship to economics, which is the science of the unintended consequences of people's attempts to obtain wealth.[19] It is not exactly that economics is deduced from ethology, for that would suggest that economics was a branch of ethology but, rather, that ethology tells us how plausible are the assumptions about people's wants and wishes from which economics starts, and that it can therefore give us some idea about where our expectations are likely to be unfulfilled.

Derivative sciences such as ethology and economics are all, therefore, expected to contribute to the grand science of general sociology. That is, the object of the study of the contributing sciences is eventually to create the science which deals with the coexistences and successions of social phenomena. This it is which explains why Mill never conceded as much in principle to Macaulay as he did in detail. For the general science of society is the last stage in the deduction of social science from individual psychology. The atomistic picture which underlies the conviction that gross regularities can be broken down into more certain regularities obtaining between particles revealed to us by analysis of the crude phenomena that we see at first sight applies with the same force to the social sphere. People's actions, if not the persons themselves, can be reduced to the play of psychological atoms; and from this starting point, we must in theory be able to construct the interplay of these atoms up to the point where the atoms compose not only a person but a whole society.

The problems which Mill should face, but does not explicitly face, in giving some account of how we deduce sociology from psychology can be brought out by briefly comparing his account with Popper's theory of "methodological individualism." This is the more profitable in that Mill is one of the targets which Popper takes in *The Poverty of Historicism*. Holism[20] and psychologism[21] are the two rocks on which the methodological individualist has to be careful not to founder, but Popper's positive statement of what methodological individualism is, is less helpful for understanding Mill than is the knowledge that it is not psychologism. However, it is clear that some kind of reductionism is intended: "it rightly insists that the 'behaviour' and the 'actions' of collectives, such as states and social groups, must be reduced to the behaviour and to the actions of human individuals." [22] This claim is itself not wholly clear, since the central idea involved, that of reduction, invites more questions than it answers. But, I take it that, for Popper at any rate, the claim is that, ontologically, *there are really no such things* as states or nations, armies, churches, and the like; and that, logically, statements about these dubious entities can all be translated into statements about nondubious entities, such as individual men and women. Thus there is no such thing as England, only a lot of Englishmen; there is no such thing as the Catholic Church, only a lot of men and women with a set of similar beliefs. Thus, Popper says: "Even 'the war' or 'the army' are abstract concepts, strange as this may sound to some. What is concrete are the many who are killed; or the men and women in uniform etc." [23] Dubious entities occupy the status of models or theoretical constructs, whose function is to explain the behavior of the people we can actually observe. We have already seen enough of Mill's views on the status of such unobservables as "forces" to be aware that he had strong leanings in this direction. It is a metaphysical inclination which is well described by Urmson, when he talks of the positivists constructing "such things as physical objects out of sense data (phenomenalism), states out of their members, persons out of the sort of things Hume said they were bundles of. . . ." [24] We have seen how Mill succeeded to his own satisfaction with the first, and failed with the third of these; the second he does not directly discuss in the same terms, but it is hardly likely that he would have conceded greater ontological security to the "average man" than to the particular man encountered in the street. But Mill's atomism goes further than Popper's individualism, since it reduces the actions of persons to the occurrence of psychic, atomic events. There is much to be said for Mill's greater boldness, for such sciences as classical economics can hardly be said to be about individuals in any straightforward sense, though they certainly rest on the dispositional laws which Mill associates with the laws of mind.

But can this reduction envisaged by Mill and to a lesser extent by Popper be performed? It is a matter of some importance to Mill, since his view of social science is so intimately bound up with the belief that sociological explanation can be backed up by laws of individual nonsocial psychology. To try to settle the "methodological individualism" controversy would be both unnecessary and ungrateful;[25] but we must throw, at any rate, some doubt on the possibility of the reduction envisaged. If we take as a statement for reduction some such statement as that Britain declared war on Germany in 1939, obvious difficulties arise. We may try rephrasing the statement by saying that Lord Halifax passed a message to Von Ribbentrop; but that is not enough until we have said what the *significance* of the message was. In explaining this, trouble begins at once; we cannot say that its significance was that Britain had declared war on Germany, since that is precisely what we are trying to subject to reductive analysis. Yet any other message will probably fail the test, since it becomes unlikely that any other message could actually be passed—say the message that "Mr. Eden, Mr. Chamberlain, Mr. Churchill . . . were at war with Germany." An indefinite number of names could appear and be absent on such a message, and still not verify or falsify the statement that Britain had declared war on Germany. Moreover, whatever message is passed, it is a declaration of war only if the person passing it is *authorized* to declare war. And the concept of authorization looks to be irretrievably buried in social institutions and not to be made sense of outside these. Indeed, it is arguable that the possibility of recognizing the relations and dispositions of individuals at all depends upon the acceptance of the framework of social rules which give to each individual the concepts with which he can organize and make sense of his behavior.[26] If this argument is accepted, then Mill's picture of a hierarchy of social sciences, resting on a more basic and nonsocial science of mind, seems to break down, for we seem to have here precisely the change of kind which Mill would have to recognize as an insuperable obstacle to deductive reasoning.

However this may be, Mill is not merely a casualty in the battle between those who think social terms are basic and those who believe them to be susceptible of reduction to descriptions of individual behavior. He is also attacked by Popper, because he does not merely subscribe to individualism, but to "psychologism." Psychologism suffers from three main defects in its efforts to reduce sociological laws to psychological ones. The first is that human nature varies considerably with different social institutions, so that its study presupposes an understanding of those institutions. In other words, people's behavior is modified by where they have been brought up, by the values they have come to accept from their social surroundings, and so on. So, for instance, Popper quotes as a convention the fear of snakes, which is not an instinct in men and anthropoid apes, but is inculcated by education.[27] The second objection is that social science deals with the *unintended* consequences of people's actions, not with the intended ones. It is not a truth of psychology, but a hard fact of nature that if everyone tries to find peace and quiet on a given mountain, then everyone will fail.[28] And the third objection is that the interest in human nature forces us to ask questions about how society originated, and this is the first step toward historicism: "If all regularities in social life, the laws of our social environment, of all institutions, etc., are ultimately to be explained by, and reduced to, the 'actions and passions of human beings,' then such an approach forces on us not only the idea of historico-causal development, but also the idea of the *first steps* of such a development. . . . Psychologism is thus forced, whether it likes it or not, to operate with the idea of a *beginning of society,* and with the idea of a human nature and a human psychology as they existed prior to society." [29]

An unconvinced critic might very well retort that he cannot make much sense of methodological individualism, except as a doctrine which reduces the laws of our social environment to the laws of individual behavior—the actions and passions of human beings, in other words. But more than this, Popper attacks Mill here at his strongest. Thus, Popper's objection that human nature varies with different societies is precisely the reason Mill adduces to explain the importance of ethology. What else can Mill mean when he says: "The circumstances in which mankind are placed, operating according to their own laws and to the laws of human nature, form the characters of the men," [30] if not that human nature is formed by basic endowment and social influence? Popper presumably cannot think that *no* basic human reactions are required for social influences to work on; and the only sense in which Mill wants to reduce social laws to the laws of individual psychology is that he wants to link the laws of man in society with the basic reactions out of which social behavior has been created. Mill himself is anxious to agree that there may be very few basic human capacities, and that circumstances may account for almost all of the diversity we observe.[31] And in all this, he is firmly on the same side as Popper. This is equally true for the issue of unintended consequences; the only person who could believe that social effects are all the desired consequences of human intentions would be an extreme adherent of the conspiracy theory of history. But Mill criticizes his father for being too willing to believe that politics is a successful conspiracy of sinister interest;[32] and as an economist Mill was very anxious to explain that such phenomena as price rises in scarce goods were not organized by anyone, but were a natural consequence of efforts devoted to quite other goals than raising prices. And as for the objection that Mill is forced to ask questions about the origins of society, this is simply absurd. The only sense in which Mill is forced to ask questions about the origins of society is if he wants to give a causal history of the development of society from its origins; but Mill is not forced to study the history of social change any more than Popper is forced to. Of course, Mill as a matter of fact was interested in trying to account for what he supposed to be long-term trends in the educational, political, and organizational character of Western society, not with an eye to the origins of that society so much as its future. But when Mill does mention the notion of an origin of society, it is to make an impeccably Popperian point, namely, that because of the mutual interaction of human nature and the institutions it creates, there could be no possibility, even in theory, of predicting the whole of human history from a knowledge of human nature and its original situation.[33] It is hard to see why Popper should seize on Mill as an opponent rather than an ally; certainly he apologizes for spending so long criticizing Mill by saying that he is "a worthier opponent than Hegel."[34] But the trouble is that he is too worthy; he does not make the mistakes which Popper wants to correct, and the general position is one which Popper adheres to himself, so that if it is mistaken, then so is Popper's individualism.

A different kind of criticism, however, is that which suggests that there is a fundamental distinction between the explanation of physical phenomena in the natural sciences and that of human behavior in history. In the next chapter we shall be concerned to see what sort of laws of social behavior Mill supposed history could provide and use. But it may be suggested that the idea that history uses *any* laws at all is mistaken; historical explanation is essentially narrative, and moreover is rational explanation, not causal explanation, so that Mill's central belief, that there is a uniform pattern of explanation in all spheres, is quite misguided. It is important to distinguish between the contention that history does not use laws, and the contention that rational explanation and causal explanation are different, although some writers have linked them, if not by explicit argument, at least by adhering to both views.[35] For we may agree that human behavior is not causally explained, but rationally justified, and still hold—as I am sure Mill would have wished to do—that rational explanation involves the use of generalizations analogous to laws about what the right or proper or prudent thing to do would be on a given occasion.

The all-out adherent of the unity of method, which is what Mill often seems to be, may either hold a simple "covering-law"[36] theory of historical explanation, or hold only that laws—perhaps a great many—are involved in any explanation. It would seem plausible to argue that strictly speaking a covering law ought to be available, even if one fabricated pretty much *ad hoc.* Thus, for example, in explaining the unpopularity of Louis XVI, we might seek a law to the effect that "Kings who engage in pointless wars, practice religious discrimination, and raise taxes are always unpopular." But the trouble with such a law is that a historian might very well be loath to accept it, even while agreeing that these specific things caused Louis XVI's unpopularity. Perhaps no law would satisfy him short of one to the effect: "To anyone in exactly the same position as Louis XVI, exactly the same things will happen"—and this is both totally lame as an ex-

planation of anything, and in grave danger of being no more
than an analytic truth. Obviously, it is much more plausible
to argue on behalf of a set of laws which contribute to the
explanation; thus we might agree willingly that high taxes
will always tend to make a king unpopular, as will pointless
wars, religious discrimination, and so on, and when we have
enough of these tendencies, without anything to offset them,
we may well be willing to say that they explain Louis's unpopularity.[37]

But some critics, notably Dray, criticize even this use of
laws to cover an explanation, not because of the difficulty of
framing the laws, which is the objection to the strict covering-
law theory, but because of the nonexplanatory nature of laws.
The way in which the law that religious persecution creates
unpopularity explains the unpopularity of Louis XVI has
nothing to do with our being able to *deduce* his unpopularity
from the law. This is plainly true; someone who said he didn't
understand why religious persecution caused unpopularity
would not be helped to understand by being told that religious persecution always precedes unpopularity. The way to
produce enlightenment is to decompose the causal sequence
into more particular elements, such as the shock to family
life, discomfort to a persecuted individual, commercial chaos,
and so on. In other words, what is needed is a causal *narrative;*
the laws are secondary to our ability to give an intelligible
narrative in terms of what Waismann called "hat-doffing"
phenomena.[38] It is, however, going too far to take this as an
objection to the account of explanation as essentially a matter of backing causal statements by laws; still, it is a valid objection to Mill's insistence that all explanation is merely sub-
stitution of one mystery for another. For it seems that, on the
contrary, what makes laws explanatory is that they show us
how to translate one kind of causal sequence into another
kind which we find intelligible. But surely the ultimate
grounds of intelligibility and familiarity are concerned with
regularity. To facts as well as people, we take off our hats

when we are thoroughly familiar with them; and this process is one of seeing the same thing and the same sort of thing happen over and over again until we know how the world, both human and inanimate, can be expected to behave. We do not express surprise and we do not demand explanations, because that sort of thing is constantly happening. To that extent, at any rate, it can be said that Mill's belief in the importance of backing explanations with laws, which in the last analysis can be reduced to statements about what can regularly be expected to happen, is justified.

The final assault on the alleged need to back explanations with generalizations can be made from the direction of drawing a distinction between causal explanation and rational explanation. Dray, again, makes this criticism of the covering-law school when he argues that in a loose sense of the term we are concerned to justify the actions of historical agents, and that this is what we mean by explanation in history.[39] That is, we want to see the situation from the inside, from the point of view of the agent, and hence to explain the action in question, together with all its consequences, as arising out of the agent's appreciation of the situation and his decision about what "the thing to do" was. To pursue this doctrine into its Collingwood form, with his emphasis on "rethinking" the past, or into the form which Weber gave it with the doctrine of *verstehen*, would be fascinating and fruitless. The justification for mentioning it at all, when I have not the least intention of discussing it in detail, is to make two points only. The first is that this type of objection is not to law-based explanation at all; to a deductivist such as Popper or Mill, the process of justification, as much as the process of explanation in the causal mode, requires the deduction of the justified course of action from a principle and the statement of the specific circumstances in a manner exactly analogous to the deduction of the effect from the causal law and the singular statement about the presence of the cause.[40] The objection, therefore, must be to the assimilation of causal explanation and the explanation of human behavior. Thus, and this is my second point, Mill is inevitably doomed to incur the displeasure of this school of thought, since his approach to human action is such as to leave no room for its central distinction between the agent's view of his own situation and the spectator's view of that situation. Mill's belief, which he halfheartedly adhered to, in spite of the difficulties which we saw force him to admit the weakness of the doctrine, to the effect that persons were susceptible of atomistic analysis, a belief which underlies his presumption that causal, deterministic explanation of human behavior must be possible, thus produces yet another problem, that of reconciling historical explanation and the requirement of a unified scientific methodology. Nonetheless, this is not a threat to Mill's more basic requirements for rationality both of belief and of behavior, which only require that belief and action should be justified by reference to general rules of one kind and another. What is more dubious is whether the principle of rationality in this weak, but anyway highly plausible, form can be employed to justify the aims which Mill sets for the science of society, as applied to history, aims which in their most extreme formulation amount to the wish for social astronomy, for a science which will be able to predict the most distant and far-reaching changes in social life and social institutions. To this sociological analogue of "celestial mechanics" we now turn our attention.

NOTES

1. *System of Logic*, VI, ix, 1; VI, x.   2. Popper, *Poverty of Historicism*, p. 136.   3. *System of Logic*, VI, ix.   4. *Ibid.*, VI, ix, 1.   5. *Ibid.*   6. *Ibid.*   7. *Ibid.*   8. *Ibid.*   9. *Ibid.*, VI, ix, 2.   10. *Ibid.*   11. *Ibid.*, VI, ix, 3.   12. *Ibid.*, VI, ix, 6.   13. *Ibid.*, VI, ix, 1.   14. *Ibid.*, VI, x, 4.   15. *Ibid.*   16. *Ibid.*   17. *Ibid.*, VI, v.   18. *Ibid.*, VI, v, 1.   19. *Ibid.*, VI, ix, 3.   20. Popper, *Poverty of Historicism*, pp. 157–158.   21. Popper,

Open Society, II, p. 91.   **22.** *Ibid.*, p. 91; Popper, *Poverty of Historicism*, p. 136.   **23.** Popper, *Poverty of Historicism*, p. 135.   **24.** Urmson, *Philosophical Analysis*, p. 38.   **25.** Cf. *British Journal for the Philosophy of Science*, 1952, 1956, 1957, 1958.   **26.** Winch, *Idea of a Social Science*, pp. 40–51.   **27.** Popper, *Open Society*, II, p. 90.   **28.** *Ibid.*, p. 92; Popper, *Poverty of Historicism*, p. 158.   **29.** Popper, *Open Society*, II, pp. 92–93.   **30.** *System of Logic*, VI, x, 3.   **31.** *Ibid.*, VI, ix, 1 and 4.   **32.** *Ibid.*, VI, viii, 3.   **33.** *Ibid.*, VI, x, 4.   **34.** Popper, *Open Society*, II, p. 99.   **35.** Dray, *Laws and Explanation in History*, cf. Chap. V *passim*.   **36.** *Journal of Philosophy* (1942), pp. 35–48; cf. Dray, *Laws and Explanation in History*, pp. 24–25.   **37.** Dray, *Laws and Explanation in History*, pp. 34–35.   **38.** *Ibid.*, p. 69.   **39.** *Ibid.*, pp. 122–126.   **40.** Popper, *Poverty of Historicism*, pp. 147–152.

SOCIAL ASTRONOMY

Toward the end of the preceding chapter we considered briefly whether the study of history seems to employ canons of explanatory adequacy similar to those of the natural sciences; and to the extent that we found no convincing objections to the view that explanations require to be backed by generalizations, we more or less accepted Mill's belief in the uniformity of rational explanation. But Mill's aim in establishing the uniformity of science is by no means confined to an interest in problems of pure logic. Like so many of his contemporaries, Mill was concerned to see why it was that such far-reaching changes as were occurring in every aspect of social life took place; he was also concerned to see their trend, to be better able to predict and control the path of social change. It is in the light of this concern that one has to understand his stricture on the historians of the eighteenth century, and his enthusiasm—much tempered by time—for Comte.[1] But paradoxically enough, Mill, who believed much less strongly than Comte in the immutability of the laws of social change, outdid him in declaring that the laws of social change are the really critical subject matter of sociology.

This emerges when Mill is characterizing what he believes to be the two sorts of social inquiry, which together form sociology: "In the first kind, the question proposed is, what effect will follow from a given cause, a certain general condition of social circumstances being presupposed. . . . But there is also a second inquiry, namely, what are the laws which determine those general circumstances themselves. In this last the question is, not what will be the effect of a given cause in a certain state of society, but what are the causes which produce, and the phenomena which characterize, States of Society generally." [2] The importance of this second study is that its conclusions limit any which we might arrive at in the first kind of inquiry. For example, we might ask what the effect on British political life would be if the party currently in power were to establish a one-party state. We might argue that the result would be revolution within a matter of months; but, were we to know that there was an accelerating process of change toward total political apathy in Britain, we should have to accept that the prediction of revolution was unsafe and would become more unsafe as time went on. The general science of society, the science which studies States of Society, has two branches, the study of social uniformities of coexistence, called by Comte "social statics," and the study of uniformities of succession, called by Comte "social dynamics." [3] The assumption behind social statics is that not absolutely any conceivable set of social conditions can coexist, since the elements of which a social situation is composed interact and depend on each other in such a way that some elements are necessary for the existence of others, and equally, of course, that some must be absent for others to be present. Mill envisages this as meaning something more interesting than such banalities—which the proposition is often only a deceptive mode of expressing—as that sophisticated technological processes cannot take place without the existence of research institutions providing the theory to back them. An example which he has in mind is Coleridge's account of the necessary conditions of a stable political order. He argues that, had his father and Bentham known about conditions outside late eighteenth-century England, they would have realized that the reconciling of good order and freedom required three major elements: "First: there has existed, for all who were accounted citizens—for all who were not slaves kept down by brute force —a system of *education*, beginning with infancy and continued through life, of which, whatever else it might include, one main and incessant ingredient was *restraining discipline*. . . . The second condition of permanent political society has been found to be, the existence, in some form or other, of the feeling of allegiance or loyalty. This feeling may vary in its objects, and is not confined to any particular form of government; but whether in a democracy or in a monarchy, its essence is always the same; viz. that there be in the constitution of the state *something* which is settled, something permanent, and not to be called in question. . . . The third essential condition [of stability in political society], . . . is a strong and active principle of nationality." [4] Of course, it is a condensed account, and not very informative about the problems of political consensus, but the example serves to show what Mill thought social statics could establish. Indeed, for Mill's own purposes social statics almost always meant the problem of what were the essential social conditions under which a given form of government could survive. The importance of this, plainly, is that it makes all questions of ideal forms of government subordinate to the problem of *possible* forms of government; the discovery that there is a necessary connection between the form of government and the state of civilization of a country "stamps the endless discussions and innumerable theories respecting forms of government in the abstract as fruitless and worthless for any other purpose than as a preparatory treatment of materials to be afterwards used for the construction of a better philosophy." [5]

But, just as the limited causal inquiry into the effects of a given cause in a given social situation is subordinate to the general inquiry about States of Society, so within the general science, social statics takes second place to social dynamics; a state of society at a given moment is simply the (rather too grand) title given to the "simultaneous state of all the greater social facts, or phenomena," [6] and the uniformity which exists among simultaneous phenomena must be, as Mill has earlier argued, the result of the coexistence of phenomena at some earlier time, in conjunction with the laws which determine the succession of phenomena. "The mutual correlation between the different elements of each state of society, is therefore a derivative law, resulting from the laws which regulate the succession between one state of society and another: . . ." [7] The basic question, then, emerges as: On what principle does one state of society follow another? And it is to this question that the appropriate chapter of the *System of Logic* is mainly devoted.

The first part of this question is: What *sort* of principle is it, on which change takes place? Mill considers two possibilities, cyclical and cumulative, or "progressive," change. Popper condemns the suggestion of a "trajectory" or cumulative change as simplistic, compared with, for example, the corkscrew motions of the dialectic.[8] But the objection is itself simple-minded. For Mill is not distinguishing between two simple patterns for history, but between two attitudes to the "recurrence" of events. A cyclical orbit in astronomy need not be regular in the sense of conforming to a simple geometrical shape; it can have as many kinks in it as we care to envisage; all that is required is that the body in orbit should return to the same place at regular intervals. Equally, a trajectory can be as complicated as we care to imagine; all that it involves is being *nonrecurrent,* a once-for-all path. Mill thinks the matter decisively settled in favor of the trajectory, though he does not think the idea of a cycle inherently absurd: "Vico, the celebrated author of *Scienza Nuova* . . . conceived the phenomena of human society as . . . going through periodically the same series of changes. Though there were not wanting circumstances tending to give some plausibility to this view, it would not bear a close scrutiny: and those who have succeeded Vico in this kind of speculations have universally adopted the idea of a trajectory or progress, in lieu of an orbit or cycle." [9] There are some well-known problems inherent in the idea of events recurring, which suggest that Mill was insufficiently stern about Vico, but our task is, rather, to see how Mill brings out the problems of his own view of historical change, and how the same problems as we met in the preceding chapter recur to trouble him.

The initial problem is whether or not there is such a trajectory; and if there is, whether or not we can discover what it is, and if we can, then how? That there is a trajectory is evident. Persons living in a given environment are molded by that environment, and they in turn create the environment which molds succeeding generations. Circumstances change people, and people change circumstances, with the result that there is a cumulative change—as Mill says: "there is a progressive change, both in the character of the human race, and in their outward circumstances so far as moulded by themselves: . . . in each successive age the principal phenomena of society are different from what they were in the age preceding, and still more different from any previous age." [10] The problem raised by this progressive change is to ascertain what the trend or tendency or law of that change is. Mill, as usual, describes two ways in which we cannot answer the question, before offering a correct solution. The first method to be rejected is that which assumes we can find a genuine law of nature in the process of change, an unalterable causal law, merely by inspecting the history of two or three nations; this method he ascribes to the French historians who have been attempting "by a study and analysis of the general facts of history, to discover (what these philosophers term) the law of progress; which law, once ascertained, must according to them enable us to predict future events, . . . I cannot but deem them . . . to be chargeable with a fundamental misconception of the true method of social philosophy." [11] The misconception, he says, "consists in supposing that the order of succession which we may be able to trace among the different states of society and civilization which history presents to us, even if that order were more rigidly uniform than it has yet been proved to be, could ever amount to a law of nature." [12] Mill, here, is insisting on Popper's distinction between a law and a trend;[13] the pattern which historians may have discerned in historical change can at best be only an empirical law, a summation of particular facts, and not a causal law at all. It *may* be the case that only one order of progression is possible, but unless we can connect the empirical law with the laws of nature on which it depends, we certainly cannot rely on it for any predictive purposes; merely because things have happened in a certain way, we cannot assume that they will continue to do so. Until we can demonstrate that the (misnamed) law of progress is the consequence of the laws of human nature and of the reaction of that nature and its environment, then both the laws of coexistence and the laws of succession must remain "in the state of empirical laws, applicable only within the bounds of actual observation, without any means of determining their real limits, and of judging whether the changes which have hitherto been in progress are destined to continue indefinitely, or to terminate, or even to be reversed." [14] That is, we cannot predict that a given pattern will continue to hold unless we know its causes; when we know these we shall then be in a position to see what likelihood there is of the pattern continuing, and also we shall be able to see what can be done to control it, to make it prevail or to alter it. Here as everywhere in his work, Mill's aim is clearly practical; we want to know what the prevailing trends are, so that we can have a greater control over social change than we have had in the past; here, also, his determinism and his activism conflict, for there is a contradiction which he neither sees nor resolves between the goals of finding unalterable natural laws governing social change, and changing the patterns of social change.

Having criticized the French historians for confusing em-

pirical laws—or trends, to use more current terminology—
with natural laws, Mill goes on to point out that the task of
constructing the empirical law of change from the laws of human nature and the original conditions of mankind is in any
case impossible. This is an argument of which we have already seen some of the consequences, and we need only recapitulate it here. Mill does not think that "any one will
contend that it would have been possible, setting out from the
principles of human nature and from the general circumstances of our species man's position in the universe, to determine à priori the order in which human development must
take place, and to predict, consequently, the general facts of
history up to the present time." [15] The reason, of course, lies
in the facts which account for the cumulative nature of
change; men are so changed by environment that within a
few steps it is acquired characteristics which determine their
behavior and not basic human nature at all; hence the least
error in calculating how men changed over time would make
the computation of the course of history utterly inaccurate.
An obvious criticism is that in Mill's determinist universe
this is only a question of computational ability and not one
of principle; but Mill seems unsure which it is. Although this
does not render the science of history impossible, owing to
the resource of *inverse* deduction, which we discussed in the
preceding chapter, Mill shows some qualms about the possibilities of offering much support, even by inverse deduction,
for whatever empirical law we may produce. "The empirical
laws must be the result of but a few instances, since few nations have ever attained at all, and still fewer by their own
independent development, a high stage of social progress. . . .
nothing is more probable than that a wrong empirical law
will result instead of the right one. . . . the most erroneous
generalizations are continually made from the course of history; . . ." [16]

All this would seem to spell more than enough in the way
of difficulties for the nascent science of history, but Mill adds

to the problems of sociology. It will be recalled that a state of society is the simultaneous state of the more important social phenomena, such as "the degree of knowledge, and of intellectual and moral culture, . . . the state of industry, of wealth and its distribution; the habitual occupations of the community; their division into classes, and the relations of those classes to one another," [17] and so on. Now, we might suppose that if a state of society can be unpacked into its elements in this way, we can follow Mill's suggestion and trace the laws which connect the former and the latter state of these various elements, and thus arrive at a series of limited empirical laws, which together will give us the empirical law of changes in states of society as a whole. But Mill denies that we can do this, on the grounds that the consensus of the parts of society is so complete that it is a mistake to believe that the analytical separation of social states corresponds to separate causal chains; the interaction of all elements in social life is such that "it is the whole which produces the whole, rather than any part a part." [18]

At this point, we may reasonably feel ourselves to have been led into an *impasse*. Direct inspection of human history cannot yield anything exact, and even if it could, it would only be an empirical law, of no predictive value; to make it more valuable is impossible because we cannot demonstrate the connections we need to between human nature and social change; and finally, we cannot unpack the grand changes between States of Society generally into less grand sets of changes between particular elements which might be more amenable to inquiry—an assertion which we may notice as being contrary to Mill's defense of such subjects as economics, which presuppose at any rate a relative independence for some of the elements. All that we seem able to achieve is a number of statements about observed low-level tendencies: "a progressive increase of some social elements and diminution of others, or a gradual change in the general character of certain elements. . . . for instance, . . . as society advances, mental tend more

and more to prevail over bodily qualities, and masses over individuals: . . ." [19] These tendencies are cited in the essay on
Civilisation,[20] and again in the review of De Tocqueville's
Democracy in America, while from the latter is extracted also
the famous theory about the irresistible tendency of the age
toward equality.[21]

But, as ever, it is when the methodological gloom is at its
deepest that Mill finds some hope for us. In this case, it is the
discovery that we can do more than enunciate low-level generalizations from observation. For, according to Mill, here following Comte and the Saint-Simonians to some extent, there
is *one* element which is of overriding importance in determining the changes which take place in States of Society as a
whole. This is the "state of the speculative faculties of mankind; including the nature of the speculative beliefs which
by any means they have arrived at, concerning themselves and
the world by which they are surrounded." [22] In explaining
this, Mill shows himself very uninclined to interpret it as
implying that human behavior is much motivated by a desire for knowledge as such. Indeed, he rates most men's affection for the truth pretty low.[23] What he does argue is
that, although the desire for knowledge is secondary in most
men to the desire for wealth or comfort, it is the determining
factor in what will happen, "all the other dispositions of our
nature which contribute to that progress being dependent
upon it for the means of accomplishing their share of the
work." [24] For example, our success in gratifying our desire for
comfort depends on having a technology capable of producing the goods we want, and this in turn depends on the existence of a science which permits the technology: "the state
of knowledge at any time is the limit of the industrial improvements possible at that time, and the progress of industry
must follow, and depend upon, the progress of knowledge." [25]
Again, according to Mill, the cohesiveness of a society depends
on the moral code it possesses, and this in turn hangs on the
beliefs of its members on all kinds of matters, so that ulti-

mately it is the state of belief which conditions the moral and the political framework. Mill thinks that this is abundantly proved both by the facts of history and by the general principles of human nature. "These conclusions, deduced from the laws of human nature, are in entire accordance with the general facts of history. Every considerable change historically known to us in the condition of any portion of mankind, has been preceded by a change, of proportional extent, in the state of their knowledge or in the prevalent beliefs." [26] This is still a very shaky principle on which to build any general theory of history; it is not at all clear that the principle will not boil down to a tautology, equivalent only to saying that men will not do what they neither know about nor know how to do. If it ceases to be a tautology, it is very dubious. For example, it is difficult to stifle doubts about the equivocation involved in accounting systems of belief in the sense of religious beliefs and systems of belief in the sense of scientific theories as equally reasonable candidates for the title of state of the speculative faculties of mankind. Or, within the area of science and technology, it is hard to see how we could have any experimental test of the hypothesis that a technology creates a pure science just a little better than it can use as opposed to what would presumably be Mill's account of the pure science creating a technology just a little inferior to the pure science, in that it cannot use quite all the knowledge available. We seem to be in danger of arguments as profitless as that concerning the priority of chickens to eggs. Mill, at any rate, sticks to his view that knowledge is the determining factor in social change quite consistently throughout his career; it forms, as we shall see, at least part of the basis of his ethical theory. And at the time of writing the relevant sections of the *System of Logic,* he was very much worried by the possibility that the growth of a uniform mass education would create a uniform set of beliefs inimical to individuality.[27]

Mill remarks on Comte's theory of the three stages through which human thought passes—the supernatural, the metaphysical, and the positive. Despite his always considerable divergences from Comte, and his increasing opposition to all Comte's political proposals, Mill never lost his admiration for this discovery. It cannot, he says, "be easily conceived, from the mere enunciation of such a proposition, what a flood of light it lets in upon the whole course of history; . . ." [28] However, the admiration is a good deal tempered by his qualification: "his predictions and recommendations with respect to the Future of society . . . appear . . . greatly inferior in value to his appreciation of the past." [29] The force of the qualification is greater than it might seem at first sight, especially when we recall that it is the goal of predicting the future and shaping it which is the prime one. But it is in the context of discussing this theory of change that Mill permits himself what amounts to his only grand statement of faith in the achievements to be expected of the positive science of society: "By the aid of these we may hereafter succeed not only in looking far forward into the future history of the human race, but in determining what artificial means may be used, and to what extent, to accelerate the natural progress in so far as it is beneficial; to compensate for whatever may be its inherent inconveniences or disadvantages," and so on.[30] The achievements of the positive science of society will be the culmination of human knowledge: "When this time shall come, no important branch of human affairs will be abandoned to empiricism and unscientific surmise; the circle of human knowledge will be complete, and it can only thereafter receive further enlargement by perpetual expansion from within." [31] It is not easy to make much sense of this; how human knowledge is to be both complete and perpetually expanding is surely inexplicable. What needs stressing, however, is that although such a manifesto as we have just quoted is a natural outcome of Mill's belief in a social science based on atomistic principles, analogous structurally to Newtonian mechanics, equally able in principle to produce predictions of a range and certainty hitherto confined to the predictions of astronomy, it is quite untypical of his usual remarks. Usually, he is concerned to stress the limited view we possess of what our future will be, and usually he is concerned to stress that we can and must act on the best available information, and not hanker after absolute certainty, a certainty which is foreign to human affairs. He points out that "historical science authorizes not absolute but conditional predictions," [32] that, in other words, it tells us what the trend is, not what must inevitably be, and he goes on to point out that "knowledge insufficient for prediction may be most valuable for guidance. It is not necessary for the wise conduct of the affairs of society, no more than of any man's private concerns, that we should be able to foresee infallibly the results of what we do." [33] So, for instance, the process whereby the mass is gaining an ascendancy over the individual is not one which we are forced to watch helplessly; a different mode of education, greater encouragement to individual initiative, may all have an effect in reversing this trend.[34]

In Chapter IX, we discussed the issue of "methodological individualism," a doctrine which is one strand of Popper's attack on what he takes to have been some fundamental misconceptions about the task of the social sciences prevalent in the nineteenth century. His attack on these misconceptions is largely contained in *The Poverty of Historicism,* and Mill is there a good deal belabored for subscribing to the impoverished doctrine under attack. In fact, Popper's attack on Mill is almost wholly misconceived, and rests on misreadings and misunderstandings; but it provides a useful set of questions against which we can set Mill's views. The three chief vices which Popper detects are "holism," a belief in "absolute" trends or tendencies which Mill confuses with genuine causal laws, and a naïve belief in progress, which stems from a yet more naïve belief in the progressiveness of human nature. The importance of making it quite clear what Mill hoped to achieve is obvious enough; Mill's account of a rational social science is designed to lay the foundations for a rational ethics.

We have spent a good deal of space on the formal analogies which Mill thinks all forms of explanation must possess; in the next chapter we shall go on to consider how this formal identity extends to justification as well as to explanation, and how the achievements of mechanics are to be mirrored not only in social explanation but also in social prescription. But there is another connection. Utilitarian ethics are social ethics, and are supposed to be based on a rational understanding of society. Popper's charges against Mill, if valid, would in the first two cases make nonsense of any claim that social science and Mill's own social and political values are related. The last charge is important in the context of Mill's essay *On Liberty*; in the last chapter of this book I shall argue that this work is indeed motivated by a concern for human progress; but if Mill were so convinced of an absolute law of progress, his defense of progress in that essay would be quite inexplicable. He would be unaccountably pessimistic at the very least, for one who believed that progress was inevitable.

First, then, as to holism. The vice of holism is to talk about States of Society as a whole. It is undeniably true that Mill does talk about them; what is not clear is why it is a vice, save in the limited sense that it is, logically, nonsense to talk about *all* the properties of anything, which logically must be infinite in number. But this esoteric point—which Popper is not above making[35]—is irrelevant to Mill, for all he is arguing is that in social matters it is in many cases impossible to ascribe to, say, economic phenomena of some kind purely economic causes, that there is such an interaction between the various aspects of social life that we cannot separate out neat causal changes. In its less exaggerated versions, this belief is surely correct; indeed it is much more nearly useless through triviality than through error. Mill's tendency to exaggerate here occurs almost always when he wants to emphasize the importance of the whole social situation for the functioning of government, and the doctrine recurs in a nonexaggerated shape in *Representative Government*.[36] But, generally, Mill leaves us in no doubt that he sees clearly that some phenomena are significant for the social scientist and others less so. The sound practical point in Popper's objection to holism is more important, and also goes even further to show Mill's innocence of the strange views he is credited with. The doctrine of holism, that every aspect of social life is intimately connected with every other, can very well be a revolutionary one, demanding that we change the whole social order to achieve our goals, and denying that they can be achieved by less than wholesale revolution. Of course, and Popper is aware of this from time to time, it can be a conservative doctrine, to the effect that we must beware of making any changes, since one change may bring about wholesale social disorder. But Mill's whole career was a lesson in trying to make piecemeal changes, though piecemeal changes at strategic points, so that they should have as many good effects as possible; it is unlikely that Mill would have revised the *System of Logic* so many times without noticing that its intention was to deny the possibility of what the *Principles of Political Economy* and *Representative Government* were advocating.

Second, Popper criticizes Mill for believing in "absolute" trends. Popper admits, of course, that there can be—indeed that there are—trends in history, and that identical trends may occur in many times and places. For example, there may in many societies at different times be a trend toward increased capital accumulation, a trend perhaps halted by a different disaster in each case.[37] But, according to Popper, the vital point about a trend is that "Its description . . . is not a law, but only a singular historical statement."[38] Mill, he says, fails to see the difference between laws and trends, because he "and his fellow historicists *overlook the dependence of trends on initial conditions.*"[39] This means they treat trends as laws, as unconditional or "absolute." Although I believe Popper is quite wrong about this, the fault is partly Mill's and is terminological; he uses the expression "empirical law" to cover too many different things; as we have said, it varies between a term to describe genuine, but low-level, laws and a term to describe merely compressed statements of observed uniformities. But in this context, it is clear that it is the latter which Mill means. He says, for example, that finding empirical laws in history consists "in finding general propositions which express concisely what is common to large classes of observed facts: . . ." [40] And the reason why they are not laws properly speaking is precisely that they are conditional, dependent on psychological and ethological laws, and upon the "collocations of facts" which happened to obtain as initial conditions. The fact that we cannot use empirical laws for purposes of prediction depends again precisely on the fact that until we know what the causes of the trend are, we cannot tell whether it will continue or not. Further support for this reading of Mill's case is to be found in the essays already mentioned, on *Civilisation* and on *Democracy in America,* where Mill is absolutely explicit that the existence of a trend is an invitation to consider whether we wish it to continue, and at what price we can reverse it if we decide we should. In all this, Mill is a paragon of Popperian virtue.

Only once does Mill give any grounds for Popper's accusation that Mill was set on "historicist prophecy," and this is in the passage quoted where he talks of looking "far into the future." [41] Otherwise, he is notably averse to committing himself to distant prophecies. The areas in which he is more willing to commit himself are easily explicable. For example, like all classical economists, he believed it to be an ineluctable law of nature that income could not rise indefinitely, and that there was nothing to be done about this. Again, he believed that so many of the psychological and social characteristics of the age would have to be reversed for there to be any change in what he saw as the egalitarian trend in all forms of social life that it was quite inconceivable that we should reverse this trend, even though it actually did lie within our power to do so.

Finally, then, the third accusation as to the rock—if it is rock

—on which Mill's historicism is said to be founded. This is his naïve belief in progress as an unconditional trend, based on the progressiveness of human nature. All we need recall to see the falsity of this accusation is our earlier discussion of Mill's problems about whether there was cyclical or progressive change in history. When Mill raises what he calls "the great and vexed question of the progressiveness of man," [42] he is not raising the question of whether things get better, but simply of whether human nature changes over time. He maintains that it does, so that we get not an orbit in human affairs, but a "trajectory or progress." [43] And then he goes on to point out that "The words Progress and Progressiveness, are not here to be understood as synonymous with improvement and tendency to improvement. It is conceivable that the laws of human nature might determine, and even necessitate, a certain series of changes in man and society, which might not in every case, or which might not on the whole, be improvements." [44] And again, in the essay on *Civilisation*, he distinguishes between two senses of the term, in one of which it does mean better, in the other of which to call a nation more civilized is only to say it has more wealth and power. And then he says, "The present age is preeminently the era of civilisation in the narrow sense; whether we consider what has already been achieved, or the rapid advances making towards still greater achievements. We do not regard the age as either equally advanced or equally progressive in many of the other kinds of improvement. In some it appears to us stationary, in some even retrograde." [45] Clearly what Mill valued was progress, in the sense of improvement in men's moral and intellectual qualities; what he thought was being achieved was an improvement in the national wealth and power; and what he thought was inevitable was cumulative change, both in man and in his environment. In none of this does Mill show a cheerful belief in the inevitability of progress.

But, of course, I do not wish to argue that Mill has properly characterized the task of sociology as the production of even a limited social astronomy; nor do I wish to argue that he is justified in thinking that the kind of historical writing we have should give way to a "scientific" approach, of which Henry Adams' history is both archetype and parody. What I do want to argue is that the ambition is consistent with the premises; it is consistent with Mill's whole picture of rationality in science. We have argued several times over that the concept of rationality and the criteria for scientific respectability that Mill adopts all rest on the atomistic picture of the universe which he inherits from Locke. This, in turn, gets much of its acceptability from the successes of the incomparable Mr. Newton; and ever since then the social sciences have sought their Newton. This, in essence, is what Mill's characterization of the historical task of sociological inquiry amounts to. The question whether social science should look for a Newton, and whether it should look for a Newton who employs a Newtonian metaphysics, is one to which much time might be devoted. My purposes, however, require that we ignore this question, and move on to the practical question of how Mill thought the transition was to be made to a Newtonian, or inductive, ethics. Many writers have felt that there is some kind of appropriateness in the connection between, say, classical economics, classical mechanics, and the principle of utility in ethics. I hope that the next two chapters will make this appropriateness more explicit in elucidating the question of what Mill regarded as rationality in ethics, and why this leads him to say that he has produced an inductive ethics.

NOTES

1. Simon, *European Positivism*, pp. 275–279. 2. *System of Logic*, VI, x, 1. 3. *Ibid.* 4. *Ibid.*, VI, x, 5. 5. *Ibid.*, VI, x, 5. 6. *Ibid.*, VI, x, 2. 7. *Ibid.* 8. Popper, *Open Society*, II, p. 87. 9. *System of Logic*, VI, x, 3. 10. *Ibid.* 11. *Ibid.* 12. *Ibid.* 13. Popper, *Poverty of Historicism*, pp.

115–119.   14. *System of Logic*, VI, x, 6.   15. *Ibid.*, VI, x, 4.   16. *Ibid.*
17. *Ibid.*, VI, x, 2.   18. *Ibid.*, VI, x, 6.   19. *Ibid.*   20. *Dissertations and Discussions*, Vol. I, p. 163.   21. *Ibid.*, Vol. II, pp. 8ff.   22. *System of Logic*, VI, x, 7.   23. *Ibid.*   24. *Ibid.*   25. *Ibid.*   26. *Ibid.*   27. *Dissertations and Discussions*, Vol. I, pp. 171–172.   28. *System of Logic*, VI, x, 8.   29. *Ibid.*   30. *Ibid.*   31. *Ibid.*   32. *Ibid.*, VI, xi, 4.   33. *Ibid.*, VI, ix, 2.
34. *Dissertations and Discussions*, Vol. I, pp. 185–186.   35. Popper, *Poverty of Historicism*, pp. 76–83.   36. *Utilitarianism, etc.*, p. 177.   37. Popper, *Open Society*.   38. Popper, *Poverty of Historicism*, p. 108.   39. *Ibid.*, p. 128.   40. *System of Logic*, VI, ix, 5.   41. *Ibid.*, VI, x, 7.   42. *Ibid.*, VI, x, 2.   43. *Ibid.*, VI, x, 3.   44. *Ibid.*   45. *Dissertations and Discussions*, Vol. I, p. 161.

XI

TOWARD RATIONALITY
IN ETHICS

We have seen that for Mill rationality is essentially bound up
with such concepts as that of proof, or evidence, with being
able to produce reasons for beliefs which one may hold; it is
also bound up with explanatory power, with the ideal of a
scientific system which is capable of explaining a great many
particular cases by inference from a relatively few laws; and
again, reasoning has much to do with inductive inference performed according to the inference rule embodied in the law of
universal causation. I have all along implied that this conception of rationality is intended to apply to rationality in ethics
as well as to rationality in the physical and moral sciences; indeed the whole purpose of this book has been to show how
light can be shed on the dark places of Mill's philosophy once
we understand how this concept of rationality holds together
his views on matters ranging from mathematics to justice. So,
our task is now to ascertain exactly what Mill was doing when
he tried to produce an inductive ethics, a rational ethics which
was appropriate to inductivists in their attack on the intuitionists. As we should expect, it is an ethics in which principles
feature very largely, since Mill was quite clear that exactly as
justification of a belief requires that we derive it from some
general principle, so also does justification of an action; again,

it is a systematic ethics, in that Mill thinks there should be some one principle on which all others hang, which stands at the center of the system. And, of course, it is an ethics which raises the problem of proof in ethics; since Moore, Mill has generally borne the greatest weight of scorn heaped on philosophers who commit what has been termed the "naturalistic fallacy," [1] the fallacy of trying to *prove* ethical propositions, of trying to derive an "ought" from an "is." [2]

Accordingly, this chapter is very largely devoted to explicating Mill's views on proof in ethics. Because so few writers have done more than echo Moore's criticisms of Mill, the interest and oddity of Mill's views have generally been overlooked. Thus, very little will be said here about the "naturalistic fallacy" or about whether Mill committed it; instead, what we shall concentrate on is the explanation that can be derived from sources other than the essay *Utilitarianism* of the doctrines which that essay is supposed to defend. And, of these doctrines, the first is the statement that there can be no proof in ethics. It has not been altogether overlooked that Mill says: "Questions of ultimate ends are not amenable to direct proof. Whatever can be proved to be good, must be so by being shown to be a means to something admitted to be good without proof." [3] On the face of it, it might seem that what I have to admit is that Mill does not believe that the criteria for rationality which hold good in the sciences hold good in ethics also, and that my thesis is simply false. But, as everyone who has read the essay will recall, Mill immediately goes on to say that the absence of proof does not mean that there can be no rational argument about ultimate ends; there are considerations capable of determining the intellect, and these he thinks tell in favor of the principle of utility. Now, from these statements, there are two ways forward. One is to dismiss Mill as essentially a muddled man; and in the context of *Utilitarianism* alone, it is not surprising that this has been a common reaction, since Mill does not explain what he means. The other way is to relate *Utilitarianism* to the *System of Logic* and to the last of the *Essays on Some Unsettled Questions of Political Economy,* out of which one can reconstruct the argument which leads him to say that proof is impossible. And what is of considerable contemporary interest is how closely Mill's account resembles that given by "prescriptivists" such as Hare.[4]

The reason why evaluative judgments are not capable of proof is that they are not factual statements; indeed they are not really statements at all. Evaluative judgments, in other words, are of a different logical order from factual statements, a difference which Mill marks by talking of the differences between *science* and *art,* between *statements* and *rules.* The distinction is made in the essay "Of the Definition of Political Economy." In this essay Mill considers the proposed definition of economics as "a science which teaches, or professes to teach, in what manner a nation may be made rich."[5] And in this definition he detects a logical flaw: "it seems liable to the conclusive objection, that it confounds the essentially distinct, though closely connected, ideas of *science* and *art.* These two ideas differ from one another as the understanding differs from the will, or as the indicative mood in grammar differs from the imperative. The one deals in facts, the other in precepts. Science is a collection of *truths;* art, a body of *rules,* or directions for conduct. The language of science is, This is, or, This is not; This does, or does not, happen. The language of art is, Do this; Avoid that. Science takes cognisance of a *phenomenon,* and endeavours to discover its *law;* art proposes to itself an *end,* and looks out for *means* to effect it."[6] In this rather remarkable passage, Mill looks both back and forward in the development of empiricist ethics; he looks back to Hume when he talks of the understanding and the will in a manner reminiscent of Hume's doctrine that morality is a matter of "feeling, not of reason";[7] and he faces forward to Hare, who argues that value judgments are to be analyzed as a species of imperative. In the *System of Logic,* Mill shows that he holds another view characteristic of recent moral philosophy. Speaking of propositions containing an "ought," he says of them: "The propositions now spoken of do not assert that anything is, but enjoin or recommend that something should be. They are a class by themselves. A proposition of which the predicate is expressed by the words *ought* or *should be,* is generically different from one which is expressed by *is* or *will be.* It is true that, in the largest sense of the words, even these propositions assert something as a matter of fact. The fact affirmed in them is, that the conduct recommended excites in the speaker's mind the feeling of approbation." [8] This is Mill's rather awkward way of saying that, although a man who says "you ought to do this" is not *stating* that he approves of the action in question, he is nonetheless *implying* it, that what he is not stating he feels, he can still be said to express.

If we may equate the inquiry into ultimate ends with the inquiry into the first principles of morality, it is clear that Mill's view that there can be no proof of ultimate ends rests on the doctrine that morality is an art, not a science, although it is an art heavily dependent on the science of human nature: "morality itself is not a science, but an art; not truths, but rules. The truths on which the rules are founded are drawn (as is the case in all arts) from a variety of sciences; but the principle of them, and those which are most nearly peculiar to this particular art, belong to a branch of the science of mind." [9] The branch to which Mill refers is the social branch— one more reason for the enthusiasm with which he defends the social sciences. If morality is an art, then it is clear that there cannot be any proof of its first principles, since no statements of fact can logically imply an imperative. So it seems that the vindication of Mill's statement that there can be no proof of ultimate ends rests in the fact that a proposition like "Happiness is the supreme good" is not, as its grammatical form suggests, a statement at all, but an imperative—"Seek happiness"—and is not susceptible of either truth or falsity but, rather, of acceptance or refusal;[10] we can follow the precept or refuse to do so, but this makes the precept neither true nor false, since these terms are inapplicable to it. The emphasis in the *System of Logic* on the inapplicability of the term "science" to any "inquiry the results of which do not express themselves in the indicative, but in the imperative mood, or in periphrases equivalent to it; . . ." [11] leaves us in no doubt that this is at the root of Mill's contention that ultimate ends are not susceptible of proof.

Judgments concerning the relation of means to end, on the other hand, are clearly scientific judgments; they state what causal steps are necessary for a given outcome; as Von Wright puts it, they are "anankastic statements." [12] To this extent, all arts must borrow from science in framing rules. But one element cannot be borrowed in this way; this is the major premise of the art, the affirmation of a goal as desirable. "Every art has one first principle, or general major premise, not borrowed from science; that which enunciates the object aimed at, and affirms it to be desirable. The builder's art assumes that it is desirable to have buildings; architecture (as one of the fine arts,) that it is desirable to have them beautiful or imposing. The hygienic and medical arts assume, the one that the preservation of health, the other that the cure of disease, are fitting and desirable ends." [13] And it is to the medical example that Mill recurs in *Utilitarianism*: "The medical art is proved to be good by its conducing to health; but how is it possible to prove that health is good?" [14] On this account, the relation between science and art is simply characterized. To declare some end desirable is to take a decision to pursue that end, rather than to describe it in any particular way; and thus this step requires no proof. Thereafter we consider the end we aim at as an effect, and ask what means must be pursued in order to achieve this effect; that is, we ask what will as a matter of fact bring about the effect we desire. It may be that a variety of courses will achieve the desired effect, in which case we have to decide on other grounds which is *the* course to pursue; or it may be that no course of action is feasible. As Mill puts it: "The art proposes to itself an end to be attained, defines the end, and hands it over to the science. The science receives it, considers it as a phenomenon or effect to be studied, and having investigated its causes and conditions, sends it back to Art with a theorem of the combination of circumstances by which it could be produced. . . . Art concludes that the performance of these actions is desirable, and finding it also practicable, converts the theorem into a rule or precept." [15] Mill sometimes accepts the term "practical science" for "art"; but he notes without comment Bain's suggestion that we should confine the term "art" to the actual body of rules, and employ the term "practical science" for "the selection from the truths of a science made for the purposes of an art." [16]

Given Mill's account of the relations of art and science, and given that he declares morality to be an art, not a science, we see why he thought himself not merely not obliged to try to *prove* the principle of utility, but obliged, rather, to point out that a proof was strictly impossible. The problem thus becomes one of finding out what sort of "considerations capable of determining the intellect" Mill did appeal to, and what weight they carry. But the preliminary point that needs to be made is a modification of our first acceptance of the identity of the first principles of morality and the principle of utility; the principle of utility is the first principle of *all* forms of assessment of conduct, and not only of moral assessment—a distinction whose practical point will emerge more clearly when we turn to Mill's defense of individual liberty. But Mill is quite clear that moral assessment is only one form of assessment, that morality is only one portion of the whole art which he calls the "Art of Life";[17] and the principle of utility is the imperative major premise of the whole Art. In the *System of Logic,* he says that the precepts we know or might discover about how to live "form (or rather might form) a body of doctrine which is properly the Art of Life, in its three departments, Morality, Prudence or Policy, and Aesthetics; the Right, the Expedient, and the Beautiful or Noble, in human conduct or works." [18] After what we have already seen of Mill's tendency to identify rationality with the creation of a systematic explanation of a set of phenomena, it is necessary only to underline the implication of the passage quoted that rationality in practical matters equally involves the systematic relation of rules of conduct to one another. As in science we try to reduce the explanatory principles to as few as possible, so in art we try to aim at one imperative major premise: "if that principle be rightly chosen, it will be found, I apprehend, to serve for the ultimate principle of Morality, as for that of Prudence, Policy or Taste." [19] In the *System of Logic* he does not try to argue his belief in utility as this first principle, but merely states his own belief that "the general principle to which all rules of practice ought to conform, and the test by which they should be tried, is that of conduciveness to the happiness of mankind, or rather, of all sentient beings: in other words that the promotion of happiness is the ultimate principle of Teleology." [20] This explains a number of otherwise rather enigmatic passages in *Utilitarianism,* such as the conclusion of the "proof" of the principle of utility: ". . . happiness is the sole end of human action, and the promotion of it the test by which to judge of all human conduct; from whence it necessarily follows that it must be the criterion of morality since a part is included in the whole." [21] In other words, the account of the matter given in *Utilitarianism* presupposes, and indeed only makes complete sense in the light of, the account in the *System of Logic.*

Before arguing *for* his first principle, Mill argues that there *must be* a first principle. Here he is arguing as so often against the intuitionists, and especially against Whewell, whose moral philosophy attracts scathing criticism in an essay devoted to the purpose.[22] But throughout Mill's works, the argument is basically the same. The only persons who think we can dispense with a first principle are the intuitionists, because they suppose "that a moral sense, or instinct, inherent in our constitution, informs us, both what principles of conduct we are bound to observe, and also in what order these should be subordinated to one another." [23] Mill's objections are threefold.

The first rests in his antipathy to all appeals to self-evidence, and the intuitionists claimed that not merely did we perceive moral principles, but also that they were perceived to be self-evident; by the end of the *System of Logic,* Mill sees no need to argue further against the concept of self-evidence. The second ground of his objection is that we do not need to suppose that we have a moral sense in order to account for moral phenomena; in this respect, Mill's account is something of an advance on Hume's. There is something distressingly *ad hoc* about the introduction of a moral sense; the only test of our possessing one is that we make moral distinctions, and yet the existence of these distinctions is itself supposed to be demonstrated by our possession of a moral sense. The final objection rests on Mill's view that morality is only *one* aspect of human conduct: "the doctrine of intuitive moral principles even if true, would provide only for that portion of the field of conduct which is properly called moral. For the remainder of the practice of life, some general principle or standard must still be sought." [24]

In any case, the intuitionists, says Mill, never live up to their claims; they claim that the "principles of morals are evident *a priori,* requiring nothing to command assent, except that the meaning of the terms be understood." [25] But they never produce a list of such principles, whereas ". . . to support their pretensions there ought either to be some one fundamental principle or law at the root of all morality, or if there be several, there should be a determinable order of precedence among them; and the one principle, or the rule for deciding between the various principles when they conflict, ought to be self-evident." [26] The fact that men have not recognized any supreme principle makes any claims to self-evidence look very feeble, should any principle be put forward. It is true that in the case of lower-level moral beliefs many people are inclined to hold that they are self-evident, but this is no more than the effect of habit. Having reduced the allegedly self-evident nature of mathematical truth to no more than habitual assent, Mill is scarcely in the mood to admit the claims of moral principles to the status of self-evident truths.

Although the intuitionists supply no first principle, and although whatever first principle we do supply will not be self-evident, Mill does not doubt that some first principle is necessary for rationally justified human conduct. Moral rules which we usually obey may turn out to conflict with each other in particular cases, and if they do, we cannot act rationally unless we have some higher principle that will tell us which rule is to give way; and if we can offer, say, two higher principles, according to both of which a given rule is to be preferred, we may still envisage situations in which there would be conflict between these higher rules also. The only resting place must lie in some single highest principle. In parallel with his account of explanation, Mill plainly holds that to justify an action, we must be able to deduce a precept enjoining that action from some imperative principle. And on such an account, it looks as if we really must look for some single highest principle from which all the rest may be inferred. "There must be some standard by which to determine the goodness or badness, absolute or comparative, of ends or objects of desire. And whatever that standard is, there can be but one: for if there were several ultimate standards of conduct, the same conduct might be approved by one of these principles and condemned by another: and there would need to be some more general principle as umpire between them." [27] The claim that there must be some one ultimate standard will be more closely investigated in the next chapter, but here we can at least point out how consistent is this claim with Mill's criteria of rationality. These tacitly presuppose that we must always be concerned to derive rules from more general rules; and while it may be true that we often do this, it is not an a priori truth that we can always find a rule to tell us what to do. Mill's retort is to say that to hold this view is to deny that every choice can be rationally justified; and perhaps many philosophers would accept that this denial of rationality is eventually forced on us. Alternatively, we may want to argue that Mill's account of what it is to be rational, though adequate for how we argue from principles to decisions in particular cases, is not adequate for arguments to high-level principles. Nonetheless, the majority of philosophers would accept the deductive picture of rationality and, for them, the choice lies between accepting Mill's argument that rationality requires an ultimate principle, or accepting that there is no rational ethics. To be a deductivist and to believe in rationality in ethics seems to commit one firmly to Mill's position on ultimate principles.[28]

Our task now is to unravel the several elements in Mill's argument that the principle of utility is the ultimate principle. The course I shall adopt is to state what seem to me the essential points in the argument, and then show how they are related to what Mill actually says. I have divided the arguments Mill actually uses into what I call a psychological proof, a logical proof, and a moral proof; and a few sentences about this division are in order here. The obvious argument for a utilitarian ethics is a Hobbesian argument about the nature of the rules which self-interested men could agree to as rules to regulate their conduct with each other, and it is this argument which I think is the major element in Mill's case. In this sense, Mill's ethics can be said to be inductively arrived at, since it is an ethics which rests on an inference from what men are basically like to what common rules they will be able to live by. In this sense, utilitarian ethics emerges as a rational contract for rational men under conditions of uncertainty, and this is certainly a fair enough picture. But, of course, there are problems about the status of the claims we make about what men want, especially when we say that they want happiness; for it is a common observation that a term like "happiness" or "pleasure" does not straightforwardly describe some mental state which men might pursue.[29] It is for this reason that I argue that part of Mill's argument anyway is less about the facts of human motivation than about the logic of motivation language. Finally, in saying that part of

Mill's argument is itself a moral argument, I hope to take account of the fact that the goal of practical argument is not mere intellectual conviction, but is action or the adoption of certain dispositions to action on the part of whoever is the target of the moral argument; to persuade someone that the principle of utility is the ultimate moral standard is thus a piece of moral persuasion. Both the persuasiveness and the weaknesses of Mill's argument seem to me directly attributable to the threefold nature of this argument; and yet, I am not wholly convinced that the blend is as intellectually shocking as it would seem to be.

The bare bones of the first element, the Hobbesian proof, are these. Men are naturally inclined to pursue each one his own happiness; each man will naturally aim at maximizing his own happiness. But the world is full of other men, and on this account of the matter, each of them is also aiming at maximizing his happiness; further, there is a rough equality between men, at least at the level that each of us could by contrivance succeed in killing another of our kind.[30] Thus, the only rules which we can mutually agree on for regulating our dealings are rules which maximize the good to be jointly produced and share it out equally. Each man has a prudential motive for joining a social system, since so much more can be done cooperatively, and since his security will be so much the greater if he can call upon the assistance of others in defending himself. This is enough to generate an identity of interest in the maintenance of rules regulating our dealings with one another, and these rules are the rules which Mill takes to be involved in either law or morality. Since the rules are intended to maximize happiness on the basis of equal distribution, it seems that the only rule which rational men in a situation of equality will accept will be the principle of utility. As a moral system it is viable, because each person has an interest in the maintenance of it and in its enforcement in cases where this is necessary. It is in each person's interest that the code should be kept, even when allowance is made for the fact that enforcement of the rules will on occasion prevent him from maximizing his own selfish interest. Each person's greatest selfish interest would, of course, lie in a code which other people kept, but which he did not, since in those circumstances he would secure the benefits of the code without incurring any of its costs in terms of opportunities forgone. But, since this is true for everyone, it follows that we can always expect a majority of all-but-lawbreaker against the lawbreaker. And as time passes, so people's sympathy and desire to be on good terms with their neighbors will lead them to feel the restraints of morality as hardly restraints at all; moral rules aim at the social good; an individual may feel both bound to and inclined to follow the rules; at any rate, they are certainly the only terms on which people *can* live together. This, of course, is Hobbes's system with the contractual element played down. But even the contractual element does appear in Mill's account; it is barely mentioned in *Utilitarianism,* but in *Liberty* Mill argues that while the idea of a social contract is, historically speaking, absurd, and that "no good purpose is served by inventing a contract in order to deduce social obligations from it," [31] it is nonetheless true that the relations of men in society are quasi-contractual: "everyone who receives the protection of society owes a return for the benefit, and the fact of living in society renders it indispensable that each should be bound to observe a certain line of conduct towards the rest." [32]

Before citing the passages in Mill's work which contain the Hobbesian argument, I want to say a little about the argument itself. It is, as it is in Hobbes, an argument from what men want for themselves to a conclusion about the sort of rules they can obey among themselves. In none of this is there any forbidden inference from "is" to "ought." The argument remains firmly in the realm of *is,* since the conclusion which it leads to is not that men ought to abide by the greatest happiness principle in regulating their dealings with one

another, but that if they do adopt any standard for their
dealings, then this is, as a matter of fact, the only one which
will work consistently with the premises. We shan't have
proved to any particular person that he ought to abide by
the rule; we have shown him that there is a good chance that
he will be made to, and also that there is no chance of any
rule more favorable to himself being adopted by rational
men. But this is all; moreover, it would be wrong to see this
as an objection, since we began with the assumption that
moral principles at the highest level could not be proved. We
might even turn on an objector and ask him what *would*
constitute a *proof* of highest-level principles. By definition,
we cannot derive the highest-level principle from some higher-
level good to which it conduces. What we can do, and have
done, is show how such a rule could work, given men as we
suppose them to be; but, of course, mankind may recognize
no supreme principle at all. Mill suggests that in general they
have not had any *explicit* supreme standard at any rate, but
that where there has been any question of referring existing
practice to any principle, the tacitly accepted principle has
tended to be that of utility. "It would be easy to show that
whatever steadiness or consistency these moral beliefs have
attained, has been mainly due to the tacit influence of a standard not recognised. Although the non-existence of an acknowledged first principle has made ethics not so much a
guide as a consecration of men's actual sentiments, still as
men's sentiments, both of favour and aversion, are greatly
influenced by what they suppose to be the effects of things
upon their happiness, the principle of utility, . . . has had a
large share in forming the moral doctrines of those even who
most scornfully reject its authority." [33] If one cannot appeal
to the principles justified by the supreme good to show that
it is good, then all one can do is show how the rules we do
regard as binding are justified by the principle, and how con-
tentious rules require to be referred to the principle, receiving

or failing to receive their justification in the light of the facts. In showing that this principle and no other will do this, we have done all that is possible.[34]

What elements in *Utilitarianism* support this reading of Mill's argument? One passage occurs in the third chapter, that dealing with the sanctions of the principle. This chapter has an avowed psychological note, since it answers the question of how people could be brought to feel obliged by utilitarian ethics; Mill sees that some people might feel that utilitarian ethics was somehow less obligatory than supernatural or intuitive ethics. The passage shows clearly that Mill believes that the only morally binding rule must be an impartial one: "Society between human beings, except in the relation of master and slave, is manifestly impossible, except on the footing that the interests of all are to be consulted";[35] and, of course, we do want to live in society: "The social state is at once so natural, so necessary and so habitual to man, that, except in some unusual circumstances, or by an effort of voluntary abstraction, he never conceives of himself otherwise than as a member of a body." [36] In other words, Mill accepts the premises of the necessity of social life and that it entails impartial and equal consideration of the interests of all. What he must go on to establish is that a person's interest is his happiness; that besides equal treatment, the members of a society require the maximization of welfare in total; in other words, that self-interest is happiness, and the general interest the general happiness.

Mill argues that there is no way of showing the desirability of happiness other than showing it is in fact desired; that men do desire happiness he thinks it quite impossible to doubt. Since this is so, it is clear that to each person his own happiness is a good, "and the general happiness, therefore, a good to the aggregate of all persons." [37] It is very usually held that this argument commits the fallacy of composition; it tries to show that the general good is a good to individuals by equivocating on the word "all." But the good of all which is the general good is the good of "all" considered collectively, whereas Mill is trying to show that it is a good to "all" considered distributively, i.e., to each.[38] But this is excessively simplistic in its view of what Mill was doing. For it was no news to Mill that universal egoism conflicts with, rather than entails, universal altruism. He shows this clearly in the previous chapter when he considers the egoist who says: "I feel that I am bound not to rob or murder, betray or deceive; but why am I bound to promote the general happiness? If my own happiness lies in something else, why may I not give that the preference?" [39] Mill's answer is largely to suggest that everyone else will simply combine to make sure that he does give the general happiness the preference. And this is surely the correct Hobbesian answer; but Mill goes on to point out that in a well-regulated society the practice of altruism will make its practitioner happy also—in other words, he adds Bishop Butler's insights to those of Hobbes. Ultimately, indeed, the very idea of not consulting the interests of other persons will be painful. Since Mill is here so clearly concerned with the problem of *getting* people to consult the public interest, he plainly cannot think that self-interest and the public interest are identical. What he is doing is arguing with a suppressed premise about what moral rules are; he thinks they are rules designed to promote the general welfare, and he is asking, therefore, what the general welfare consists in. His answer is that it is happiness; each individual's interest lies in his own happiness, and the point of moral rules, the rules which aim at the general welfare, is to maximize the general happiness; and, of course, the point of sanctions, of punishment, of the inculcation of feelings of obligation, of the capacity to feel guilt, is precisely to *make* it the individual's interest to do what is in the general interest.

Much more dubious than the proposition that the general happiness is the general interest is the statement that the *only* thing which can be an interest is happiness. Is this not straightforwardly untrue? That is, is it not false that all a man can desire is happiness, and that all moral agents can wish for is the general happiness? We talk of a miser who hoards money and is made no happier; we talk of a man who sacrifices *his* happiness to his children's and we are surely correct to do so. It is surely true that the miser has forgotten how to be happy, and simply collects money; and it is surely true that the father does sacrifice his happiness. In other words, accepting Mill's equation of our interests and what we desire—an equation which there is much to be said against[40]—it is surely false that all we desire, we desire for the sake of happiness. Mill's reply is that whatever we desire *for its own sake,* we desire for the sake of happiness. The miser who seeks gold for its own sake is properly described as seeking happiness; the point is that the gold which was merely a *means* to happiness is now part of it. It is possible that the miser really does not know what he is doing; but generally to be a miser is just to be someone whose happiness consists in possessing money. Equally the father who, for example, refrains from spending money on food for himself to buy clothes for his child can be said to find his happiness in the child's welfare, and is properly described as seeking happiness. In other words, there is no clash between saying that a man seeks his happiness and saying that he seeks the welfare of someone else. "The principle of utility does not mean that any given pleasure, as music, for instance, or any given exemption from pain, as for example health, is to be looked on as a means to a collective something termed happiness, and to be desired on that account. They are desired and desirable in and for themselves; besides being means, they are part of the end." [41] In short, to object that not everything that is done must be done for the sake of happiness, either private or general, must assume that happiness is the name of a distinct thing, whereas the fact is that particular goods, both public and private, are *parts* of happiness, where they are not means. And this leads Mill to conclude that "there is in reality nothing desired except happiness." [42] The conclusion that this eliminates any other candidate for the *summum bonum* is at once drawn by Mill. "We have now, then, an answer to the question, of what sort of proof the principle of utility is susceptible. If the opinion I have now stated is psychologically true, if human nature is so constituted as to desire nothing which is not either a part of happiness or a means to happiness, we can have no other proof, and we require no other, that these are the only things desirable." [43] And Mill is convinced that "to desire anything, except in proportion as the idea of it is pleasant, is a physical and metaphysical impossibility." [44] Recapitulating the argument, then, we see that what Mill has argued is that to be motivated to action a man must see something as part of his own happiness; and that moral rules are rules restraining and assisting men in the pursuit of this happiness. A man must rationally desire the existence of moral rules, since they are indispensable to social life; to be motivated toward actually keeping the rules, it must be in his interest to keep them on particular occasions, and this is achieved in part by sanctions and in part by the force of habit working on our need for the affection and approval of other people. The force of Mill's remarks about happiness is psychological; it is true that he calls the impossibility of desiring anything other than happiness a "metaphysical" impossibility; but to him metaphysical very often meant psychological. Thus, when Mill argues that happiness is the only object of desire, what he is pointing to is a fact about human motivation, namely, that men will only do what makes them more happy than any of the alternatives. It follows, therefore, that any moral code will be accepted to the extent that it maximizes the goods available which contribute to our happiness, and that it will only be obeyed to the extent that the happiness of individuals can be bound up in keeping it. This is clearly the best argument which Mill can put forward for the principle of utility, and it is a good one. The usefulness of it, of course, will depend very largely on the extent to which men agree on what will make them happy, and Mill himself is not willing to make large claims for much better than basic agreement about matters such as the preservation of life, liberty, and the means of subsistence.

To my mind, the above Hobbesian argument is at the very least a large part of Mill's case. It is an argument which is central to the long utilitarian tradition in English thought, and it is unnecessary to demonstrate at length the parentage of the utilitarianism of the nineteenth century in the thought of Hobbes; at the very least it was no accident that it should have been Molesworth who produced the great edition of Hobbes's works. But, it is not the only argument in Mill's case, even if it is the best, and even though it would have been much more persuasive had it been put more clearly. For, the doctrine that men seek only pleasure or the means of it has logical overtones which must be attended to. When Mill argues as he does that men can only desire happiness or the means to happiness, he seems often not to be appealing to a contingent fact about what men happen to want but, rather, to a logical truth about how we are to describe what people want. There are two positions to distinguish here: the first is what Mill *says* he is doing; the second, what he actually does. Undoubtedly, what he says and presumably thinks is that he is dealing with a matter of fact, with an empirical question concerning the laws of mind, the answer to which can be inductively arrived at. What he actually does is to appeal to logical considerations; and the fact that he calls them psychological is not a hindrance to seeing them as in reality logical, for many of the "laws of thought" have decided leanings toward truths of logic. And Mill's equation of psychology and metaphysics makes sense, not because what he called metaphysics we should now call psychology, but because what he thought of as psychological considerations we should consider logical or metaphysical ones. The slide toward an appeal to logical truths is most apparent in the following passage: ". . . desiring a thing and thinking it pleasant, aversion to it and thinking of it as painful, are phenomena entirely inseparable, or rather two parts of the same phe-

nomena; in strictness of language, two different modes of naming the same psychological fact: that we think of an object
as desirable (unless for the sake of its consequences), and to
think of it as pleasant, are one and the same thing." [45] Here
we can see a steady movement in Mill's case from regarding
desiring and thinking pleasant as logically distinct but psychologically connected conditions to regarding them as two
names for one state of affairs. To say that a man thinks something will make him happy is identical in force to saying that
he desires it for its own sake. Mill even begins to use the language of the formal object of desire when he talks, not of seeking pleasure, but of seeking something "as pleasant." But our
problem is less to show that Mill appeals to logical truths
than to see what assistance they are. *Prima facie,* it seems implausible to argue that merely redescribing our actions can
achieve anything in the way of moral proof.

What perhaps the argument can do is this. It can uncover
the formal structure of moral and prudential rules by showing
the logical connection between happiness and these rules.
Thus, when we come to the answer that a man does something
because it makes him happy, we can see that we have come
to the end of a certain series of questions about why he behaves in a certain way. We may ask why he plays cricket and
be told that he does it to earn money, and we may go on to
ask why he wants the money; but if we are told he does it
for pleasure we cannot sensibly go on to ask why he wants
pleasure. To say something is done for pleasure is to point
out that further questions are ruled out. And, if this is true
of explanations of·behavior where no moral obligation is at
issue, we might go on to argue that, logically, the concept of
moral reasons for actions is linked to the promotion of common goods, of general happiness. Prudential rules, we might
say, tell us how to secure our own happiness, while moral
rules, the interpersonal rules, which we have to obey in common with everyone else, are designed to promote interpersonal
goods. To ask for the point of a moral rule is to ask what

H

common good, what object of Humian impartial desiring, it promotes. A moral rule which cannot be represented as serving some such goal cannot be a moral rule at all. And, if this answer were adequate, it would at any rate rule out some other answers as adequate; thus, it could not be an answer to a request for moral justification to say merely: "It is God's will"—we should have to show how doing God's will advances our common interests. Of course, this does not rule out God as a moral legislator in the sense of an authority on what rules we should adopt; and it does not rule out God acting as a source of moral sanctions, ensuring that the good flourish and the evil do not. What it does rule out is giving the answer that God wills such-and-such as the answer to a request for moral justification. But even if the logical explication of moral discourse will tell us so much, it has not told us enough. For the argument in favor of the principle of utility to be useful to the advocate of moral enlightenment, such as Mill, we shall need a much more adequate characterization of what it is for a person to seek his own good, or happiness, in terms of what sort of things really satisfy a man; and again we shall need to know what sort of things form the common good. It may be the case that, once we see what the logic of moral discourse is, we shall in fact reach agreement on moral rules; but it does not seem very likely. It is this more adequate argument which we really require, and which the Hobbesian argument with its implicit view of what constitutes basic human welfare more readily supplies.

The last argument which can be discerned is in some ways the most interesting, since it raises the question which the next chapter discusses, namely, whether moral rationality does involve appealing to a single value. For this last argument seems itself to be a moral argument, an argument from "is" to "ought." If this is indeed the case, then we shall have to ask what sort of rule of inference it implies; if, as seems logically implied, this rule of inference is some kind of moral principle, then it would seem that there is at least one principle other than the principle of utility, which is at least as ultimate as it. The argument proceeds almost as if Mill were addressing himself to each individual reading *Utilitarianism;* What, he asks us, do you want? And presumably we reply that we want our own happiness. Then he draws our attention to the fact that there may often be competition with other men for the means of happiness; the question is whether we believe we have any greater right to our happiness than they have to theirs; i.e., the question is whether we can produce a moral justification for self-preference. If we cannot, and the presumption is that we cannot in the abstract do so, Mill can reasonably ask us whether we can think of any rule other than that of maximizing happiness and distributing it equally which we can put forward as a moral rule for all of us to obey. In other words, Mill wants to get us to agree that we *ought* to live by utilitarian principles. In a way, this is the moral face of our Hobbesian proof; that proof was entitled to the name of proof because it stayed on the "is" side of the logical divide; but here the question is one of adopting a principle and the question cannot be one of proof. And what Mill says at the beginning of *Utilitarianism* strongly suggests that he thinks his task is one of securing our adoption of the principle, for no sooner has he declared that the principle is not amenable to proof than he goes on to say: "We are not, however, to suppose that its acceptance or rejection must depend on blind impulse or arbitrary choice," [46] which seems to imply clearly enough that it is acceptance which is at issue, of getting us to adopt a rule, not to believe something or other to be the case. On the other hand, he continues: "The subject is within the cognisance of the rational faculties; and neither does that faculty deal with it solely in the way of intuition. Considerations may be presented, capable of determining the intellect either to give or withhold its assent to the doctrine, and this is equivalent to proof." [47] The trouble here is that the faculty Mill should be interested in is not the reason but the will, since it is to the latter that "ought" has been assigned; nor can he be wholehearted in thinking that it is the intellect alone which he must gain. For he speaks only of the determining considerations as "equivalent to proof." If they were meant for the intellect only, they would not be merely equivalent to proof, they would be proof, since the only thing that determines a well-ordered intellect is proof. All this tends to suggest that Mill thought that both the will and the intellect were involved, that the adoption of a principle involves being reasonable in what one wills, and perhaps that once people saw clearly what was involved in moral issues they simply would become utilitarians. In effect what is envisaged is that, if the intellect is given enough information of one kind and another, the will will be determined in a utilitarian direction, and this is why it is worth asking "what rational grounds can be given for accepting or rejecting the utilitarian formula." [48]

This view of Mill explains why he should be so concerned with the problems of the sanctions of the principle; in trying to prove the principle, as we can now see, Mill is offering us motives which will induce us to live by it. Mill remarks that the question is often—and entirely properly—asked of a moral principle: "What is its sanction? What are the motives to obey it? Whence does it derive its binding force?" [49] This question, he says, "arises whenever a person is called on to *adopt* a standard" [50] where the question, therefore, is not one of asking why someone else does something, but of asking: Why should I do this? The considerations Mill presents are, as we saw, to a large extent prudential, although he adds appeals to such nonprudential motives as self-respect. Mill sets out to persuade us that we have to live in society, and that we cannot hope to live selfishly, so that we shall do as well as we can reasonably hope to do, if we abide by equitable rules for maximizing happiness. More than this, he points out how much happier we shall be when we are not at odds with our fellows and when we make their welfare the object of our spontaneous concern.

But all this is open to the Kantian objection that it may be an argument that will get us to *want* to do what, it may be, is right, but it cannot get us to see that we *ought* to do what is right. He can persuade us that we should do well in a utilitarian society; he can persuade us that because of the interest which everyone else has in having the rules obeyed, it will probably be prudent to obey the rules even where we do not feel inclined to do it. He can perhaps even persuade us that we shall eventually like obeying the rules, that we shall feel no conflict between our own and the general welfare. Is this the same as persuading us that we are under an obligation to keep the rules? It seems that Mill believes, or half-believes, that it is, because he tends to analyze the notion of obligation as equivalent to feelings of discomfort at the thought of not doing an action. Thus, "I am obliged to do X" is analyzed as "the thought of not doing X causes me pain." But this analysis confuses the feelings which a man may have when he thinks he is under an obligation with the obligation itself. Clearly, neither Mill nor anyone else thinks that a man who hardens his heart enough to avoid feeling any pangs of conscience is thereby absolved of obligations. In fact, when Mill is not analyzing, but simply using, the concept of obligation, he makes what looks much more like the correct move—to appeal to impartiality, consistency, universalizability,[51] or whatever name we should give the considerations in question. Mill's reasoning on this point arises out of considering the obligation not to make exceptions to rules for the purpose of doing what we want. He sees that the essential point about obligation is that it condemns our making exceptions in our own favor, and indeed condemns making exceptions except with good reasons shown. Thus, in the essay on Whewell's moral philosophy, Mill considers the case of a man wanting to make an exception to the rule forbidding murder. The justification for the rule is that "if it were thought allowable that any one might put to death at pleasure any human being whom he thought the world would be well rid of, nobody's life would be safe";[52] and the objection to making exceptions is: "If one person may break through the rule on his own judgment, the same liberty cannot be refused to others." [53] In other words, the principle of impartial consideration demands that if we want the rule kept at all, we must accept it in all cases; what we think we are entitled to do, we cannot refuse other people's right to do also. If preferring our happiness to the general happiness is all right for us, it must be all right for everyone; but this would contradict our initial acceptance of the desire for social life and moral rules. That this is at the back of Mill's mind is evident from his references to Kant in *Utilitarianism*; his objection to Kant is that his principle of impartiality does not by itself produce moral rules, because on its own it cannot move people to action as the desire for happiness can—or as desire for, or aversion to, consequences can. But that impartiality is absolutely required for a moral judgment, Mill never doubts; a man who does not make his judgment impartially does not make a moral judgment at all. So deeply embedded in Mill's concept of morality is the principle of impartiality that Mill quotes the Golden Rule as a brief summary of utilitarianism: "in the golden rule of Jesus of Nazareth, we read the complete spirit of the ethics of utility. To do as you would be done by, and to love your neighbour as yourself, constitute the ideal perfection of utilitarian morality." [54] And this comes as a gloss on the statement that "As between his own happiness and that of others, utilitarianism requires him to be as impartial as a disinterested and benevolent spectator." [55]

The problem which all this poses is the status of the principle of impartiality on which it is based. If this is a logical principle, then we can say that Mill shows how a compelling moral argument to the principle of utility can be produced; if it is a moral principle, then we have to admit that a moral *petitio principii* has been committed. My argument in the next chapter is largely devoted in fact to arguing that aggregative moral goals, such as that of creating more happiness, cannot be reduced to, and cannot generate, distributive moral aims, such as justice and impartiality. But, before doing this, I should like to conclude this chapter by pointing out how very much like a formal principle the impartiality principle is. In that it points out the irrationality of discriminating without differences, it *is* a logical principle, and of course not peculiar to moral argument; it would be irrational to call two indistinguishable colors by different names, and it looks very plausible to say that the same sort of irrationality is involved in distinguishing between cases where we are prepared to accept a moral rule and cases where we are not, if we can give no reason.[56] But I do not think that this position holds up, and therefore the next task that awaits us is to try to explain how it is that Mill's view of rationality in ethics, though very plausible and attractive, is nonetheless incorrect.

NOTES

1. G. E. Moore, *Principia Ethica*, pp. 9–10.   2. Hume, *Treatise of Human Nature*, III, i, 1.   3. *Utilitarianism*, etc., p. 4.   4. Hare, *Language of Morals*, Chap. XI; *Freedom and Reason*, Chap. VI.   5. *Essays on Some Unsettled Questions*, p. 123.   6. *Ibid.*, pp. 123–124.   7. Hume, *Treatise of Human Nature*, III, i, 2.   8. *System of Logic*, VI, xii, 6.   9. *Essays on Some Unsettled Questions*, p. 135.   10. Day, *Critical History of Western Philosophy*, p. 364.   11. *System of Logic*, VI, xi, 1.   12. Von Wright, *Norm and Action*, pp. 10–11.   13. *System of Logic*, VI, xii, 6.   14. *Utilitarianism*, etc., p. 4.   15. *System of Logic*, VI, xi, 2.   16. *Ibid.*, VI, xi, 5n.   17. *Ibid.*, VI, xii, 6.   18. *Ibid.*, VI, xii, 6.   19. *Ibid.*, VI, xii, 7.   20. *Ibid.*, VI, xii, 7.   21. *Utilitarianism*, etc., p. 36.   22. *Dissertations and Discussions*, Vol. II, pp. 450–509.   23. *System of Logic*, VI, xii, 7.   24. *Ibid.*, VI, xii, 7.   25. *Utilitarianism*, etc., p. 2.   26. *Ibid.*, p. 3.   27. *System of Logic*, VI, xii, 7.   28. Hare, *Freedom and Reason*, pp. 203–224.   29. E.g., Ryle, *Dilemmas*, pp. 57–63.   30. Hobbes, *Leviathan*, p. 63.   31. *Utilitarianism*, etc., p. 132.   32. *Ibid.*   33. *Ibid.*, p. 3.   34. *System of Logic*, III, xxi, 4; cf. *Utilitarianism*, etc., p. 3.   35. *Utilitarianism*, etc.,

p. 29.   **36.** *Ibid.*   **37.** *Ibid.*, p. 33.   **38.** Plamenatz, *English Utilitarians,* p. 140.   **39.** *Utilitarianism, etc.,* p. 25.   **40.** Barry, *Political Argument,* pp. 174–176.   **41.** *Utilitarianism, etc.,* p. 34.   **42.** *Ibid.*, p. 35.   **43.** *Ibid.,* p. 36.   **44.** *Ibid.*   **45.** *Ibid.*   **46.** *Ibid.*, p. 4.   **47.** *Ibid.*   **48.** *Ibid.*   **49.** *Ibid.*, p. 24.   **50.** *Ibid.*   **51.** Hare, *Freedom and Reason,* pp. 7–50.   **52.** *Dissertations and Discussions,* Vol. II, p. 476.   **53.** *Ibid.*   **54.** *Utilitarianism, etc.,* p. 16.   **55.** *Ibid.*   **56.** Hare, *Freedom and Reason,* pp. 10–12.

❊XII❊

UTILITY AND JUSTICE

In Chapter XI, we extracted from Mill's account of utilitarian ethics several criteria for the rationality of utilitarian ethics. In the first place, he holds that it is possible, if not exactly to prove utilitarian ethics, then certainly to produce rational arguments for the adoption of utilitarian standards. In the second place, the principle of utility can, he maintains, account for our moral rules in a tidy deductive fashion. And, finally, the principle of utility provides us with a principle for settling conflicts of obligation. In a manner of speaking, the last two claims are involved in Mill's conception of proving utilitarian ethics, for just as we have for a long time made inferences, not *from* but *according to,* the law of universal causation, which thus strengthens, and is strengthened by, these inferences, so we have for a long time made moral judgments according to the unexpressed standard of utility.[1] So, any failure of the principle to validate moral judgments, or any complications in the manner of validating them, will have serious effects on Mill's claim. And, equally, any failure to provide validation of *all* our moral judgments will have serious effects.

Thus, the burden of this chapter is, in the first place, to explain how the several portions of the Art of Life, of which morality is one, are related to each other. In the second place, we must ask what the relation of morality to the greatest-happiness principle is conceived to be—what the process is by which we validate moral judgments. In the last place, we must see how Mill tries to account for the concept of justice in utilitarian terms. In doing this, we can see how much Mill depends on an analogy between the rules of morality and the laws of a natural science. This analogy is both a source of strength and a source of weakness. It lends strength to Mill's account in giving it a coherence not usually associated with his name; but its weakness is that ultimately it is a misleading analogy.

In the *System of Logic,* Mill explains what an art is in contrast to a science. An art is defined by the goal to be achieved, as for example, building is defined by the goal of erecting buildings, and architecture by the goal of erecting beautiful ones. And this raises the question of the relation of the practical arts and the fine arts to the Art of Life. It is easy enough to see how a practical art or a fine art is to be defined; but it is much harder to see what is involved in the definition of the Art of Life. All we have from Mill is a couple of sections in the *System of Logic;*[2] but they offer enough guidance to reconstruct his views with some plausibility. Particular arts, like medicine, building, architecture, rest on the assumption that what they aim at is desirable; this is the major premise on which the imperatives of the art depend. But what of the establishment of this major premise? What of premises like "health is desirable" or "buildings are desirable"? At this point, the Art of Life comes in. People may like or dislike whatever is proposed as a goal, but this is not enough: "For the purposes of practice everyone must be required to justify his approbation, and for this there is need of general premisses, determining what are the proper objects of approbation, and what the proper order of precedence among these objects."[3] These general premises are what form the body of doctrine about ends, which Mill calls Teleology or the Art of Life.[4] Normally, there is little need of it: ". . . the various subordinate arts form a misleading analogy. In them, there is seldom any visible necessity for justifying the end, since in general its desirableness is denied by no-one, and it is only when the question of precedence is to be decided between that end and some other, that the general principles of Teleology have to be called in."[5] Thus, we might have to decide how far the beauty of a building should outweigh its impracticality, or how far the health of a patient warranted subjecting him to some discomfort. We don't deny that health is good and discomfort bad; what we want is some way of measuring the good of one against the bad of the other. It is to settle this kind of issue that we call in teleology; but how? Mill does not say, and in the short space he had, he hardly could have said. I think the answer runs as follows. The Art of Life has three divisions, which Mill usually calls "morality," "prudence," and "aesthetics," though in the essay on Bentham, he talks, rather, of actions possessing "a *moral* aspect, that of its *right* and *wrong;* its *aesthetic* aspect, or that of its beauty; its *sympathetic* aspect or that of its *lovableness.* The first addresses itself to our reason and conscience; the second to our imagination; the third to our human fellow-feeling."[6] This argues a rather different division, which leaves out prudence. The account in the *System of Logic* seems at any rate the one to stand by.

Morality, prudence, aesthetics—these are the divisions of the Art of Life; according to them, we may assess conduct as right and wrong, wise and foolish, noble and base. And the principles of each are to be derived from the principle of maximizing utility. Prudential rules are hypothetical commands: "If you don't want to get burned, stay clear of fires," for example. Moral rules are categorical commands, and are backed by sanctions, both those of general opinion and those of the agent's own conscience. They differ from prudential commands in that they apply only to other-regarding actions or to the other-regarding *aspects* of actions, where prudential rules apply only to the self-regarding aspects or to self-regarding actions. Thus a moral rule might be "Don't tell lies" or "Keep your promises." There is no question here of what the agent feels like doing, only of what he must do. This, says Mill, is involved in the very meaning of the word "right," as he is at pains to inform Whewell: "Dr Whewell announces it as *his* opinion, as the side *he* takes in this great controversy, 'that we must do what is right, at whatever cost of pain and loss.' As if this was not everybody's opinion: as if it was not the very meaning of the word right." [7] Finally, there is aesthetic assessment. Its rules are elusive; we do not seem inclined to utter hypothetical imperatives, such as "If you want to act nobly, do such-and-such." The explanation seems to be connected with the kind of evidence on which we call to back up an aesthetic judgment. In the case of both moral and prudential judgments, calculation is in place: in the former case, about good and evil done to persons other than the agent; in the latter case, about good and evil done to the agent. But, if prudence is about the agent's happiness, and morals is about that of other people, then aesthetics cannot be on a level with them; the human race is exhaustively divisible into the agent and those other than the agent. To what, then, do we appeal? Mill gives as an example, judging of a lie that it is *"mean* because it is cowardly—because it proceeds from not daring to face the consequences of telling the truth—or at best is evidence of want of that *power* to compass our ends by straightforward means, which is conceived as belonging to every person not deficient in sense or in understanding." [8] And this is said to be a matter for the imagination; it is not a matter of calculation, but of trying to visualize life in a certain way. I do not think Mill's concern with this element in appraising human conduct has been adequately understood, and in the final chapter I try to show how vital it is to Mill's argument in *Liberty*. But here all we need to notice is how it explains, as nothing else can, what Mill says about higher and lower forms of pleasure.[9] The difference between a man's happiness

and the pig's is not a matter of morality; for, if that were the
test, then the man who shrank from human contact would be
the most securely guarded against the danger of wickedness.
Equally it cannot be a matter of prudence, since a man who
wanted nothing would be most securely protected against
failure in that line. It is, rather, that men are, and pigs are
not, susceptible to appeals of a different kind, such as "the
sense of *honour,* and personal dignity—that feeling of exalta-
tion and degradation which acts independently of other people's opinion, or even in defiance of it; the love of *beauty,* the
passion of the artist; the love of *order,* of congruity, of consistency in all things, and conformity to their end." [10] This
is why, for all its inadequacy, Mill's statement that the best
judge of these matters[11] is the man with the wider experience
is at least the foundation of a correct answer.

The relation of these elements of the Art of Life to the
subordinate practical arts is not difficult to outline. The logical structure of a practical art is the same as that of a science.
Thus, corresponding to a low-level empirical law we have
either a rule of low generality—"Put windows in walls about
half way along and half way up"—or else a set of particular
precepts—"Put that window six feet along and three feet up,"
"Put that window nine feet along and two-feet-six up," and
so on. As with the low-level statements of a science, these
could be known as rules of thumb, without any sort of ra-
tionale. The middle-level rules, or axiomata media, are those
from which particular precepts and low-level rules can be
derived, as, for example, "Put nonload-bearing features in a
position equidistant from major load-bearing features." The
rules about windows and doors would appear as specifications
of such rules. The major premise of the building art, however, rests on the Art of Life. Thus the desirability of buildings is easily derived from the prudential consideration that
we need to keep warm and dry; the desirability of beautiful
buildings is easily derived from our wish to have both the
warmth and comfort of buildings and their attractiveness to

the eye as well. The relation between the end of a practical art and the goals of a portion of the Art of Life is not itself a means-end relation. Rather, to say that prudence validates the art of building is simply to say what sort of appeal to happiness is involved when someone justifies our erecting buildings. There is no *end* called prudence; "prudence" is simply the way we have or might have of arranging secondary ends, or subordinating some of these to others, as contributing to the agent's happiness. The relation of the elements of the Art of Life to the *summum bonum,* or the greatest happiness is, again, not one of means to ends. If it were such, then we might ask whether morality or prudence were the better means to the greatest general happiness, and this seems an odd question. On our account of the way we classify conduct, it would indeed be an odd question. If we look for prudential rulings, we look for justification of self-regarding action; if for moral ruling, for the justification of other-regarding action. Aesthetics, again, is a different matter altogether.

But presumably we can conceive of clashes between morality, prudence, and aesthetics. A given action might be both prudent, unaesthetic, and immoral, and we might need a rule to cover the clash. Thus, we might hold that a bank clerk who is threatened by a gunman may reasonably hand over the money in the till, even though the spectacle of a man who scorned the gunman's threats might be admirable, and even though in general the effect of diminishing the general welfare will result from handing over other people's money. Now, in effect, we have moral, prudential, and aesthetic rules applying to the same action, rules which conflict with each other. Thus, we have the proposition that it is wrong to hand over money in one's keeping, and this is a moral proposition. We also have the proposition that if faced with a man with a gun, it is wise to do what one is told. And, finally, we have the aesthetic proposition that it is noble to ignore threats. The moral rule thus says, Do not hand over the money; the aesthetic principle says, Do not yield to threats; the prudential principle says, Do not get shot. The point is, however, that the rule we produce is not exactly like any of these precepts, for it is *about* these precepts, and will in fact be a rule about when not to hold someone guilty of a *prima facie* breach of duty.

In effect, what we say is that when the alternative is extreme danger to the agent, he should not be held responsible, and equally that it is silly to dwell on the nobility of resistance when the danger is very extreme. On our analysis of moral rules as essentially other-regarding rules, what we have produced is a moral rule. Mill's dictum is always that "responsibility means punishment"; [12] and what we have here is a rule about when not to punish people either by legal or by moral sanctions. Punishing, holding responsible, these are essentially other-regarding actions. So it seems that the thing to say about the validation of the various rules is this. They can be demonstrated to be *prima facie* rules if it can be shown that the observance of such principles would tend to maximize general happiness, achieved either via the agent's welfare, other people's welfare, or by the increase in aesthetic satisfaction. Where the *prima facie* rules conflict with one another, we consider which rules should take precedence; and this is a decision whether or not we should intervene in favor of one or another rule. And this is to take a moral decision. Thus morality is both other-regarding and ultimate, and these are two features of morality which we should try to maintain on any account of it. [13]

But the problem still remains of how we are to relate our obligations to the greatest-happiness principle. We have suggested that there is a clear and simple line to be drawn between morality and prudence, so that not everything becomes a matter of obligation. But the other difficulty may be that we cannot show *enough* things, or the right things, to be matters of obligation. Plainly it would be a defect in the principle of utility if it proved too much to be our duty.[14] It would be another if it proved too little or the wrong things to be our duty.

One of the obvious objections to the principle of utility is that it places too great a strain on the capacity of the average man to calculate the effects of his actions on the general welfare of "all sentient beings." [15] Yet, of course, Mill remains emphatic that the "morality of an action depends upon its forseeable consequences." [16] If we cannot foresee consequences, then the principle of utility cannot be applied. Mill's answer is to argue that, in general, obligation is a matter of following secondary rules, axiomata media, which are both necessary to moral judgments and on which agreement can be reached more readily than it can on the highest-level principles: "As mankind are much more nearly of one nature, than of one opinion about their own nature, they are more easily brought to agree in their intermediate principles, *vera illa et axiomata media* as Bacon says, than in their first principles." [17] In *Utilitarianism* he pours scorn on those who adduce the difficulties of calculation; mankind has had long enough to see what are the good and bad consequences of actions by now: "People talk as if the commencement of this course of experience had hitherto been put off, and as if, at the moment when some man feels tempted to meddle with the property or life of another, he had to begin considering for the first time whether murder and theft are injurious to human happiness . . . but, at all events, the matter is now done to his hand. It is truly a whimsical supposition that if mankind were agreed in considering utility to be the test of morality, they would remain without any agreement as to what *is* useful. . . . There is no difficulty in proving any ethical standard whatever to work ill, if we suppose universal idiocy to be conjoined with it." [18] We *can* work out why the rules which we have are in general obligatory as conducive to general welfare; but the going rules are at any rate *prima facie* obligatory. Mill also insists that the rules are open to improvement: "that the received code of ethics is by no means of divine right; and that mankind still have much to learn as to the effects of actions on the general happiness I admit, or rather, earnestly maintain." [19] In general, then, we are content to rely on secondary rules, and it is "when two or more of these principles conflict that a direct appeal to some first principle becomes necessary." [20] And this is, I think, Mill's stance throughout his career. For when he defends Bentham against the strictures of Whewell, he is quick to say that Bentham neither invented nor pretended that he had invented the principle of utility. Bentham's great claims to fame rest on his patient and detailed derivation of secondary, and more frequently usable, rules.[21]

Mill's picture of the substantiation of moral rules, on the analogy of axiomata media in the natural sciences, however, has one fatal flaw in it. This is the ambiguity which permeates his account as to whether he is always defending the performance of the class of actions or abstentions which directly maximize utility, so that the actions are simply means to the end of the greatest general happiness. For this defense is inextricably mixed up with an account that closely resembles Hume's·derivation of the "artificial virtues," [22] that is, of the actions which are virtues, not because they directly enhance general utility, but because they are essential to the maintenance of a *convention* which is itself primarily intended to secure that people do *not* calculate the utilitarian merits of their actions. Promising is the paradigm of this case, in virtually all discussions of the matter; if we merely considered whether to hand someone five dollars, knowing he would spend it on drink, after which he would beat his wife, then clearly utility demands that we do not hand it to him. But, if we have promised to give it to him, we seem at any rate *prima facie* under an obligation to hand it to him, or, should we decide in the other direction, under an obligation to explain why we have not given it to him. Here we cannot justify the action of handing over the money merely as the action of handing over the money; any utilitarian justification it may get comes only from the fact that a *promise* has been made. This, of course, means that the relation of utility to particular actions is no longer direct and tidily deductive, but is indirect and mediated by social conventions of one kind and another. And this, of course, makes utility a much less reliable test than it was before, since now we have to assess the consequences, not simply of actions, but also of whole nonutilitarian conventions.[23]

Mill sees a certain part of this; at any rate, he is certainly concerned to justify the existence of *rules* as such, in a manner reminiscent of Hume. The case he takes is that of the suggestion that we might murder someone, were we sure that his death would increase general utility; Mill's objection is that if there were no general presumption against our being able to decide for ourselves whether someone was entitled to go on living, then nobody's life would be safe. And this is a matter not so much of the worth of particular actions as of the rule: "Rules are necessary, because mankind would have no security for any of the things which they value, for anything which gives them pleasure and shields them from pain, unless they could rely on one another for doing, and in particular for abstaining from, certain acts." [24] That is, we are concerned to know what to expect, and particularly concerned to be able to expect abstention from actions directed at our harm, and more concerned with this than with maximizing utility in a simple sense. Or perhaps it would be better to say that certainty is a large element in welfare. The value of clear and certain rules is so enormous that we are more than ready to forgo the possible advantage of making exceptions now and then. Even here, of course, Mill is resolutely consequentialist; the primacy of rules still permits us to calculate the consequences of having and not having such rules. "The portion of the tendencies of an action which belong to it not individually, but as a violation of a general rule, are as certain and as calculable as any other consequences; only, they must be examined not in the individual case but in classes of case." [25] Here Mill talks of classes of cases, and I think it is this which enables him to disguise from himself the conflict between justice and utility, which he does not resolve; for the point here is not that we have to consider classes of cases, merely because there is a rule at issue, but because what we argue is, roughly, "What if everyone were to do that?" and it is this only which introduces classes of cases. Presumably, the person who wants to make an exception is going to say that he only wants to make an exception, and not a new rule; i.e., he does not wish to establish a new rule, but merely make one break in the existing rule. The effect of classes of action is wholly irrelevant to his case.

Let us take the example of a proposal to punish an innocent man; we have made the necessary concession to Mill—even though it makes a large dent in his view of rational action—that we count indirect appeals to utility. Thus we justify punishment, and we justify the general rule that no one who is not guilty of a breach of known rules is to be punished. Now, we propose to punish an innocent man to avert a considerable disaster, say a revolution with the certainty of extreme bloodshed. We do not propose to make a habit of punishing the innocent; indeed, so concerned are we that people should not lose their belief that the innocent are not punished that we will go to extreme lengths to make sure he is believed guilty. For all this, some writers would say that this is an utterly inadmissible argument; Kant speaks for many of them when he says that no man may be treated as a means,[26] for others, the slogan *Fiat justitia et ruat caelum* sums up their feelings. On the other hand, many people would feel that, regrettable and unpleasant as it might be, if the alternative really is that the heavens would fall, then injustice had better be done. But what is patently the case is that both the defenders of the exception and the objectors to it agree on one thing which is fatal to Mill's case—that there are two considerations involved, that of justice and that of utility.

If Mill's defense of utility is to be successful, and his account of rationality is to be complete, then he must be able to .how how utility justifies the principles of justice.

The importance of this issue is twofold. As we have seen, if utility cannot account for the requirements of justice, then the principle has failed. And second, we argued in Chapter XI that one of the best candidates for a "proof" of the principle of utility rested on what I labeled, fairly tentatively, the impartiality principle. The argument seems to rest on the principle that, given we each want to maximize our own welfare, the only *fair* or *equitable* rules we can have are such as will maximize welfare and distribute it equally. If the principle of impartiality is a moral principle, and amounts to the principle that it is unjust or unfair—and not straightforwardly illogical—to try to shelter behind rules which we do not want to keep, then it seems that, so far from justice being derived from utility, the greatest-happiness principle, in this form at any rate, rests on the prior claims of justice.

In *Utilitarianism* Mill gives, as if aware of the dangers of his position, a long account of the relations between justice and utility. His procedure is to list the sorts of consideration which normally are adduced when we discuss justice, and then to ask what the common characteristic of these considerations is. The inquiry leads at length to the view that justice is concerned with security, which is a peculiarly important aspect of utility; and thus that justice is a division of utility. Mill's initial list of the requirements of justice is certainly reasonable enough. Thus it is just to respect and unjust to violate someone's legal rights, unless they have forfeited them in some way;[27] but, of course, a law may itself be unjust because it infringes someone's moral rights.[28] The element of *desert* is an important one: "Speaking in a general way, a person is understood to deserve good if he does right, evil if he does wrong; and in a more particular sense to deserve good from those to whom he does or has done good, and evil from those to whom he does or has done evil. The requirement of returning good for evil has never been regarded as a case of the fulfillment of justice, but as one in which the claims of justice are waived, in obedience to other considerations." [29] A fourth element is not to break faith with anyone with whom we have entered into an agreement, or whose expectations we have knowingly and deliberately aroused.[30] Fifth, it is just to be impartial and unjust to be partial, although Mill rather erodes the stringency of this requirement by saying it is merely instrumental to giving everyone his due.[31] And finally, he adds equality, a notion which in many people's eyes is not just part of justice but "constitutes its essence." [32] He discounts this by arguing that we regard equality as unjust only if it is expedient. Thus a man may agree that the few and trivial rights of slaves should be protected with equal rigor as those of their masters, but see nothing unjust in the existence of the vast inequality in their rights, because he believes the class difference to be expedient.[33]

Although Mill's examples of the considerations comprehended under justice are unexceptionable, he begins to confuse the issue both in his discussion of equality and in that of impartiality. Thus, when discussing impartiality, he says it cannot be a dictate of justice in any simple way, because we are blamed if we do *not* show some partiality to our friends or to our family. But this is beside the point, for surely the counter is that it is not a case of partiality to prefer these persons in doing good; they are persons whose expectations we have probably aroused, we probably owe them a great deal of good in one way and another, and are only giving them what is due. Mill reverts to a wiser view when he concludes that impartiality involves only the principle of no discrimination without relevant reasons being adduced.[34] But as regards equality, he fails to rescue himself: "Those who think that utility requires distinctions of rank, do not think it unjust that riches and social privileges should be unequally dispersed; but those who think this inequality inexpedient think it unjust also." [35] This, of course, is not wholly false; but it is not the point at issue. The person who agrees that *some* inequalities are expedient may still deny that the existing ones are just; for the question as to whether they are just is a question about why the particular people who have done well or badly have done so. In other words, we don't deny that there should be a distribution, but what we want to know is whether it is a fair one. And this question, as to why social benefits have been distributed in a particular way, is not one to be answered simply by saying that *some* inequalities are expedient; what we are asking is, usually, Are *these* inequalities fair? And this is a different matter.

Mill tries to unravel the concept of justice by tracing its connections with law, with which it is certainly etymologically connected. But this clue is rejected on the ground that all obligation is essentially the same in involving punishment and other sanctions. What Mill eventually argues is that the duties of justice are duties of perfect obligation—"those duties in virtue of which a correlative *right* resides in some person or persons." [36] Thus, whenever the issue is one of justice, it is one where the right is vested in some assignable person. "It seems to me," says Mill, "that this feature in the case, a right in some person correlative to the moral obligation, constitutes the specific difference between justice and generosity and beneficence." [37] Mill maintains that the distinction has to be made along these lines, since otherwise all morality will be turned into justice; the moralist who maintains that the rest of mankind have a right to my good will must represent this as my return for theirs, as my fulfilling a debt of gratitude for what they have done for me.[38] Unfortunately Mill does not explain in any sort of detail why the moralist cannot argue like this; since it would represent a way of subsuming utility under justice, it is a threat to Mill's position which he ought to meet.

But he goes on to merge justice in utility, by giving an account of what it is to have a *right* against someone; and in doing this, he shows how the distributive side of ethics simply cannot be accommodated in any obvious way under an aggregating concept such as that of utility. Mill distinguishes between cases where we merely say that someone has done wrong, and cases where we say an injustice has been committed on the grounds that, although punishment or outrage is involved in both, in the sentiment of justice the desire to punish is linked to the fact that "there is some definite individual or individuals to whom harm has been done." [39] But this is surely quite inadequate. If a man well known to all of us has been murdered, we may certainly want the murderer brought to book. But, if we were to argue that it was a case of *injustice* to murder the man, we should have to tell a rather special kind of story—perhaps that they were well-known crooks who had agreed to leave certain territory neutral, and that the murdered man had been taken unfair advantage of. The mere fact that someone specific has been harmed is not an adequate account of what we mean by saying someone's rights have been infringed; the statement that rights have been infringed seems to involve, in a way which merely talking of wrong does not, either the existence of a distributive system for pains and pleasures or the claim that there should be such a system.

Mill certainly manages to smuggle in part of what is needed. For he declares that the categorical imperative has a vital place in justice;[40] and in this he is right, for the one thing that it does rule out is injustice—its defect is that it *only* rules out injustice, and does not rule out more substantial moral evils. The crook's *unfairness* is simply that he takes advantage of a rule, so sheltering under a rule he will not prescribe to himself. But this element is not what Mill seizes on; the element he is concerned with is the point of why we have rules and general principles at all. As we have already seen, he accounts very plausibly for this in terms of the "extraordinarily important and impressive kind of utility" [41] which is possessed by "security, to everyone's feelings the most vital of interests. All other earthly benefits are needed by one person, not needed by another; and many of them can, if necessary, be cheerfully forgone, or replaced by something else; but security no human being can possibly do without." [42] The echoes of Hobbes are at their strongest; man alone among the animals has the capacity to fear the future, to be alarmed about uncertainty, and it is this which lies at the root of both his social and his antisocial inclinations. It is, to say the least, an impressive kind of utility.

Nevertheless, it is not justice. For Mill fails to show, and must fail to show, how a distributive ideal can be subsumed under an aggregative one. In this dilemma he is at one with the classical economists whose doctrine always assumed that the greatest good was maximum total income; and who failed to devote themselves to the awkward question of what we were to do, should it become clear that maximizing social income involved extreme inequality in its distribution. The utilitarian principle of utility maximization is clearly intended as analogous to the income-maximization principle. But what if maximizing total happiness involves extreme inequality in its distribution? If, to revert to our original question, the general welfare will be increased if we punish an innocent man, why do we think it unfair to punish the man? It is true that, were people to lose their assurance that justice would be observed in general, they would be made unhappy. But so what? Let us assure people that nothing would happen to them if they did not break the rules of society. We are making just *one* exception; indeed we may persuade everyone that the victim is guilty. Yet, there is something wrong; and Mill would agree. To behave in this fashion is to infringe the rule of "everybody to count for one, nobody for more than one." [43] For here someone would be counting for less than one, would be being used as a means to our ends. But the objection to this is not utilitarian. It is based on something else, and that something else seems to me to be a very primitive principle that unless there are good reasons why the rule should be breached, everyone ought to be treated equally. Mill's explanation of the principle of equality is extremely feeble. He says that the principle that everyone has an equal right to happiness "may be more correctly described as supposing that equal amounts of happiness are equally desirable whether felt by the same or different persons." [44] This, I fear, is exactly the wrong answer, for it raises all the objections made to simple aggregative utility as a moral principle. What if nine people are very bad at turning external goods into subjective utility quantities, and a tenth person is immensely good at this; should we hand over the goods of the nine to the tenth? Are we not much more likely to feel that the poor people who are unhappy should be helped to become happier?

It seems to me significant, in the light of our strictures on Mill's account of personal identity, that Mill's ethics fails precisely where he loses sight of the priority of persons over their psychological states. In the account of action, persons disappear, to be replaced by chains of psychological atoms; in the ethics, also, personal happiness disappears, to be replaced by bundles of pleasure sensations. Again, the concept of responsibility, as it emerges from Mill's treatment, becomes a forward-looking notion, because justice again becomes merged in utility. Mill's analysis of what we mean when we say a man was responsible is that the man will tend to change his mind about crime in future if he is punished. But, of course, it may be true that a man who has so far done nothing wrong may become more socially acceptable if he is ill-treated now; but this is not the same as saying he is justly punished. We might, that is, agree it would be *useful*, but we could not say it was *fair*.

We must now recapitulate the results of this discussion for Mill's attempt to "prove" the principle of utility, and for the concept of rationality in ethics. I take it that the argument above has shown that justice is a principle independent of, and in some ways opposed to, that of maximizing general happiness. To desire an equal, or a fair, distribution of goods is not the same thing as desiring to maximize goods. The most morally compelling argument which Mill puts forward for the principle of utility seems in the end to rest on a principle of justice, a principle which may be basic to moral reasoning, but one which is clearly a moral principle. Mill's "proof" rests also on the analogy between the logical structure of the natural sciences and the art of morality; and this analogy we have seen to be defective.

It cannot be concluded that rational ethics cannot be otherwise accounted for. Mill's problem is that he cannot conceive of rational choice save on the basis of the maximization of a single value; and, in general, this is true of welfare economics prior to Pareto. But from Pareto we can borrow a picture of rationality which does not require some ultimate single value whose maximization is at issue. We may take utility or welfare, and justice, as our paradigms of incommensurable goods. For a rational man to make ethical choices, it is only necessary that two things should be true. The first is that an indifference curve can be constructed to show how he would trade off utility against justice; the other, that he should prefer to be on an indifference curve which allows for more of both values rather than less.[45] Consistency and transitivity of choice may seem limited criteria for rationality, compared with those of Mill, but it only needs a tinge of Mill's optimism about the basic identity of human nature and human needs for us to believe that if choices are made explicit, and the Paretian criteria are followed, then rational argument and eventual agreement are more than possible.

NOTES

1. *Utilitarianism*, etc., p. 3; cf. *System of Logic*, III, xxi, 2.   2. *System of Logic*, VI, xii, 6–7.   3. *Ibid.*, VI, xii, 6.   4. *Ibid.*   5. *Ibid.*   6. *Dissertations and Discussions*, Vol. I, p. 387.   7. *Ibid.*, Vol. II, pp. 459–460.   8. *Ibid.*, Vol. I, p. 387.   9. *Utilitarianism*, etc., pp. 6–9.   10. *Dissertations*

and Discussions, Vol. I, p. 360. **11.** *Utilitarianism,* etc., p. 9. **12.** *Examination of Hamilton,* p. 571. **13.** Hare, *Freedom and Reason,* pp. 151–157. **14.** Urmson, in *Philosophical Quarterly* (1953), p. 35. **15.** *System of Logic,* VI, xii, 7. **16.** *Dissertations and Discussions,* Vol. I, p. 387. **17.** *Ibid.,* p. 384. **18.** *Utilitarianism,* etc., p. 22. **19.** *Ibid.* **20.** *Dissertations and Discussions,* Vol. I, p 385. **21.** *Ibid.,* Vol. II, p. 461. **22.** Hume, *Treatise of Human Nature,* III, ii, 5. **23.** Urmson, in *Philosophical Quarterly* (1953), p. 35; cf. Mabbott, in *Philosophical Quarterly* (1956), pp. 115–120. **24.** *Dissertations and Discussions,* Vol. II, p. 495. **25.** *Ibid.,* p. 476. **26.** Kant, *Groundwork of the Metaphysic of Morals,* p. 101. **27.** *Utilitarianism,* etc., p. 40. **28.** *Ibid.* **29.** *Ibid.,* p. 41. **30.** *Ibid.* **31.** *Ibid.,* p. 42. **32.** *Ibid.,* pp. 42–43. **33.** *Ibid.,* p. 43. **34.** *Ibid.,* p. 42. **35.** *Ibid.,* p. 43. **36.** *Ibid.,* p. 46. **37.** *Ibid.* **38.** *Ibid.,* pp. 46–47. **39.** *Ibid.,* p. 47. **40.** *Ibid.,* pp. 48–49. **41.** *Ibid.,* p. 50. **42.** *Ibid.* **43.** *Ibid.,* p. 58. **44.** *Ibid.,* p. 58n. **45.** Barry, *Political Argument,* pp. 3–8.

❦XIII❦

ON LIBERTY:
BEYOND DUTY TO
PERSONAL AESTHETICS

The title of this chapter indicates, I hope, accurately enough, the relation of this chapter to what has gone before. The intention of the preceding chapters has been to show how Mill's conception of what it is to be rational holds together his account of the philosophy of science, the philosophy of the social sciences, and his justification of utilitarian ethics. I have argued that utilitarian ethics is essentially a system of social rules, the object of which is to secure the security and welfare of self-interested men. What I wish to conclude by doing is to show what the goals of individual life are, which lie beyond duty, which it is the function of the existence of moral rules to protect, but not to force upon men. In a manner of speaking, what I wish to discuss in this chapter is what lies beyond rationality, in the sphere of imagination, self-culture, personal aesthetics, and with which rationality is only concerned to the extent that a rational ethics will be concerned to secure to the individual an area within which his individuality may be exercised to the full.

It may seem, stated simply, that this goal is not a startling one. But I think it calls for something of a reappraisal of the essay *On Liberty,* a reappraisal which can only make sense in the light of the account of the Art of Life which I have given in the preceding chapters. For the discussion of the famous essay has been confused by a misunderstanding of its purpose; from Fitzjames Stephen to Lord Devlin, the assumption has been that the purpose of the essay is to consider "What is the function of the state." [1] And this question has been mostly understood as that of whether the state should by law suppress "private immorality." Thus, when the Wolfenden Committee recommended that the laws against homosexual behavior should be changed, they appealed to Mill in arguing that "there must remain a realm of private morality and immorality which is, in brief and crude terms, not the law's business. To say this is not to condone or encourage private immorality." [2] It is, of course, true enough that Mill would have been amenable to the argument that even if a thing is wrong, it may nonetheless be impolitic to legislate against it. But it is still a fundamental error to represent Mill's concern as a concern with the enforcement of morals.

The first reason why I say this is that for a utilitarian there can be no problem of principle here. To see if an action is wrong, we have to see whether it is an other-regarding action which tends to diminish other people's welfare. Once we see it is wrong, the question whether to employ the sanctions of law rather than those of opinion is another question of the social costs of enforcement. To utilize the complicated apparatus of the law is expensive, and the use of this apparatus can only be justified if the costs of its use are lower than the costs of putting up with the more frequent occurrence of the wrong action that will result from not using the machinery of the law. Thus Mill says: "It would always give us pleasure and chime in with our feelings of fitness that acts which we deem unjust should be punished, though we do not always think it expedient that this should be done by the tribunals. . . . If we see that its enforcement by law would be inexpedient, we lament the impossibility, we consider the impunity given to injustice an evil, and strive to make amends for it by bringing a strong expression of our own and the public disapprobation to bear upon the offender." [3]

My second reason rests on what Mill himself said, namely, that he was not concerned only with political freedom, with the problem of state interference, but with *all* forms of social pressure. This is stated in two letters to Villari.[4] In June, 1857, he wrote: "Il ne s'agit pas cependant de liberté politique dans ce livre, autant que de liberté sociale, morale et réligieuse." And in March, 1858: "Il traite de la liberté morale et intellectuelle, en quoi les nations du Continent sont autant au-dessus de l'Angleterre qu'elles lui sont inférieures quant à la liberté politique." What he saw as his problem was to stop the "likings and dislikings of society" [5] from being the determining factor in the rules of conduct which society enforced by opinion or by law. This was a problem which he thought was so peculiar to Victorian England that he told Villari: "Il n'a guère de valoir que pour l'Angleterre." [6] Mill's attack is entirely at one with that on what he took to be the tendency of intuitionist moral philosophy, to sanctify existing prejudices and emotional reactions by misdescribing them as the immediate perceptions of moral truth. "People are accustomed to believe, and have been encouraged in the belief by some who aspire to the character of philosophers, that their feelings on this subject are better than reasons and render reasons unnecessary." [7] This echoes his objection in the essay on Whewell where he says that people have difficulty in believing that "the feelings of right and wrong which they have from infancy received from all around them, can be sincerely thought by anyone else to be mistaken or misplaced. This is the mental infirmity which Bentham's philosophy tends especially to correct, and Dr Whewell's to perpetuate." [8] The course of the argument in *Liberty* corroborates my statement of Mill's aims, for it is much more concerned with the intrusion of social pressures on the individual in matters which are not strictly matters of right and wrong than with the legal enforcement of morals.

Given, then, that Mill had in mind something other than the limiting of the activity of the state through the law, there seem to be four tasks confronting us. The first is to establish that Mill is concerned to limit *compulsion* and *coercion* on the part of the society he lives in, and only concerned to limit these—i.e., that he is not concerned to limit warning, advice, education, and exhortation. Second, we have to show how the limitation of compulsion and coercion to other-regarding actions links up with his account of the Art of Life, and particularly with the distinction between moral appraisal, on the one hand, and aesthetic or prudential appraisal, on the other. Third, we have to see whether a distinction can be maintained between self-regarding and other-regarding actions, since such a distinction is at the heart of the distinction between the moral and the nonmoral appraisal of actions. Fourth, we have to look briefly at some allegedly hard cases where Mill is often accused of admitting coercion inconsistently with his own principles. And the intention is that in the course of dealing with these issues, we shall become clear on what in Mill's eyes are the ends of life and how they are related to individual liberty.

That Mill was concerned only to eliminate compulsion, and not all forms of concern with other individuals has escaped practically all his critics, beginning as usual with Stephen, who had a bizarre account of motivation which forced him to count advice and warning as a form of coercion, and thus assumed that the only attitudes open to society were coercion in the most literal sense and utter indifference. And in this view he is followed by Devlin. But Mill goes to great lengths to explain that it is only *coercion* that he wishes to eliminate, and that the motive for doing so is in part to allow the use of more appropriate ways of showing our concern for other persons' well-being. Thus, having stated clearly that the "object of this Essay is to assert one very simple principle as entitled to govern absolutely the dealings of society with the individual in the way of compulsion and control, whether the means used be physical force in the form of legal penalties, or the moral coercion of public opinion," [9] which indicates clearly that the concern is with *all* forms of coercion, he states, of conditions which are not such as to justify coercion, that they may be "good reasons for remonstrating with him, or reasoning with him, or persuading him, or entreating him, but not for compelling him, or for visiting him with any evil in case he do otherwise" [10]—in other words, that it is *only* coercion that is at issue. Later the doctrine is spelled out in detail. If a man behaves with a grave lack of prudence, we are not to compel him; but we should, out of human fellow feeling, offer advice or assistance. "It would be a great misunderstanding of this doctrine to suppose that it is one of selfish indifference, which pretends that human beings have no business with each other's conduct in life. . . . But disinterested benevolence can find other instruments to persuade people to their good, than whips and scourges, either of the literal or metaphorical sort." [11] Mill goes further, and criticizes the current canons of politeness as inhibiting our telling each other what we think of each other's behavior: "It would be well indeed if this good office were much more freely rendered than the common notions of politeness permit, and if one person could honestly point out to another that he thinks him in fault, without being considered unmannerly or presuming." [12] Thus, advice, entreaty, exhortation are all in order; but coercion is not. The question this raises is: What are we to count as coercion, and what the proper expression of opinion?

It seems that coercion is involved where harm is *organized* to deter someone from an action, or in retribution for action. Thus, natural ill-consequences are not a case of coercion; only those ill-consequences which are organized by other persons with a view to deterrence or retribution count as compulsion. Mill admits our right to avoid the company of a man who is a habitual drunkard; he agrees that we should warn him that he will lose our friendship if he gets drunk. But these are natural ill-consequences; they are not calculated to stop him doing

I

whatever he wants; they are not, in other words, cases of punishment. A man may "suffer very severe penalties at the hands of others, for faults which directly concern only himself; but he suffers these penalties only so far as they are the natural, and, as it were, the spontaneous consequences of the faults themselves, not because they are purposely inflicted on him for the sake of punishment." [13] The importance of this emphasis on punishment as distinct from natural ill-consequences is that it forms the bridge between Mill's views on ethics and his defense of freedom.

Stephen saw the difference between natural ill-consequences and punishment, but not its importance. "What is the difference between such inconveniences and similar ones organised, defined and inflicted upon proof that the circumstances which call for their infliction exist? This organisation, definition and procedure make all the difference between the restraints which Mr Mill would permit and the restraints to which he objects." [14] Stephen misunderstands the distinction, because he thinks the distinction is between "social and legal penalties," [15] where in fact Mill is distinguishing between all kinds of *penalty* and natural ill-consequences. Stephen is quite right that organization is crucial, however, for Mill's point about punishment is that society either *has* or *should* organize ill-consequences for those whom it is desired to deter or punish. So, Mill's principle that coercion is only in place where an individual's behavior foreseeably damages other people, amounts to arguing that we should only organize ill-consequences in such cases, i.e., in cases of moral wrong. The crucial point about ill-consequences which are contrived and organized is that they are inflicted on the individual *because* he has done whatever it is, and not simply as a causal consequence of the action. That is, the idea of desert comes in, and the moment this idea comes in, it is clear that the ideas of punishment and wrong are intrinsically connected. Thus, to punish someone is to inflict harm because he has done wrong. And punishment is, strictly speaking, impartially inflicted harm, inflicted on behalf of mankind collectively.[16] Revenge is not exactly punishment for this reason. It is also the reason why natural ill-consequences are not punishment; they are not inflicted by nature deliberately with the object of promoting general welfare. They occur simply because we neglect some law of nature which we should have taken more account of. The only sense in which we can see the imprudent as deserving the evil they suffer is that they could have avoided it with more sensible behavior. If they succeed by cleverness or ingenuity in avoiding the ill-consequences, then they do not deserve to suffer them. With punishment, it is different; a man deserves punishment not because he is foolish but because he is wicked; and if he succeeds in escaping punishment, it makes him no less *deserving* of it.

Mill makes the connection between punishment and wrong very explicit only in the last chapter of *Utilitarianism*. "We do not call anything wrong, unless we mean to imply that a person ought to be punished in some way or other for doing it, if not by law, by the opinion of his fellow creatures; if not by opinion, by the reproaches of his own conscience." [17] And this is why Mill is so extremely concerned to object to those who assume that their "likings and dislikings" are all that is involved; for when we call a thing wrong we are invoking society to assist us in punishing whoever does that thing. But to say merely that we do not like it is to do nothing of the sort—we invoke no one's assistance, encourage no one in organized hostility.

On Mill's account, moral and legal rules are logically similar in that they are sanction-backed rules designed to make social life possible: "All that makes life valuable to anyone depends on the enforcement of restraints upon the actions of other people. Some rules, therefore, must be imposed, by law in the first place, and by opinion on many things which are not fit subjects for the operation of law." [18] These rules, on the account of Chapters XI and XII, are general imperatives addressed impartially to no-matter-whom, which are backed by the sanctions of law or organized dislike. As we have said, they cannot exactly be true or false, but they can be "well-grounded" if it is true that the following of the rule is necessary to social life. Thus "Lying is wrong" is a categorical imperative "Don't lie," which is grounded in the fact that widespread lying would make communication difficult; and its sanction is, or should be, general disapproval of liars. A legal rule is similar, save that its validity is a matter of convention; but its goodness is a utilitarian question, and its sanction is simply more organized and clearer than that of a moral rule. Prudential rules, on the other hand, are only hypothetical imperatives, which are not grounded in the welfare of anyone other than the agent. And, as we have said, in the case of prudence, if the agent does not mind the consequences or can escape them, then so much the better, and the prudential rule fails. But in the case of moral or legal rules, if the agent either does not mind the punishment or can evade it, we do not think how lucky this is; rather, we step up the punishment, so that he will mind, or else we make sure he will suffer it. Certainly we do not think the moral rule weakened or the law unneeded.

After this preamble, I can now state what I believe to be the essence of Mill's argument in *Liberty*. People have failed to distinguish between acts which really are wrong and those which are foolish or unaesthetic, and of this confusion, with its attendant confusion about where punishment is in order, intuitionism is one cause, since it encourages people to believe that their moral views need no justification. Mill's point is that moral judgments must be grounded on the harm the agent knowingly does to others; what lies outside this realm is a matter for prudence and aesthetics, fit matter for entreaty, expostulation, exhortation, but not compulsion, not punishment. To miss the distinction is to behave thoroughly irrationally, for if we punish actions which are simply imprudent, we are in the ridiculous position of trying to rescue or patch up a judgment by *making it* come true, when the whole ground for our originally uttering it was that it was true anyway, simply because of the way nature happens to be organized.

That this is the core of Mill's doctrine appears, very obviously, in Chapter IV of *Liberty*. There he refers to the "self-regarding faults previously mentioned, which are not properly immoralities, and to whatever pitch they may be carried, do not constitute wickedness." [19] Adhering closely to the lines of division we have explored, he goes on: "They may be proofs of any amount of folly, or want of personal dignity and self-respect, but they are only a subject of moral reprobation when they involve a breach of duty to others, for whose sake the individual is bound to have care for himself." [20] Mill amplifies this with some picturesque examples: "George Barnwell murdered his uncle to get money for his mistress, but if he had done it to set himself up in business he would equally have been hanged." [21] In other words, what we punish is the breach of duty, the doing of wrong, and not the self-regarding faults of the criminal. The soldier who gets drunk on duty is not to be punished for intemperance, but for neglect of his duties as a soldier.[22] "Whoever fails in the consideration generally due to the interests and feelings of others, not being compelled by some more imperative duty, or justified by allowable self-preference, is a subject of moral disapprobation for that failure, but not for the errors merely personal to himself, which may have remotely led to it." [23] And earlier Mill states the doctrine in terms which explicitly refer back to the Art of Life and its divisions: "What are called duties to ourselves are not socially obligatory, unless circumstances are such as to render them at the same time duties to others. The term duty to oneself, when it means anything more than prudence, means self-respect or self-development." [24]

At this point, it is necessary to point to one ambiguity in Mill's account of where punishment *is* in order, which stems from an uncertainty in his doctrines about the distinction between conduct which is *right,* and conduct which is obligatory

because others have *a right* against us. The passage quoted
from *Utilitarianism,* where Mill distinguishes between what
we mean when we call conduct "right" and "wrong," [25] is the
source of this ambiguity. A man who gives away some large part
of his wealth to those in need has done what on utilitarian
grounds is right; it is patently an other-regarding action which
tends to maximize welfare. But it is not an action whose performance is morally obligatory, one to which someone has *a
right,* one the omission of which is a case calling for punishment. Men are not to be blamed for not being saintly or
heroic.[26] We punish people for not doing what is obligatory,
for doing what is disobligatory; but not for merely not doing
what it would be virtuous to do. But, in *Liberty,* Mill confines
himself clearly enough to cases where we should want to say
that it was a question of doing what society has a right to expect us to do. The obligation is to refrain from damaging the
interests of others, and to perform some positive actions,
summarized as "each person's bearing his share [on some equitable principle] of the labours and sacrifices incurred for defending the society from injury and molestation." [27] Thus he
says: "If anyone does an act hurtful to others, there is a *prima
facie* case for punishing him, by law, or where legal penalties
are not safely applicable, by general disapprobation." [28] People
have a right to our abstaining from harming them. There are
also some positive benefits which society can fairly compel us to
confer on the community, "such as to give evidence in a
court of justice; to bear his fair share in the common defence,
or in any other joint work necessary to the interest of the
society of which he enjoys the protection." [29] There are, too, a
number of acts of preventing harm to individuals which are
culpably neglected: "certain acts of individual beneficence,
such as saving a fellow creature's life, or interposing to protect
the defenceless against ill-usage, things which whenever it is
obviously a man's duty to do, he may rightfully be made responsible to society for not doing." [30] In short, society has a
right to demand from us abstentions from doing definite harm

and also the positive performance of certain essential duties, necessary to any sort of social life.

We must now reconsider the position of punishment in all this. For we have to show that an adequate distinction can be drawn between punishment and natural ill-consequences, adequate that is to Mill's case. Mill discusses this problem when talking of how we might behave toward a man who was persistently drunk. He might do nothing which a utilitarian could call wicked, but be so generally deficient in pleasing qualities that virtually everyone would find his company unpleasant. This, according to Mill, is a natural ill-consequence and not a penal sanction; the naturalness lies in the fact that our distaste for his company lies in the impossibility that we should "have the opposite qualities in due strength without entertaining these feelings." [31] And, as free men ourselves, "We have a right also in various ways to act upon our unfavourable opinion of anyone, not to the oppression of his individuality, but in the exercise of ours." [32] Thus, we may shun his company, and prefer other people in our good offices, and in this way he may suffer great discomfort and misery, but only "in so far as they are the natural and, as it were, the spontaneous consequences of the faults themselves, not because they are purposely inflicted on him for the sake of punishment." [33] Stephen objected to this, that we could, no doubt, learn to live with drunkards; but this point Mill has met, for as he says, a man whose idea of a good life involves diverse interests, clearly contemplated, cannot want to spend his time with drunkards, and the outcome of his free choice of his way of life will be the avoidance of the drunkard's company. Punishment involves the intention to inflict harm; in this case the harm is a side effect of each person exercising his freedom. Moreover, when Mill says, "we are not bound to seek his company; we have a right to avoid it," he at once adds "(though not to parade the avoidance)" [34]—thus pointing out that avoiding his company is merely suiting ourselves, while parading the avoidance is going beyond what is just in encouraging other people to gang up against the man in question, a thing for which there is no moral warrant.

To the question of whether it matters to draw so sharp a line between natural ill-effects and punishments, Mill answers with a clear affirmative. "It makes a vast difference both in our feelings and in our conduct towards him, whether he displeases us in things in which we have a right to control him, or in things in which we know that we have not." [35] It may, of course, be that a man alienates everyone so thoroughly that he is as badly off as if they had deliberately ostracized him. But if this is true in extreme cases, it will very often not be so. For whereas moral judgments should be impartial, collective, and unanimous, likings and dislikings will be, and hopefully will remain, partial, individual, and diverse. If we say we do not like something, we do not beg the question of how other people should react. Moreover, even if we all do not like something, it does not follow that the action should be abstained from, nor if we merely say we do not like it, do we incite ourselves to take action against it. As Mill said, people are loath to admit that what they think is a moral judgment is in fact merely an expression of liking or disliking, but "an opinion on a point of conduct, not supported by reasons, can only count as one man's preferences; and if the reasons, where given, are a mere appeal to a similar preference felt by other people, it is still only many people's liking instead of one." [36] Thus, what Mill is saying is that if people recognize that what they are doing is not making a fully fledged moral judgment, then their behavior will reflect an awareness of what they are doing. If we "stand aloof" from someone we dislike, we still shall not "feel called on to make his life uncomfortable." [37] We shall see that his life is grim enough already, and that such dealings as we do have with him should be such as will help him out of trouble, not such as will plunge him into more. Mill does not say that because we are intending our own good, we cannot be blamed for another's harm; rather, he says that if we and he are each seeking our own good in our own way, some clashes

cannot be helped. And he stresses almost beyond the point of
realism that we should not opt out but, rather, help out.

The part of Mill's doctrines, however, that has always received the most criticism has been his distinction between self-
regarding and other-regarding actions. We have all along been
assuming that the distinction could be drawn readily enough,
since we have been talking in terms of a distinction between
moral and prudential rules along precisely this line. Indeed,
in the previous chapter we have tried to draw the line. But
from Stephen to Devlin, it has been argued that no such line
can be drawn. I think that there is no point in this context
in discussing the views of the Idealists such as Green or Bradley
on this issue; given their concept of the self, which was identical with the self of all other persons, it is clear both that they
will refuse to draw the distinction Mill is making, and that
their grounds for the refusal rest on a metaphysics which would
take us too far out of the stream of current debate. For the
current debate is couched in the terms which the English ju-
diciary have employed with remarkable consistency from
Stephen to Devlin, in terms of the private and public morality of individuals. What Mill would assign to the category of
"self-regarding actions" under the heading of personal aesthetics or prudence, Devlin calls "private morality"—as does
the Wolfenden Report. And what I want to show is how Mill's
terminology is adequate to the task he wants it to perform, and
how much clearer it is than that of his liberal and illiberal
successors. A typical argument for the indivisibility of social
life occurs in Devlin's *The Enforcement of Morals*. He says:
"I do not think óne can talk sensibly of a public and private
morality any more than we can of a private or public high-
way." [38] Nor, of course, did Mill, on his reading of what the
word "morality" means. The distinction between public and
private can mean two things; in the first place it might mean
much the same as the distinction between official and unoffi-
cial: a lie to the House of Commons is a breach of public
morality, where a lie to one's friends is a breach of private

morality. But the second distinction is between self-regarding and other-regarding behavior; to lie to one's friends is public morality in this sense, while to pursue private goals, such as the establishment of a happy and stable homosexual relationship with another man, is a matter of private morality, or a self-regarding action. What Devlin argues is that we cannot draw this line. My reply, which I take to be Mill's, is that we do draw it. But it is worth showing how misleading is Devlin's terminology compared with Mill's. The force of Devlin's argument is that it rests on the covert assumption that when we call an action immoral, we are always using the same criterion, namely social damage, but when he comes to try to make this explicit, his argument is embarrassingly poor.

The test for social intervention is when it is required to maintain the social fabric; in what does this consist? He says: "an established morality is as necessary as good government to the welfare of society. Societies disintegrate from within more frequently than they are broken up by external pressure. There is disintegration when no common morality is observed and history shows that the loosening of moral bonds is often the first stage of disintegration, so that society is justified in taking the same steps to preserve its moral code as it does to preserve its government and other essential institutions." [39] But does he really mean that we are in imminent danger of civil war, mob violence, or foreign domination, if we do not share a common horror of, say, masturbation? Such a suggestion is so ludicrous that it must be rejected as soon as it is made. But it is much harder to see what Devlin does mean. At one point he says, "What makes a society of any sort is a community of ideas, not only political ideas but also ideas about how its members should behave and govern their lives; these latter ideas are its morals." [40] In other words "society" is now *defined* as, in Mill's terminology, the sum total of our views on prudential, moral, and aesthetic matters; so it becomes not a disputable causal consequence that dissent creates the collapse of society, but a necessary truth. But the conclusion to be drawn surely is not that individual views may be regulated without limit, but that society as redefined is no longer very important, and it is no cause for alarm should it collapse and be replaced by another society. For if it is true by definition that "society" in this odd sense is destroyed when there is dissent about the good and bad of masturbation, and yet, as we have argued, no obvious damage is done, then it is clear that the collapse of society as thus defined has lost all its terrors. In short, what Devlin does is to redefine what is meant by a society in such a way that its survival depends on self-regarding behavior being in conformity with public opinion, and then slides into the usual meaning of the word to persuade us that the collapse of society would be very alarming. These two disparate pieces of the case are held together by a very bad argument. Devlin seems to believe that people will "drift apart" [41] unless they hold common views about self-regarding behavior. If homosexuality is disliked by most people, their views must prevail if we are not to drift apart. But this is both illiberal to a degree, and founded on a very simple error. It is illiberal when it means that the mere fact of someone's disliking—or even being disgusted by the thought of—what I do in private is good ground for coercion. From this Devlin shies away; he says that the only sort of dislike or disgust that is a good ground for coercion is when it is founded on a "deliberate judgment that the practice is injurious to society." [42] Thus Devlin first says that the wrongness of an action is simply that it upsets other people; but then he says that this upset cannot be considered unless it is an upset caused by the judgment that social damage will be caused by the action. If he argues this, there are only two conclusions; the first is that anything is wrong if it is thought wrong, because all we need to do to show that someone is immoral is to show that someone else dislikes what he does; alternatively, we are told that a thing is wrong if it tends to damage society (in the usual sense of the word), so that the dislike people happen to feel for that sort of private behavior cannot be added in as part of the social damage done. The latter position amounts to a complete capitulation to Mill.

What, then, does the position adopted by Mill rest on? We might say that the test of an action being self- or other-regarding depends on the intention of the agent. Thus to say, "Jones lied to Smith" is to describe an other-regarding action, since it involves the assertion that Jones intended Smith to receive what was said untruly as a true statement. It is important to add in here the qualification to the scope of morality made by Mill, that actions are still self-regarding if others are involved "only with their free, voluntary and undeceived consent and participation." [43] To show the usefulness of these criteria we must show how they cover this case. Thus, when we say that Jones lied to Smith, we should not want to say it was a lie if, for example, Jones had been rehearsing lines to a play and Smith had mistakenly thought it was a reply to a question. Or again if Jones had mistaken Smith for Brown and had said what would have been true, had it been Brown ("Your wife left a message for you"). Again, we shouldn't call it a case of lying if Smith had joined in freely; indeed it is very odd to suppose there could be a case of undeceived consent to being lied to. Equally, if Smith takes Jones's watch with his free and undeceived consent, the case is one of gift, not theft. Thus our gloss on Mill's case amounts to saying that the only sort of conduct which *can* be morally wrong, and thus fall within the scope of social coercion, is that by which the agent intends to bring harm upon other persons; if this cannot be shown, we have no case of immorality at all. As Mill puts it, before punishment is in order "the conduct from which it is desired to deter him, must be calculated to produce evil to someone else." [44]

The objection to this, I think, is to argue that there is no *one* description of an action which we are bound to accept. A man who drinks so much that there is no money left for the housekeeping can be variously described. We may just say: "He spends all his money on drink"—describing the action in merely self-regarding terms and not invoking any kind of judgment on it. We may say: "He is drinking himself to death," where again the description is self-regarding, but lines up the action for prudential condemnation; or we might say: "He is neglecting his wife and children," and here we have an other-regarding action, which is squarely morally condemned. It may be that he does not *want* to harm them; but he is clearly doing so, and Mill would clearly want us to intervene to pro-tect the assignable rights of the family. Mill indeed holds with a good deal of severity that violations of the rights of others are to be punished; this he holds as firmly as that this is *all* that we are to punish. But if there is no *one* thing we can say about the action, then how can we drawn the line we wish to draw? The answer, I think, is to say that although intention is not the only element in the description of an action, it has claims to be thought both the first and the most vital element. If punish-ment is to be deterrent, intention must be considered, since a man can only be deterred from what he knows how to avoid doing; and equally, we should be loath to accept a moral equiv-alent of the doctrine of strict liability. Thus, we may rephrase Mill's principle so that it requires us to leave alone those ac-tions of other persons where they intend no harm to others, and where it is not readily foreseeable that such harm will fol-low. This is plainly what he means when he qualifies the statement that "whenever, in short, there is a definite damage or a definite risk of damage, either to an individual or to the public, the case is taken out of the province of liberty and placed in that of morality or law" [45] by saying, "But with regard to the merely contingent, or, as it may be called, con-structive injury which a person causes to society, by conduct which neither violates any specific duty to the public, nor occasions any perceptible hurt to any assignable individual except himself; the inconvenience is one which society can afford to bear, for the sake of the greater good of human free-dom." [46]

The fourth task we set ourselves was to deal briefly with some of the cases where Mill is said to admit coercion on paternalist grounds. These are legislation for shorter hours in factories, sanitary regulations, the regulation of prostitution, and education. In all these cases, Mill is accused of being paternalistic and of "enforcing morality." We have said the latter charge is inaccurate. The first charge, also, is often misconceived, especially in connection with factory work, because it is thought that Mill's grounds for nonintervention in society are the same as the grounds of free trade.[47] But Mill says explicitly of free trade that it "rests on grounds different from, though equally solid with, the principle of individual liberty asserted in this Essay. Restrictions on trade, or on production for purposes of trade, are indeed restraint, and all restraint *qua* restraint is an evil; but the restraints in question affect only that part of conduct which society is competent to restrain, and are wrong solely because they do not really produce the results which it is desired to produce by them." [48]

Mill discusses the case of legislation designed to provide a maximum working day in the *Political Economy*.[49] The case is one of whether a combination of workers who could achieve a shorter working day, were they to combine, should be able to enforce the agreement on one of their members. Mill does not see the argument at all as one of coercing the odd individual for his own good; the argument is very different. If the workers agree together, they can obtain their present wages for less work; but if one or more individuals can work for longer, these will receive higher wages, and if all can do so, and try to do so, the agreement will collapse and they will all again be working a longer day for the same pay as before. It is a Hobbesian situation; we can all be better off, if we agree to restraints. Some can be better off if everyone, except them, is bound by the agreement, and they are able to use it to secure greater gains than the rest. But this, of course, means that some sanctions will be needed to stop the selfish taking advantage of the unselfish. It is not that we are being coerced for our own good; but, rather, that we are being coerced out of taking more than our fair share of the benefits available for those who combine to obtain them. This is no stranger a situation than is the case of the private individual being able to ask for social help in seeing that after his death his wishes about his property are met via the legal enforcement of his will.

Devlin is of the opinion that Mill's principles rule out sanitary regulations. In saying this, he unconsciously echoes Whewell; and the answer to Devlin is Mill's cold reply to Whewell. Mill quotes Whewell and then says where he goes wrong: " 'What is the meaning of restraints imposed for the sake of public health, cleanliness and comfort? Why are not individuals left to do what they like with reference to such matters? Plainly because carelessness, indolence, ignorance would prevent their doing what is most for their own interest.' —Say, rather, would lead them to do what is contrary to the interest of other people. The proper object of sanitary laws is not to compel people to take care of their own health, but to prevent them from endangering the health of others. To prescribe by law, what they should do for their own health alone, would by most people be regarded as something very like tyranny." [50]

The case of prostitution worries Mill, because essentially it is the pimp who is to suffer, not the prostitute or the man who seeks her services, and it seems like a case of punishing the accessory where the principal is allowed to go free.[51] It is clear that neither the prostitute nor the client is wicked or behaving wrongly, even if we want to say they are foolish, indecorous, or lamentable in some other way. But Mill's question is: "What the agent is free to do, ought other persons to be equally free to counsel and instigate?" [52] Once more this is often taken to be a case of the state intervening to protect private morality.[53] But this is nonsense. Mill is clear that what is wrong with being a pimp—as with selling drink, distributing narcotics, or keeping a gambling den—is that the seller of these services has an interest in committing a fraud. The pimp offers an illusory satisfaction, and this is a fraud, as is the cigarette

advertiser's failure to point out that cigarettes give some pleasure and do much damage to your health. Mill makes himself
look shifty, because he seems to invoke an independent principle of excluding interested advice.[54] But this is silly, since
it would exclude all advertisement whatever. The appropriate
principle is to hold responsible for such damage as the agent
suffers whoever instigates him to the action, unless the insti-
gator represents the case accurately—and it is hard to see
many pimps remaining in business under those conditions.
Equally, a man who sells a bottle of methylated spirits to
someone whom he has no reason to suppose likely to drink
it cannot be blamed. But someone who persuaded a man to
drink methylated spirits would be just as responsible for the
harm that resulted as a salesman selling a car with defective
brakes.

Finally, education. This is a subject which could well do
with a book to itself. Here all I want to deal with is the contention that Mill is on weak ground in requiring parents to
provide education for their children. Children, for some reason
I have never seen declared, are thought to be less than assignable individuals with claims against those who brought them
into the world. But a man's behavior toward his children is
a clear and important case of other-regarding behavior, one
in which the chances of the other party to give anything de-
scribable as free and undeceived consent are very slight. The
very minimum of obligation contracted to a child when it is
brought into the world is that of giving it as good a chance
of being happy as can be fairly obtained. In fact, so un-
paternalist is Mill in this context that he makes the very
optimistic—and to my mind quite unrealistic—assumption
that once we secure that people send their children to school
we can leave the provision of education very largely in individual hands.

I hope that in the course of this chapter something will
have emerged of why Mill so values freedom. Now, however,
I should like to summarize the case. The obvious question

we could ask is: Why is it wrong to coerce men into being better people? Why is it legitimate only to coerce people out of harming others, and not into doing all the good they can? And why can we not coerce them into being better specimens of humanity? The answers to the questions are to a large extent founded on the same considerations, but let us look at them separately. Mill's first answer is that the damage caused by coercion far outweighs the extra benefits of compelling people to do all they can for society. In time of war, the case may be different; but this is always felt to be a temporary expedient, and not a tolerable situation in normal life. A second consideration is that part of the utility of spontaneously beneficent behavior lies precisely in its spontaneity. If a man out of the kindness of his heart gives assistance to another, then among the benefits the latter receives is the assurance that he is the object of sympathy and concern on the part of one of his fellows. If the money, or whatever assistance it may be, is forced out of the helper, this assurance— and it is clearly one which matters very deeply—cannot be had. So the evils of coercion are wider than they seem at first, in that it appears that a large part of the benefits which we want are not contingently connected with their being given freely. A further consideration against coercion is that, beyond a limited point, it is much less clear what benefits people than it is what harms them, and hence it is very difficult to establish general rules. It may not be hard for a reasonable and sensitive individual to see what would assist some other individual; but in the sphere of law and morality we need general rules, and it looks much harder to find rules which would make people do all the good they can to others than it is to establish rules which forbid them doing the harm they might. But the major element undoubtedly is Mill's concern for diversity, spontaneity, and individuality; so it is time to conclude by considering why self-regarding virtues should not be forced on people.

It will be remembered that in the essay on Bentham, Mill

gave a list of the springs of action which Bentham never mentioned.[55] It is these which for Mill are the ends of life. To be silly, to be trivial, to lead a life which conforms to no aesthetic standards, all mean that we reject the appeals which can be made on the basis of honor, beauty, order, power, energy, and so on. The whole object of *Liberty* is to argue that we must safeguard these goods, the ultimate goods of individual life, and that we must safeguard them by leaving people the room to experiment and inquire into them. This is not to say we are to create an environment where no one cares about anyone else; part of the character of Mill's ideal is that we will care greatly about the quality of life of other persons; but we will not take this as a license for coercion. Mill has been criticized for appealing here to "utility in the largest sense, grounded in the permanent interests of man as a progressive being." [56] But, on my account of the matter, this is exactly the right appeal, because the permanent interest of a being who can change himself, explore his nature and the nature of the world, discover and invent new ways of expressing himself is precisely freedom. No other single thing matters so much.

And this explains why the self-regarding goods should not be forced on men. First, of course, the odds are that the evils of coercion will outweigh the goods achieved. Second, individuals are so diverse in their needs and in their capacities for happiness that coercion will almost certainly be ill-directed.[57] The person with the best information about his own wants is the owner of them, and he is also the person with the greatest incentive to satisfy them. The third reason is that diversity is in itself a good, so that, other things being equal, we should encourage it rather than limit it. But in the final analysis, freedom is a necessary ingredient in anything that Mill can recognize as the life which a rational man would choose. The good society is one made up of happy people, and Mill's picture of what makes a man happy is not unclear. It is the possession of a character which is self-reliant, rational in its assessment of the world, tolerant, wide-ranging in its interest, and spontaneous in its sympathies. Not merely can we not make men like this by coercing them; coercion is logically at odds with the creation of such a character. To be self-reliant, for example, is to be able to do what we want without being helped—and certainly without being forced; and the case is the same for the other virtues. To be a saint or a hero by order is just a nonsensical idea. The whole point of saintliness and heroism is that they establish new goals, new standards of what man can do when he tries. Without freedom, there can be no such moral progress as this leads to. And, however much at odds it sometimes is with his determinist universe, Mill's concern with self-development and moral progress is a strand in his philosophy to which almost everything else is subordinate. And this is why, once we have established the rational society, scientifically understood, controlled according to utilitarian principles, the goals we aim at transcend these, and can only be described as the freely pursued life of personal nobility—the establishment of the life of the individual as a work of art.

NOTES

1. McCloskey, in *Philosophical Quarterly* (1963), p. 144. 2. *Wolfenden Report*, para. 61. 3. *Utilitarianism*, etc., p. 44. 4. *Letters* (ed. Elliot), I, pp. 196, 203. 5. *Utilitarianism*, etc., p. 70. 6. *Letters* (ed. Elliot), I, p. 203. 7. *Utilitarianism*, etc., p. 69. 8. *Dissertations and Discussions*, Vol. II, pp. 471–472. 9. *Utilitarianism*, etc., p. 72. 10. *Ibid.*, p. 73. 11. *Ibid.*, p. 132. 12. *Ibid.*, p. 134. 13. *Ibid.* 14. Stephen, *Liberty, Equality, Fraternity*, p. 13. 15. *Ibid.*, p. 15. 16. *Utilitarianism*, etc., pp. 48–49. 17. *Ibid.*, p. 45. 18. *Ibid.*, p. 69. 19. *Ibid.*, p. 135. 20. *Ibid.* 21. *Ibid.*, p. 138. 22. *Ibid.* 23. *Ibid.* 24. *Ibid.*, p. 135. 25. *Ibid.*, pp. 45–46. 26. Urmson, in *Modern Essays in Moral Philosophy*, pp. 202–203. 27. *Utilitarianism*, etc., p. 132. 28. *Ibid.*, p. 74. 29. *Ibid.* 30. *Ibid.* 31. *Ibid.*, p. 134. 32. *Ibid.* 33. *Ibid.* 34. *Ibid.*

35. *Ibid.,* p. 136.   **36.** *Ibid.,* p. 69.   **37.** *Ibid.,* p. 136.   **38.** Devlin, *The Enforcement of Morals,* p. 16.   **39.** *Ibid.,* p. 13.   **40.** *Ibid.,* p. 9; cf. p. 10. **41.** *Ibid.,* p. 10.   **42.** *Ibid.,* p. 17.   **43.** *Utilitarianism,* etc., p. 75.   **44.** *Ibid.,* p. 73.   **45.** *Ibid.,* p. 138.   **46.** *Ibid.*   **47.** McCloskey, in *Philosophical Quarterly* (1963), pp. 151–152.   **48.** *Utilitarianism,* etc., pp. 150–151.   **49.** *Principles of Political Economy,* V, i, 2.   **50.** *Dissertations and Discussions,* Vol. II, p. 504.   **51.** *Utilitarianism,* etc., p. 155.   **52.** *Ibid.,* p. 153.   **53.** McCloskey, in *Philosophical Quarterly* (1963), pp. 149–150. **54.** *Ibid.,* pp. 154–155.   **55.** *Dissertations and Discussions,* Vol. I, p. 360. **56.** *Utilitarianism,* etc., p. 74.   **57.** *Ibid.,* p. 140.

BIBLIOGRAPHY

WORKS CITED

The standard bibliography of the works of John Stuart Mill is: *Bibliography of the Published Writings of John Stuart Mill* by Ney MacMinn and others (Evanston, Ill., 1945). For works on Mill, readers should refer to the bibliography in progress in *The Mill Newsletter* (University of Toronto Press). I list below only those works of Mill actually referred to in the text, giving the source employed in the text together with the date of first publication.

For secondary works, the source employed in the text is given. Where a separate American edition exists, that is listed in parentheses if it was not the source employed in the text.

WORKS BY MILL

Autobiography. New York: Columbia University Press, 1924 (London, 1873).

Essays on Some Unsettled Questions of Political Economy. London: John W. Parker, 1948 (London, 1844).

An Examination of Sir William Hamilton's Philosophy. London, 1865 (London 1865).

Principles of Political Economy. London and Toronto: University of Toronto Press, 1965 (London, 1848).

St. Andrew's Address. London, 1867.

A System of Logic, Ratiocinative and Inductive, 8th ed. London, 1961 (London, 1843).

Utilitarianism, Liberty and Representative Government. London, 1962 (New York: E. P. Dutton). (*Utilitarianism* in Fraser's Magazine, 1861; *Liberty*, London, 1861; *Considerations on Representative Government*, London, 1861).

Dissertations and Discussions, 4 vols. London, 1859–1875 (London, 1859–75), for:

"Civilisation," I, pp. 160–205 (*London and Westminster Review*, 1836).

"Bentham," I, pp. 330–392 (*London and Westminster Review*, 1838).

"De Tocqueville on Democracy in America," II, pp. 1–83 (*Edinburgh Review*, 1840) .

"Michelet's History of France," II, pp. 120–180 (*Edinburgh Review*, 1844).

"Dr. Whewell on Moral Philosophy," II, pp. 450–509 (*Westminster Review*, 1852).

"Berkeley's Life and Writings," IV, pp. 154–187 (*Fortnightly Review*, 1871).

"Archbishop Whately's Elements of Logic," (*Westminster Review*, 1828).

The Earlier Letters of John Stuart Mill, 1812 to 1848, ed. F. E. Mineka. London and Toronto: University of Toronto Press, 1963.

The Letters of John Stuart Mill, 2 vols. ed. H. S. R. Elliot, London and New York: Longmans, Green, 1910.

SECONDARY WORKS

Anschutz, R. P. *The Philosophy of J. S. Mill.* New York: Oxford University Press, 1953.

Austin, J. L. *Philosophical Papers,* ed. Urmson and Warnock. New York: Oxford University Press, 1961.

Bambrough, J. R. "Principia Metaphysica," *Philosophy* (1964). London.

Barry, B. M. *Political Argument.* London, 1965 (New York: Humanities Press, 1965).

Berkeley, George. *A New Theory of Vision.* London, 1910 (New York: E. P. Dutton).

Bradley, F. H. *Ethical Studies.* Oxford, 1927 (New York: Oxford University Press, 1929).

Braithwaite, R. B. *Scientific Explanation.* Cambridge: University Press, 1955.

Brodbeck, May. "Explanation, Prediction, and 'Imperfect' Knowledge," *Minnesota Studies in the Philosophy of Science, Series III.* Minnesota, 1962.

Day, J. P. "John Stuart Mill," *A Critical History of Western Philosophy,* ed. D. J. O'Connor. London, 1964 (Glencoe: Free Press, 1964).

——. "Mill on Matter," *Philosophy* (1964). London.

Devlin, Patrick. *The Enforcement of Morals.* New York: Oxford University Press, 1965.

Dray, W. *Laws and Explanation in History.* Oxford, 1965 (New York: Oxford University Press, 1957).

Einstein, A. *The World as I See It.* London, 1935.

Feyerabend, P. "Explanation, Reduction, and Empiricism," *Minnesota Studies in the Philosophy of Science, Series III.* Minnesota, 1962.

Flew, A. G. N. and MacIntyre, A. C. *New Essays in Philosophical Theology.* London, 1955 (New York: Macmillan Co., 1964).

Frege, G. *Foundations of Arithmetic,* trans. J. L. Austin. Oxford, 1953.

Geach, P. T. and Anscombe, G. E. M. *Three Philosophers.* Oxford, 1961 (Ithaca: Cornell University Press, 1961).

Hare, R. M. *Freedom and Reason.* New York: Oxford University Press, 1963.

——. "The Freedom of the Will," *Aristotelian Society, Proceedings, Supplementary Volume* (1951). London.

——. *The Language of Morals.* New York: Oxford University Press, 1952.

Hempel, C. G. "Deductive-Nomological vs. Statistical Explanation," *Minnesota Studies in the Philosophy of Science, Series III.* Minnesota, 1962.

——. "The Function of General Laws in History," *Journal of Philosophy* (1942). New York.

Hempel, C. G. and Oppenheim, P. "The Logic of Scientific Explanation," *Readings in the Philosophy of Science,* ed. H. Feigl and M. Brodbeck. New York, 1953.

Hobbes, Thomas. *Leviathan.* London, 1914 (New York: E. P. Dutton, 1950).

Hume, David. *A Treatise of Human Nature,* ed. L. A. Selby-Bigge. Oxford, 1960 (New York: Oxford University Press, 1941).

Jackson, R. "Mill on Geometry," *Mind* (1941). Edinburgh.

——. "Mill's Joint Method," *Mind* (1937, 1938). Edinburgh.

Jevons, W. S. *Pure Logic and Other Minor Works*. London, 1890.

Kant, Immanuel. *Groundwork of the Metaphysic of Morals*, trans. and ed. H. J. Paton. London, 1959 (New York: Harper Torchbook).

Locke, John. *An Essay on the Human Understanding*. London, 1948 (New York: E. P. Dutton).

Mabbott, J. B. "The Interpretation of the Philosophy of J. S. Mill," *Philosophical Quarterly* (1956). Dundee.

Macaulay, T. B. *Miscellaneous Writings*, 2 vols. London, 1860.

McCloskey, H. "Mill's Liberalism," *Philosophical Quarterly* (1963). Dundee.

Melden, A. I. *Free Action*. London, 1961 (New York: Humanities Press).

———. (ed.). *Essays in Moral Philosophy*. Seattle: University of Washington Press, 1958.

Mill, James. *An Essay on Government*. Cambridge, 1937 (Indianapolis and New York: Bobbs Merrill, 1955).

Moore, G. E. *Ethics*. London, 1963 (Gloucester, Mass.: Peter Smith).

———. *Principia Ethica*. Cambridge, 1959.

Nagel, E. *The Structure of Science*. London, 1963 (New York: Harcourt, Brace and World, 1961).

Nagel, E. (ed.). *Mill's Philosophy of Scientific Method*. New York: Harper & Row, 1950.

Nowell-Smith, P. H. *Ethics*. Harmondsworth: Penguin Books, 1954.

Plamenatz, J. P. *The English Utilitarians*. Oxford, 1958 (New York: Humanities Press).

Popper, K. R. *Conjectures and Refutations*. London, 1965 (New York: Basic Books, 1963).

———. *The Logic of Scientific Discovery*. London, 1959 (New York: Basic Books, 1963).

———. *Open Society and Its Enemies*. London, 1954.

———. *The Poverty of Historicism*. London, 1961 (New York: Basic Books, 1966).

Rescher, N. "Fundamental Problems in the Theory of Scientific Explanation," *Delaware Seminar for the Philosophy of Science*, Vol. 2. New York, 1963.

Ryle, G. *The Concept of Mind*. Harmondsworth, 1963 (New York: Barnes & Noble, 1950).

———. *Dilemmas*. Cambridge: University Press, 1954.

Simon, W. M. *European Positivism in the Nineteenth Century*. Ithaca: Cornell University Press, 1963.

Stephen, J. F. *Liberty, Equality, Fraternity*. London, 1874 (Cambridge: University Press, 1968, ed. R. J. White).

Toulmin, S. E. *The Philosophy of Science.* London, 1962 (New York: Harper & Row, 1960).

———. *The Uses of Argument.* Cambridge: University Press, 1958.

Urmson, J. O. "The Interpretation of the Philosophy of J. S. Mill," *Philosophical Quarterly* (1953). Dundee.

———. *Philosophical Analysis.* Oxford, 1958.

———. "Saints and Heroes," in A. I. Melden (ed.), *Essays in Moral Philosophy.* Seattle: Washington University Press, 1958.

Winch, P. G. *The Idea of a Social Science.* London, 1958 (New York: Humanities Press).

Wolfenden, John (chairman). *Report of the Committee on Homosexual Offences and Prostitution* (Command Paper 247). London, 1957.

Wootton, B. *Social Science and Social Pathology.* London, 1959 (New York: Humanities Press).

Wright, G. H. von. *The Logical Problem of Induction.* Oxford, 1957 (New York: Barnes & Noble, 1965).

———. *Norm and Action.* London, 1963 (New York: Humanities Press).

———. *A Treatise on Induction and Probability.* London, 1951.

WORKS CITED IN THE PREFACE TO THE SECOND EDITION

Berger, Fred R. *Happiness, Justice and Freedom.* Berkeley: University of California Press, 1985.

Godwin, William. *An Enquiry Concerning Political Justice*, ed. K. Codell Carter. Oxford University Press, 1971.

Gray, John. *Mill On Liberty: A Defence.* London: Routledge and Kegan Paul, 1983.

Hollis, Martin. *Models of Man.* Cambridge: University Press, 1977.

Lessnoff, Michael. *The Structure of Social Science.* London: George Allen & Unwin, 1974.

Mackie, J. L. *The Cement of the Universe.* Oxford University Press, 1974.

Quine, W. V. O. "Two Dogmas of Empiricism", in *From a Logical Point of View.* Cambridge, Mass.: Harvard University Press, 1961.

Rawls, John. *A Theory of Justice.* Cambridge, Mass.: Harvard University Press, 1971.

Sumner, L. W. "The Good and the Right", in *New Essays on John Stuart Mill and Utilitarianism, Canadian Journal of Philosophy*, Suppt. V, 1979, pp. 99–114.

Williams, Bernard. *Ethics and the Limits of Philosophy*. London: Collins/Fontana, 1985.

Wollheim, Richard. "John Stuart Mill and Isaiah Berlin", in Alan Ryan (ed.), *The Idea of Freedom*. Oxford University Press, 1979, pp. 253–69.

(I have employed the same editions of Mill's work as before: but readers will be aware that *The Collected Works of John Stuart Mill* (University of Toronto Press, 1963) have superseded them for all scholarly purposes.)

ADDITIONAL SELECT BIBLIOGRAPHY,
1 9 7 1 – 8 5

Duncan, Graeme. *Marx and Mill*. Cambridge: University Press, 1973.

Frey, R. G. (ed.), *Utility and Rights*. Oxford: Basil Blackwell, 1985.

Halliday, John. *John Stuart Mill*. London: George Allen and Unwin, 1976.

Himmelfarb, Gertrude. *On Liberty and Liberalism: The Case of John Stuart Mill*. Knopf, 1974.

McCloskey, H. J. *John Stuart Mill: A Critical Study*. London: Macmillan, 1971.

Miller, Harlan B. and Williams, William H. (eds.), *The Limits of Utilitarianism*. University of Minnesota Press, 1982.

Quinton, A. M. *Utilitarian Ethics*. London: Macmillan, 1973.

Rees, John C. *John Stuart Mill's On Liberty*. Oxford University Press, 1985.

Robson, John M. and Laine, Michael. (eds.), *James and John Stuart Mill*. London and Toronto: University of Toronto Press, 1976.

Ryan, Alan. *J. S. Mill*. London: Routledge and Kegan Paul, 1975.

Sen, Amartya and Williams Bernard. (eds.), *Utilitarianism and Beyond*. Cambridge: University Press, 1982.

Smart, J. J. C. and Williams, Bernard. *Utilitarianism For and Against*. Cambridge: University Press, 1973.

Ten, C. L. *Mill on Liberty*. Oxford University Press, 1980.

Thomas, William. *Mill*. Oxford University Press, 1985.

INDEX